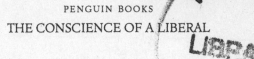
PENGUIN BOOKS

THE CONSCIENCE OF A LIBERAL

Paul Krugman, who was named Columnist of the Year by *Editor* and *Publisher* magazine, writes a twice-weekly column for the op-ed page of *The New York Times*. A winner of the John Bates Clark Medal, the most prized award given to American economists, he teaches economics

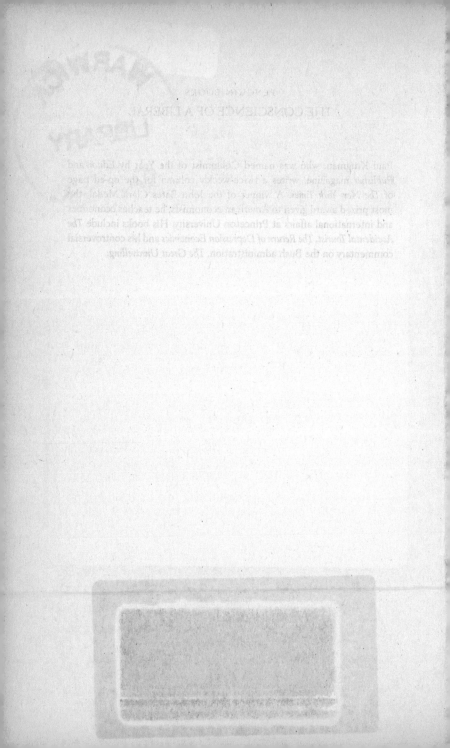

Paul Krugman

THE CONSCIENCE

OF A LIBERAL

Reclaiming America from the Right

PENGUIN BOOKS

PENGUIN BOOKS

Published by the Penguin Group
Penguin Books Ltd, 80 Strand, London WC2R 0RL, England
Penguin Group (USA) Inc., 375 Hudson Street, New York, New York 10014, USA
Penguin Group (Canada), 90 Eglinton Avenue East, Suite 700, Toronto, Ontario, Canada M4P 2Y3
(a division of Pearson Penguin Canada Inc.)
Penguin Ireland, 25 St Stephen's Green, Dublin 2, Ireland (a division of Penguin Books Ltd)
Penguin Group (Australia), 250 Camberwell Road,
Camberwell, Victoria 3124, Australia (a division of Pearson Australia Group Pty Ltd)
Penguin Books India Pvt Ltd, 11 Community Centre,
Panchsheel Park, New Delhi – 110 017, India
Penguin Group (NZ), 67 Apollo Drive, Rosedale, North Shore 0632, New Zealand
(a division of Pearson New Zealand Ltd)
Penguin Books (South Africa) (Pty) Ltd, 24 Sturdee Avenue,
Rosebank, Johannesburg 2196, South Africa

Penguin Books Ltd, Registered Offices: 80 Strand, London WC2R 0RL, England

www.penguin.com

First published in the United States of America by W. W. Norton & Company, Inc., 2007
First published in Great Britain by Allen Lane 2008
Published in Penguin Books 2009
004

Printed in Great Britain by Clays Ltd, St Ives plc

978-0-141-03577-2

www.greenpenguin.co.uk

Penguin Books is committed to a sustainable
future for our business, our readers and our planet.
This book is made from Forest Stewardship
Council™ certified paper.

ALWAYS LEARNING   **PEARSON**

To my parents

Contents

Introduction to the Paperback Edition

T he core of this book is the assertion that America is ready for a new, progressive political agenda—a "new New Deal." There was already a lot of evidence for that position in the summer of 2007, when the hardcover edition went to press: polling data showed that American voters had been shifting to the left on a number of issues, and the 2006 congressional elections were a stunning victory for the Democrats, who brought an abrupt end to the supposedly permanent Republican majority. Yet there was also room for doubt: maybe the 2006 election was really a referendum on the Iraq war and on the leadership of George W. Bush rather than a wholesale rejection of the principles of movement conservatism, which had dominated American politics since the 1970s.

Skeptics about the prospects for a new New Deal argued, in particular, that drastic changes in domestic policy don't happen unless there's an economic crisis. And in the summer of 2007 the economy wasn't doing too badly, at least as long as you focused only on the headline numbers: unemployment was low by historical standards; the Dow was hitting new highs. True, under the surface of this apparent prosperity ran a deep undercurrent of economic anxiety: the number of Americans without health insurance was rising; wages were barely keeping up with inflation; and the purchasing power of the median American household was still below its 2000 level, even though six years had passed since the official end of the 2001 recession. But the public's economic anxiety arguably didn't rise to the level needed to provoke a fundamental change in the nation's direction.

Needless to say, a few things have happened since then, both to the economy and to the political scene. Like the original Gilded Age, which this book argues didn't really end until the 1930s, the New Gilded Age—with conservatives dominating our political life and inequality at levels not seen since 1929—was followed by a vast financial and economic crisis. And Democrats won another stunning electoral victory, at least in part thanks to a public perception that conservative economic policies helped create that crisis. As a result, we're now living in an environment with a strong family resemblance to the environment in which FDR and the original New Deal came to power. The claim that America is ready for a new New Deal—which some readers considered quixotic when the hardcover edition was published—is now more or less conventional wisdom.

But how justified is this conventional wisdom? To answer that question, let's look at the economic and political developments that took place between the two editions of this book.

The Economic Crisis

As I've already pointed out, even at its best the "Bush boom" didn't feel like prosperity to most Americans. Still, for a while profits, stock prices, and the incomes of the best-off Americans did do fairly well, leading to claims of success from the Bush administration. Indeed, on July 19, 2007, the Dow rose above 14,000 for the first time. Two weeks later the White House released a "fact sheet" boasting about the economy's performance on the Bush administration's watch: "The President's Pro-Growth Policies Are Helping Keep Our Economy Strong, Flexible, and Dynamic," it declared.

Some economists, myself included, warned that the economy's success, such as it was, rested on shaky foundations—that much of the economy's growth was driven by an unsustainable bubble in housing prices, and that the economy would experience major problems when that bubble burst. And by the summer of 2007 the housing bubble was already starting to deflate. But administration officials made light of the risks: the problems in housing and in subprime mortgages were "largely contained," said Treasury Secretary Henry Paulson in an August 1, 2007, speech in Beijing.

They weren't. On August 9, 2007, BNP Paribas, a French bank, suspended withdrawals from three of its funds. This event is generally considered to have marked the beginning of the current financial crisis, which is already the worst such crisis since the banking collapse of the early 1930s—a collapse that, most economists agree, was what turned a nasty recession into the Great Depression.

As in the 1930s, the crisis in the financial system is wreaking havoc with the real economy: the disruption of normal channels of borrowing and lending has plunged the United States into a recession that will clearly be deep and may be prolonged. Unemployment will almost certainly rise to its highest level since the early 1980s, and possibly to levels not seen since World War II. And bear in mind that, for most Americans, health insurance is tied to employment, meaning that most of the newly unemployed will lose their medical coverage as well. In addition, millions of families will lose their homes and many others will see most of their savings wiped out.

What made this disaster possible? The answer is that over the past quarter century the financial protections established by the New Deal were gradually eroded. In response to the banking crisis of the early 1930s, Congress enacted legislation that created a financial safety net: on one side, bank deposits were insured; on the other, banks were regulated to keep them from taking excessive risks. The combination of insurance and regulation was designed to prevent a return of the contagious bank runs that were a regular feature of the pre–New Deal economy and that wreaked havoc in 1931–32. Since the 1980s, however, our financial system has become increasingly dependent on what is widely known as the "shadow banking system": institutions that in effect carry out the functions of banks but are structured so as to evade regulation.

The rise of the shadow banking system should have caused great concern: bank regulations were created for a very good reason, and the growing importance of unregulated financial institutions should have set alarm bells ringing. But the changes in the financial system took place while the American political landscape was dominated by those who were committed to undermining the New Deal's legacy. To them, regulatory restraints and government safety nets were the enemy, and their mission was to deregulate and privatize as much as they could. From their point of view, the fact that ever more of the financial system was operating without a safety net was a good thing, and they certainly had no interest in extending regulation to keep up with the economy's changing realities.

Not incidentally, the deregulation of financial markets helped the rich get richer. Financial repackaging of assets created a flood of profits for Wall Street, as dubious accounting inflated the value of corporate assets and drove share prices higher. Higher asset prices fed higher levels of debt, more transactions, and more fees, in a seemingly nonstop expansion of wealth on Wall Street.

And then the music stopped.

The housing bubble was inflated by "subprime" lending: mortgages issued to borrowers who didn't meet the normal criteria for getting credit. As subprime lending soared, some people, including senior officials at the Federal Reserve such as the late Ned Gramlich, warned about the dangers. But they were ignored by those in power, particularly Alan Greenspan. When the attorneys general of all fifty states sought to investigate subprime lending practices, they were blocked by a coalition of the major banks and the Bush administration, which invoked the little-used National Banking Act of 1863 to prevent state-level action. Then the housing bubble burst, and defaults on home mortgages soared. Since most mortgages had been "securitized"—sliced and diced into complex financial claims that were sold to investors who had little idea of the risks they were taking—the losses from these defaults spread far and wide, undermining the capital of many financial institutions and sapping confidence throughout the system. Conventional banks, protected by a New Deal–vintage safety net, held up fairly well—but the unregulated shadow banking system largely collapsed.

A troubled economy is always bad for the party that holds the White House, even if the troubles are the result of factors beyond the incumbent's control—as was arguably the case for Jimmy Carter, whose presidency was undermined by events in the Middle East that disrupted the world's oil supply. The crisis of 2008, however, really was an object lesson in the wrong-headedness of conservative economic philosophy.

Republicans opposed regulation of any kind because they believed in Reagan's dictum from his first inaugural address: "Government is not the solution to our problem; government is the problem." But when disaster struck, it became clear that Reagan had been wrong and that Franklin Delano Roosevelt had been right. In his 1936 speech accepting the Democratic nomination, FDR declared, "We have always known that heedless self-interest was bad morals; we know now that it is bad economics." And that line has never rung truer.

The Election

Those of us who hoped for a new New Deal had some anxious moments over the course of the 2008 campaign. First, there were questions about whether the Democratic nominee actually believed in our agenda: Barack Obama initially ran on a "post-partisan" platform, blaming left and right equally for our problems. During the fight for the Democratic nomination he repeatedly attacked Hillary Clinton, his main rival, from the right—in particular, attacking her health care proposal for mandating that everyone have coverage, which, as explained in Chapter 11, is an integral part of our best-hope strategy for achieving universal health care. And after winning the nomination, Obama initially seemed unwilling to make straightforward denunciations of conservative economic policies.

All this raised fears about whether Obama would pursue progressive policies if he won. Furthermore, there were real doubts about whether he would win: by September 2008 Obama's once-formidable lead in the polls had evaporated, and betting markets were predicting a McCain victory.

Why did Obama trail, even briefly, in such a favorable year for the Democrats? His initial reluctance to make a strong case for a change in economic policy may have been part of the problem. I had conversations with senior Democrats who said, despairingly, that Obama refused to hit hard on the issues, preferring instead to give "hopey-changey" speeches that threw away the party's best arguments against Republicans.

There was also the undeniable issue of race. The GOP's electoral dominance from 1980 to 2004 can be explained almost entirely in five words: Southern whites started voting Republican. A key argument of this book is that the GOP's Southern strategy is losing its effectiveness. But to say that race is an issue of diminishing force is not to say that it is completely gone. And Democrats were, one has to say, tempting fate by nominating an African American presidential candidate.

Indeed, the election results showed the clear fingerprint of racial politics. Nationally, there was a large swing to the Democrats between 2004 and 2008, but this swing was largely absent or even went the other way in a number of states, including Louisiana, Arkansas, Oklahoma, Alabama, Mississippi, Kentucky, and Tennessee. Enough said. Overall, a rough guess is that the candidate's race cost the Democrats two or three percentage points nationally and could have cost them the White House if it hadn't been such a Democratic year.

But it was a Democratic year, and everything went right for the Democrats in the last seven weeks of the campaign. The financial crisis intensified abruptly with the failure of Lehman Brothers on Sept. 15, 2008, and Obama responded superbly to the changed environment. He managed to combine calmness with a sense that he understood the gravity of the situation—in sharp contrast to his opponent, who oscillated wildly between pronouncements that the fundamentals were sound and calls for a suspension of campaigning. Furthermore, the crisis seemed to bring an abrupt sharpening of Obama's economic message: hopey-changey gave way to hard-hitting speeches about the costs of a "failed philosophy," which had progressives cheering.

In the end, Obama took the White House easily. There were also large gains for the Democrats in Congress, building on their 2006 victory. Indeed, the combined results of the 2006 and 2008 congressional elections add up to an awesome reversal of fortune, from a supposedly permanent Republican majority to an overwhelming Democratic dominance. Democrats went from a 29-seat deficit in the House to a more than 80-seat majority; they went from a 10-seat deficit in the Senate to a majority of at least 14. (At the time of this writing, several races were still unresolved, and Democrats seemed likely to take at least one more Senate seat.)

A Center-Left Nation

Even before the results of the 2008 election were in, many commentators were warning Democrats not to imagine that they had a mandate for major changes. America, proclaimed a *Newsweek* cover story, is a "center-right nation." And Bill Clinton's failures in 1993–94, when he was unable to pass health care reform even though his party had congressional majorities approximating those resulting from the 2008 election, were held up as a cautionary tale.

A serious look at the polling evidence, however, refutes the claim that the center-right owns voters' allegiances. While it's true that Americans are much more likely to describe themselves as conservatives than as liberals, these labels turn out to be misleading. When self-proclaimed moderates, the largest group, are questioned about their views on actual policy issues, those views turn out to be largely indistinguishable from those of self-proclaimed liberals. The results of the 2008 election, in which voters generally saw Obama as a liberal and chose him anyway, confirms it: we're not a conservative country, we're a center-left country.

Meanwhile, about that congressional majority: the numbers are similar to those of 1993, but that's as far as the resemblance goes. The old Democratic majority was a weak coalition of Northern liberals and Southern conservatives. The new majority is much more solidly progressive, largely because it was achieved despite the disappearance of the Dixiecrats. Meanwhile, the Republican Party, having taken over the South, has lost the rest of the country and has largely been reduced to a Southern rump—a development predicted in Chapter 10 of this book. Indeed, it's a good bet that the remaining non-Southern Republicans in Congress, especially in the Senate, will prove relatively accommodating out of fear for their own reelection prospects. Barack Obama will have a much better chance of achieving a progressive agenda than Bill Clinton ever did.

The Agenda

This book argues that health care reform should be at the core of the next administration's agenda—that universal health coverage should be to the new New Deal what Social Security was for the original New Deal. The case for health care reform as the centerpiece of a new progressive agenda is as strong as ever. However, the incoming administration will also have another urgent task: rescuing the economy.

In ordinary times, most of the burden of fighting recessions falls on monetary policy, which is the province of the largely nonpolitical Federal Reserve Board. We are not, however, living in ordinary times: as of late 2008, the Fed had cut the interest rates it controls almost to zero, without managing to pull the economy out of its tailspin. Massive bailouts of troubled financial institutions have also failed to stop the economy's slide. This leaves, as the only remaining policy option, large-scale fiscal stimulus. In other words, the Obama administration will have to try to spend America out of its slump.

What form will the spending take? It will probably be a combination of public works projects, aid to the unemployed, aid to state and local governments, and much more. And the expense will be huge: reasonable estimates by independent economists suggest that the extra spending in 2009 alone should be $500 billion or more. (My own estimate is $600 billion.)

This raises the question: does the cost of rescuing the economy leave room for the longer-term agenda? In particular, is this a good time to be pushing for universal health care? Yes.

The political arguments for a quick push on health care, laid out in Chapter 11, are as compelling as ever. In fact, they may be even more compelling. It's not just that Democrats have the momentum of a big election win behind them. As millions of American workers have lost their jobs, the weakness of employer-based health insurance has become devastatingly obvious. FDR used the instability of the 1930s economy to argue for the necessity of unemployment insurance and Social Security; his successors can use the instability of the twenty-first-century economy to argue for the necessity of guaranteed health insurance.

While the Democrats should push for passage of fundamental health care reform as soon as possible, that doesn't mean that the program will or should start up immediately. In fact, that was never part of the plan. All of the Democratic plans for reform were based on the premise that the expiration of the Bush tax cuts at the end of 2010 would provide the funds for health insurance subsidies to lower-income Americans. So health care reform should be enacted in 2009 but should take effect around two years later. This offers at least a partial answer to the question of how the nation can afford both massive economic stimulus and major health care reform: if all goes well, the economy will be on the road to recovery and no longer on life support by the time health care reform kicks in.

Can we really do all of this? Can we save the economy, bring universal health care to America, and make this a fundamentally more democratic nation? Yes, we can. Right now the prospects for a dramatic progressive turn in American policy, for a bold reassertion of liberal values, are even better than I thought they'd be when the hardcover edition went to the printers. The new New Deal starts now.

THE CONSCIENCE
OF A LIBERAL

1

THE WAY WE WERE

I was born in 1953. Like the rest of my generation, I took the America I grew up in for granted—in fact, like many in my generation, I railed against the very real injustices of our society, marched against the bombing of Cambodia, went door to door for liberal political candidates. It's only in retrospect that the political and economic environment of my youth stands revealed as a paradise lost, an exceptional episode in our nation's history.

Postwar America was, above all, a middle-class society. The great boom in wages that began with World War II had lifted tens of millions of Americans—my parents among them—from urban slums and rural poverty to a life of home ownership and unprecedented comfort. The rich, on the other hand, had lost ground: They were few in number and, relative to the prosperous middle, not all that rich. The poor were more numerous than the rich, but they were still a relatively small minority. As a result, there was a striking sense of economic commonality: Most people in America lived recognizably similar and remarkably decent material lives.

The equability of our economy was matched by moderation in our politics. For most but not all of my youth there was broad consensus between Democrats and Republicans on foreign policy and many aspects of domestic policy. Republicans were no longer trying to undo the achievements of the New Deal; quite a few even supported Medicare. And bipartisanship really meant something. Despite the turmoil over Vietnam and race relations, despite the sinister machinations of Nixon and his henchmen, the American political process was for the most part governed by a bipartisan coalition of men who agreed on fundamental values.

Anyone familiar with history knew that America had not always been thus, that we had once been a nation marked by vast economic inequality and wracked by bitter political partisanship. From the perspective of the postwar years, however, America's past of extreme inequality and harsh partisanship seemed like a passing, immature phase, part of the roughness of a nation in the early stages of industrialization. Now that America was all grown up, we thought, a relatively equal society with a strong middle class and an equable political scene was its normal state.

In the 1980s, however, it gradually became clear that the evolution of America into a middle-class, politically middle-of-the-road nation wasn't the end of the story. Economists began documenting a sharp rise in inequality: A small number of people were pulling far ahead, while most Americans saw little or no economic progress. Political scientists began documenting a rise in political polarization: Politicians were gravitating toward the ends of the left-right scale, and it became increasingly possible to use "Democrat" and "Republican" as synonyms for "liberal" and "conservative." Those trends continue to this day: Income inequality today is as high as it was in the 1920s,[1] and political polarization is as high as it has ever been.

The story of rising political polarization isn't a matter of both parties moving to the extremes. It's hard to make the case that Democrats have moved significantly to the left: On economic issues from welfare to taxes, Bill Clinton arguably governed not just to the right of Jimmy Carter, but to the right of Richard Nixon. On the other side it's obvious that Republicans have moved to the right: Just compare the hard-line conservatism of George W. Bush with the moderation of Gerald Ford. In fact, some of Bush's policies—like his attempt to eliminate the estate tax—don't just take America back to the way it was before the New Deal. They take us back to the way we were before the Progressive Era.

If we take a longer view, both the beginning and the end of the era of bipartisanship reflected fundamental changes in the Republican Party. The era began when Republicans who had bitterly opposed the New Deal either retired or threw in the towel. After Harry Truman's upset victory in 1948, the leadership of the GOP reconciled itself to the idea that the New Deal was here to stay, and as a matter of political self-preservation stopped trying to turn the clock back to the 1920s. The end of the era of bipartisanship and the coming of a new era of bitter partisanship came when the Republican Party was taken over by a radical new force in American politics, movement conservatism, which will play a large role in this book. Partisanship reached its apogee after the 2004 election, when a triumphant Bush tried to dismantle Social Security, the crown jewel of the New Deal institutions.

There have, then, been two great arcs in modern American history—an economic arc from high inequality to relative equality and back again, and a political arc from extreme polarization to bipartisanship and back again. These two arcs move in parallel: The golden age of economic equality roughly corresponded to the golden age of political bipartisanship. As the political scientists Nolan McCarty, Keith Poole, and Howard Rosenthal put it, history suggests that there is a kind of "dance" in which economic inequality and political polarization move as one.[2] They have used a sophisticated statistical technique to track the political positions of members of Congress. Their data show the Republicans moving left, closer to the Democrats, when income inequality declined, producing the bipartisanship of the fifties and sixties. Then the Republicans moved right, creating today's bitter partisanship, as income inequality rose. But what makes the dancing partners stay together?

One possibility is that inequality takes the lead—that, to change metaphors, the arrow of causation points from economics to politics. In that view the story of the last thirty years would run like this: Impersonal forces such as technological change and globalization caused America's income distribution to become increasingly unequal, with an elite minority pulling away from the rest of the population. The Republican Party chose to cater to the interests of that rising elite, perhaps because what the elite lacked in numbers it made up for in the ability and willingness to make large campaign contributions. And so a gap opened up between the parties, with the Republicans becoming the party of the winners from growing inequality while the Democrats represented those left behind.

That, more or less, is the story I believed when I began working on this book. There's clearly something to it. For example, a close look at the campaign to repeal the estate tax shows that it has largely been financed by a handful of families with huge estates to protect. Forty years ago there weren't many huge estates, and the country's superrich, such as they were, weren't rich enough to finance that kind of campaign. So that's a case in which rising inequality has helped pull Republicans to the right.

Yet I've become increasingly convinced that much of the causation runs the other way—that political change in the form of rising polarization has been a major cause of rising inequality. That is, I'd suggest an alternative story for the last thirty years that runs like this: Over the course of the 1970s, radicals of the right determined to roll back the achievements of the New Deal took over the Republican Party, opening a partisan gap with the Democrats, who became the true conservatives, defenders of the long-standing institutions of equality. The empowerment of the hard right emboldened business to launch an all-out attack on the union movement, drastically reducing workers' bargaining power; freed business executives from the political and social constraints that had previously placed limits on runaway executive paychecks; sharply reduced tax rates on high incomes; and in a variety of other ways promoted rising inequality.

The New Economics of Inequality

Can the political environment really be that decisive in determining economic inequality? It sounds like economic heresy, but a growing body of economic research suggests that it can. I'd emphasize four pieces of evidence.

First, when economists, startled by rising inequality, began looking back at the origins of middle-class America, they discovered to their surprise that the transition from the inequality of the Gilded Age to the relative equality of the postwar era wasn't a gradual evolution. Instead, America's postwar middle-class society was *created*, in just the space of a few years, by the policies of the Roosevelt administration—especially through wartime wage controls. The economic historians Claudia Goldin and Robert Margo, who first documented this surprising reality, dubbed it the Great Compression.[3] Now, you might have expected inequality to spring back to its former levels once wartime controls were removed. It turned out, however, that the relatively equal distribution of income created by FDR persisted for more than thirty years. This strongly suggests that institutions, norms, and the political environment matter a lot more for the distribution of income—and that impersonal market forces matter less—than Economics 101 might lead you to believe.

Second, the timing of political and economic change suggests that politics, not economics, was taking the lead. There wasn't a major rise in U.S. inequality until the 1980s—as late as 1983 or 1984 there was still some legitimate argument about whether the data showed a clear break in trend. But the right-wing takeover of the Republican Party took place in the mid-1970s, and the institutions of movement conservatism, which made that takeover possible, largely came into existence in the early 1970s. So the timing strongly suggests that polarizing political change came first, and that rising economic inequality followed.

Third, while most economists used to think that technological change, which supposedly increases the demand for highly educated workers and reduces the demand for less-educated workers, was the principal cause of America's rising inequality, that orthodoxy has been gradually wilting as researchers look more closely at the data. Maybe the most striking observation is that even among highly educated Americans, most haven't seen large income gains. The big winners, instead, have been members of a very narrow elite: the top 1 percent or less of the population. As a result there is a growing sense among researchers that technology isn't the main story. Instead, many have come to believe that an erosion of the social norms and institutions that used to promote equality, ultimately driven by the rightward shift of American politics, has played a crucial role in surging inequality.[4]

Finally, international comparisons provide a sort of controlled test. The sharp rightward shift in U.S. politics is unique among advanced countries; Thatcherite Britain, the closest comparison, was at most a pale reflection. The forces of technological change and globalization, by contrast, affect everyone. If the rise in inequality has political roots, the United States should stand out; if it's mainly due to impersonal market forces, trends in inequality should have been similar across the advanced world. And the fact is that the increase in U.S. inequality has no counterpart anywhere else in the advanced world. During the Thatcher years Britain experienced a sharp rise in income disparities, but not nearly as large as the rise in inequality here, and inequality has risen modestly if at all in continental Europe and Japan.[5]

Political change, then, seems to be at the heart of the story. How did that political change happen?

The Politics of Inequality

The story of how George W. Bush and Dick Cheney ended up running the country goes back half a century, to the years when the *National Review*, edited by a young William F. Buckley, was defending the right of the South to prevent blacks from voting— "the White community is so entitled because it is, for the time being, the advanced race"—and praising Generalissimo Francisco Franco, who overthrew a democratically elected government in the name of church and property, as "an authentic national hero." The small movement then known as the "new conservatism" was, in large part, a backlash against the decision of Dwight Eisenhower and other Republican leaders to make their peace with FDR's legacy.

Over the years this small movement grew into a powerful political force, which both supporters and opponents call "movement conservatism." It's a network of people and institutions that extends far beyond what is normally considered political life: In addition to the Republican Party and Republican politicians, movement conservatism includes media organizations, think tanks, publishing houses and more. People can and do make entire careers within this network, secure in the knowledge that political loyalty will be rewarded no matter what happens. A liberal who botched a war and then violated ethics rules to reward his lover might be worried about his employment prospects; Paul Wolfowitz had a chair waiting for him at the American Enterprise Institute.

There once were a significant number of Republican politicians who weren't movement conservatives, but there are only a few left, largely because life becomes very difficult for those who aren't considered politically reliable. Just ask Lincoln Chafee, the moderate former senator from Rhode Island, who faced a nasty primary challenge from the right in 2006 that helped lead to his defeat in the general election, even though it was clear that the Republicans might well need him to keep control of the Senate.

Money is the glue of movement conservatism, which is largely financed by a handful of extremely wealthy individuals and a number of major corporations, all of whom stand to gain from increased inequality, an end to progressive taxation, and a rollback of the welfare state—in short, from a reversal of the New Deal. And turning the clock back on economic policies that limit inequality is, at its core, what movement conservatism is all about. Grover Norquist, an antitax activist who is one of the movement's key figures, once confided that he wants to bring America back to what it was "up until Teddy Roosevelt, when the socialists took over. The income tax, the death tax, regulation, all that."[6]

Because movement conservatism is ultimately about rolling back policies that hurt a narrow, wealthy elite, it's fundamentally antidemocratic. But however much the founders of the movement may have admired the way Generalissimo Franco did things, in America the route to political power runs through elections. There wouldn't be nearly as much money forthcoming if potential donors still believed, as they had every reason to in the aftermath of Barry Goldwater's landslide defeat in 1964, that advocating economic policies that increase inequality is a political nonstarter. Movement conservatism has gone from fringe status to a central role in American politics because it has proved itself able to win elections.

Ronald Reagan, more than anyone else, showed the way. His 1964 speech "A Time for Choosing," which launched his political career, and the speeches he gave during his successful 1966 campaign for governor of California foreshadowed political strategies that would work for him and other movement conservatives for the next forty years. Latter-day hagiographers have portrayed Reagan as a paragon of high-minded conservative principles, but he was nothing of the sort. His early political successes were based on appeals to cultural and sexual anxieties, playing on the fear of communism, and, above all, tacit exploitation of white backlash against the civil rights movement and its consequences.

One key message of this book, which many readers may find uncomfortable, is that race is at the heart of what has happened to the country I grew up in. The legacy of slavery, America's original sin, is the reason we're the only advanced economy that doesn't guarantee health care to our citizens. White backlash against the civil rights movement is the reason America is the only advanced country where a major political party wants to roll back the welfare state. Ronald Reagan began his 1980 campaign with a states' rights speech outside Philadelphia, Mississippi, the town where three civil rights workers were murdered; Newt Gingrich was able to take over Congress entirely because of the great Southern flip, the switch of Southern whites from overwhelming support for Democrats to overwhelming support for Republicans.

A New New Deal

A few months after the 2004 election I was placed under some pressure by journalistic colleagues, who said I should stop spending so much time criticizing the Bush administration and conservatives more generally. "The election settled some things," I was told. In retrospect, however, it's starting to look as if the 2004 election was movement conservatism's last hurrah.

Republicans won a stunning victory in the 2002 midterm election by exploiting terrorism to the hilt. There's every reason to believe that one reason Bush took us to war with Iraq was his desire to perpetuate war psychology combined with his expectation that victory in a splendid little war would be good for his reelection prospects. Indeed, Iraq probably did win Bush the 2004 election, even though the war was already going badly.

But the war did go badly—and that was not an accident. When Bush moved into the White House, movement conservatism finally found itself in control of all the levers of power—and quickly proved itself unable to govern. The movement's politicization of everything, the way it values political loyalty above all else, creates a culture of cronyism and corruption that has pervaded everything the Bush administration does, from the failed reconstruction of Iraq to the hapless response to Hurricane Katrina. The multiple failures of the Bush administration are what happens when the government is run by a movement that is dedicated to policies that are against most Americans' interests, and must try to compensate for that inherent weakness through deception, distraction, and the distribution of largesse to its supporters. And the nation's rising contempt for Bush and his administration helped Democrats achieve a stunning victory in the 2006 midterm election.

One election does not make a trend. There are, however, deeper forces undermining the political tactics movement conservatives have used since Ronald Reagan ran for governor of California. Crucially, the American electorate is, to put it bluntly, becoming less white. Republican strategists try to draw a distinction between African Americans and the Hispanic and Asian voters who play a gradually growing role in elections—but as the debate over immigration showed, that's not a distinction the white backlash voters the modern GOP depends on are prepared to make. A less crude factor is the progressive shift in Americans' attitudes: Polling suggests that the electorate has moved significantly to the left on domestic issues since the 1990s, and race is a diminishing force in a nation that is, truly, becoming steadily less racist.

Movement conservatism still has money on its side, but that has never been enough in itself. Anything can happen in the 2008 election, but it looks like a reasonable guess that by 2009 America will have a Democratic president and a solidly Democratic Congress. Moreover, this new majority, if it emerges, will be much more ideologically cohesive than the Democratic majority of Bill Clinton's first two years, which was an uneasy alliance between Northern liberals and conservative Southerners.

The question is, what should the new majority do? My answer is that it should, for the nation's sake, pursue an unabashedly liberal program of expanding the social safety net and reducing inequality—a new New Deal. The starting point for that program, the twenty-first-century equivalent of Social Security, should be universal health care, something every other advanced country already has. Before we can talk about how to get there, however, it's helpful to take a good look at where we've been. That look—the story of the arc of modern American history—is the subject of the next eight chapters.

2

THE LONG GILDED AGE

Looking at the political economy of the United States before the New Deal from the vantage point of the Bush years is like looking at a sepia-toned photograph of your grandfather and realizing that he looked a lot like you—in fact, that in some ways you resemble your grandfather more than you resemble your father. Unfortunately the family features that seem to have reemerged in your face after skipping a generation are deeply unattractive.

Pre–New Deal America, like America in the early twenty-first century, was a land of vast inequality in wealth and power, in which a nominally democratic political system failed to represent the economic interests of the majority. Moreover the factors that let a wealthy elite dominate political life have recognizable counterparts today: the overwhelming financial disadvantage at which populist political candidates operated; the division of Americans with common economic interests along racial, ethnic, and religious lines; the uncritical acceptance of a conservative ideology that warned that any attempt to help the less fortunate would lead to economic disaster.

You might be tempted to say that I'm overstating the resemblance, that America today isn't as unequal as it was before the New Deal. The numbers, however, say otherwise. As Table 1 shows, the concentration of income in the hands of a narrow elite today matches its concentration in the 1920s.

Table 1. Share of High-Income Groups in Total Income, Excluding Capital Gains

	Highest-income 10%	Highest-income 1%
Average for 1920s	43.6%	17.3%
2005	44.3%	17.4%

Source: Thomas Piketty and Emmanuel Saez, "Income Inequality in the United States, 1913–1998," *Quarterly Journal of Economics* 118, no. 1 (Feb. 2003), pp. 1–39. Updated data available at http://elsa.berkeley.edu/~saez/.

Now, it's true that the oligarchic nature of pre–New Deal politics and the often bloody way the power of the state was used to protect property interests were more extreme than anything we see today. Meanwhile, though the inequality of income was no greater than it is now, the inequality of living conditions was much greater, because there were none of the social programs that now create a safety net, however imperfect, for the less fortunate. All the same, the family resemblance between then and now is both striking and disturbing.

Before I say more about that resemblance, however, I need a better name for the period I'll be discussing than "pre–New Deal," which defines the era only by what it wasn't. Historians generally say that the Gilded Age gave way to the Progressive Era around 1900, and they have a point. The cultural and political tone of the country shifted considerably around 1900. Theodore Roosevelt, who became president in 1901, was less reliably proplutocrat than his predecessors; the Food and Drug Administration was created in 1906; the income tax was reintroduced in 1913, together with a constitutional amendment that prevented the Supreme Court from declaring, as it had before, that it was unconstitutional. These changes, however, had little impact on either the inequality of income and wealth in America or the minimal role that the U.S. government played in mitigating the effects of that inequality. As best we can tell, America in the 1920s, although richer than it had been in the late nineteenth century, was very nearly as unequal, and very nearly as much under the thumb of a wealthy elite.

So at the risk of annoying historians, I'll refer to the entire period from the end of Reconstruction in the 1870s to the coming of the New Deal in the 1930s as the Long Gilded Age. It was a period defined above all by persistently high levels of economic inequality.

The Persistence of Gilded Age Inequality

We don't have detailed statistics on the distribution of income and wealth in America during most of the Long Gilded Age. There's enough evidence, however, to show that America was a vastly unequal society circa 1900—an observation that won't surprise anyone. Perhaps more surprisingly, the evidence also suggests that the level of inequality remained almost unchanged through the twenties.

That's important to know. The persistence of extreme inequality right through the Jazz Age is a first piece of evidence for one of this book's central points: Middle-class societies don't emerge automatically as an economy matures, they have to be *created* through political action. Nothing in the data we have for the early twentieth century suggests that America was evolving spontaneously into the relatively equal society I grew up in. It took FDR and the New Deal to bring that society into being.

What's the evidence that the Gilded Age persisted, in crucial respects, right through the 1920s? One useful number that we can compute, even lacking extensive statistical data, is the number of extremely rich Americans. J. Bradford DeLong, an economist and economic historian at Berkeley, has calculated the number of "billionaires," whom he defines as those with wealth greater than the annual output of twenty-thousand average American workers. (That was about a billion dollars in the mid-1990s, when he devised the measure, but close to $2 billion today.) In 1900 there were, by DeLong's count, twenty-two American billionaires. By 1925 there were thirty-two, so the number of billionaires more or less kept up with population growth right through the Progressive Era. It was only with the New Deal that the billionaires more or less vanished from the scene, dropping in number to sixteen in 1957 and thirteen in 1968.[1] (Around 160 Americans meet DeLong's criterion now.)

The Gilded Age billionaires were exactly who you'd expect: the robber barons, the men who made fortunes off railroads, manufacturing, and extractive industries such as oil and coal. In 1915 John D. Rockefeller topped the list. Behind him were two steel magnates, Henry C. Frick and Andrew Carnegie, then an array of railroad builders and financiers, plus Henry Ford.

The count of billionaires fits with other evidence, such as the sizes of large estates, suggesting that the concentration of wealth at the very top was about the same at the end of the 1920s as it was in 1900. That concentration then declined dramatically with the coming of the New Deal. During the first few decades after World War II, the inequalities of the Gilded Age became a thing of myth, a type of society that nobody thought would return—except that now it has.

The high level of inequality during the Long Gilded Age, like high inequality today, partly reflected the weak bargaining position of labor. For most of the era, large employers were free to set wages and working conditions based on whatever the job market would bear, with little fear of organized opposition. Strikes were often broken up by force—usually involving strikebreakers hired by employers, but sometimes, as in the 1892 strike at Carnegie's Homestead steelworks and the 1894 Pullman strike, by state militias or federal troops. Unionization rates and union influence gradually rose after 1900, temporarily reaching a peak soon after World War I. But a counterattack by employers pushed labor into retreat again. By the late 1920s union membership, which reached more than 17 percent of the labor force in 1924, was back below 11 percent—about what it is now.

High inequality didn't mean that workers failed to share any of the fruits of progress. While inequality was great, it was more or less stable, so that the growth of the U.S. economy during the Long Gilded Age benefited all classes: Most Americans were much better off in the 1920s than they had been in the 1870s. That is, the decline in real earnings for many workers that has taken place in America since the 1970s had no counterpart during the Long Gilded Age. Urban workers, in particular, saw a vast improvement in the quality of life over the course of the Long Gilded Age, as diets and health improved, indoor plumbing and electricity became standard even in tenements, and the emergence of urban mass transit systems enlarged personal horizons.*

These improvements, however, shouldn't lead us to gloss over the persistence of real deprivation. At the close of the twenties many American workers still lived in grinding poverty. For the unlucky—those who got thrown out of work, were injured on the job, or simply grew old without children to support them—there was great misery in the midst of opulence for the few. For before the 1930s there were no significant government income redistribution policies such as welfare or food stamps, nor were there any government provided social insurance programs such as Social Security or Medicare. Government at all levels was very small, and as a result taxes on all but the very richest were extremely low. For example, in the mid-1920s $10,000 bought as much as about $120,000 today, and people with incomes of $10,000 a year were in the top 1 percent of the income distribution—but they paid less than 1 percent of their income in income taxes, compared with around 20 percent for similarly situated people today. So it was a very good time to be rich. On the other hand, since income support programs currently account for most of the income of the poorest fifth of Americans, being poor in the 1920s was a far harsher experience than it is today.

This leads to an obvious question: Given the great wealth being generated during the Long Gilded Age, the great disparities in income, and a democratic system in which poorly paid workers vastly outnumbered the minimally taxed elite, what explains the absence of effective demands that the government do more to soak the rich and help the less well off?

---

*The improving quality even of slum living can be seen by comparing restored apartments from different eras in New York City's Lower East Side Tenement Museum.

It's not that the concepts of progressive taxation and the welfare state had yet to be invented, or even implemented in other places. In Germany, Otto von Bismarck introduced old-age pensions, unemployment insurance, and even national health insurance in the 1880s. Bismarck acted out of political calculation, not compassion—he wanted to head off potential opposition to the Kaiser's rule. But in so doing he showed that more compassionate government was, in fact, possible. Here in the United States the system of benefits introduced after the Civil War for veterans and their survivors was, in important ways, a forerunner to Social Security. The Populist platform of 1896 called for a progressive income tax and public works programs to provide jobs in times of depression —not qualitatively very different from what FDR would finally do almost forty years later.

Nor was America too poor a country to afford such programs. The United States in the 1920s was substantially richer than European countries, yet France, Germany, and the United Kingdom all had substantial programs of public aid several times as large as those in America.[2] In fact the United States in 1925 was about as rich as Britain would be in the early post–World War II years, the years in which Britain established a full-fledged welfare state, including national health care—a welfare state that was in some ways more extensive than the United States has now.

So why wasn't there an effective demand to, as Huey Long would later put it, "soak the rich and help the little man"?

The Politics of Plutocracy

Republicans, who began as the party of free labor but by the 1870s had undeniably become the party of big business and the rich, won twelve of the sixteen presidential elections between the Civil War and the Great Depression. They controlled the Senate even more consistently, with Democrats holding a majority in only five of the era's thirty-two Congresses. While the House of Representatives was somewhat more competitive, even there the Republican Party was usually in control.

Furthermore, party comparisons understate the conservative dominance of politics during this era, because one major wing of the Democratic Party—the so-called Bourbon Democrats, who included both reactionary Southerners and probusiness Northerners—was just as supportive of the interests of the wealthy and opposed to government help for the poor as the Republicans. The Bourbon Democrats did differ from the Republicans on some issues: They believed in free trade rather than high protective tariffs, and they decried corruption in politics. But it would be wrong to characterize the Bourbons as being in any meaningful sense to the left of the GOP. And on the rare occasions when a Democrat did take control of the White House, it was always a Bourbon: Grover Cleveland, the only Democrat to win the presidency between the Civil War and Woodrow Wilson's victory in 1912,[3] was a Bourbon, and so were Democrats who got anywhere near the White House, like Samuel Tilden in 1876.

What accounts for this prolonged conservative dominance in a country in which demands to tax the rich and help the needy should, by the numbers, have had mass appeal? The explanation involves several factors that are all too familiar from today's political scene, but were present in an exaggerated form.

First there was the effective disenfranchisement of many American workers. In 1910 almost 14 percent of adult males were non-naturalized immigrants, unable to vote. Meanwhile Southern blacks were effectively disenfranchised by Jim Crow. Between the immigrants and the blacks, about a quarter of the population—and by and large, the poorest quarter—were simply denied any role in the political process. As we'll see later in this book the problem of disenfranchisement has returned in contemporary America, thanks to large-scale illegal immigration and the continuing low voting participation of blacks—aided by systematic vote suppression that is more subtle than that of Jim Crow days, but nonetheless can be decisive in close elections.

Then there was the matter of campaign finance, whose force was most vividly illustrated in the 1896 election, arguably the only time between the Civil War and 1932 that a challenger to the country's ruling economic elite had a serious chance of winning the White House. Fearful of what William Jennings Bryan might do, the wealthy didn't crucify him on a cross of gold—they buried him under a mountain of the stuff. William McKinley's 1896 campaign spent $3.35 million, almost twice as much as the Republicans had spent in 1892, and five times what Bryan had at his disposal. And bear in mind that in 1896 three million dollars was a lot of money: As a percentage of gross domestic product, it was the equivalent of more than $3 billion today, five times what the Bush campaign spent in 2004. The financial disparity between the parties in 1896 was exceptional, but the Republicans normally had a large financial advantage. The only times the Democrats were more or less financially competitive between the Civil War and Woodrow Wilson's election in 1912 were in 1876, an election in which the Democrat Samuel Tilden actually won the popular vote (and essentially had the electoral vote stolen, in a deal in which Rutherford B. Hayes got the White House in return for his promise to withdraw federal troops from the South), and in Grover Cleveland's two victories in 1884 and 1892. Not coincidentally Tilden and Cleveland were Bourbon Democrats. When the Democratic Party nominated someone who wasn't a Bourbon, it was consistently outspent about three to one.[4]

Finally there was pervasive election fraud.[5] Both parties did it, in a variety of ways. For much of the period secret ballots were rare: Most voters used ballots printed by the parties themselves, and these ballots were easily distinguishable by size and color. As a consequence, vote buying was feasible, easy—there was no problem verifying that the votes were actually cast as purchased—and widespread. In 1888 the *New York Times* acquired a letter sent by William Dudley, the treasurer of the Republican National Committee, to Republican county chairmen in Indiana. It read, in part:

> Your committee will certainly receive from Chairman Huston the assistance necessary to hold our floaters and doubtful voters . . . divide the floaters into blocks of five, and put a trusted man, with the necessary funds, in charge of those five, and make him responsible that none get away, and that all will vote our ticket.[6]

As the *Times* editorialized, this letter was "a direct incitement to criminal acts . . . an official handbook for the voter buyers and bribery corps of the Republicans in Indiana." And it wasn't unusual. In fact there's reason to believe that high rates of voter participation in the Gilded Age largely reflected financial incentives. Vote buying was, inevitably, most prevalent in swing states: One widely cited estimate is that during the Gilded Age and the Progressive Era up to a third of voters in New Jersey, which was very much a swing state at the time, regularly took cash for their votes.

Ballot-box stuffing was also widespread—and not just in areas dominated by urban machines, though most box stuffers were too bashful to say bluntly, as William Marcy Tweed did, "The ballots made no result; the counters made the result." There was also extensive use of intimidation to keep the other party's voters away from the polls. And as a last resort entrenched political groups sometimes simply overruled the will of the voters. For example, in 1897 the Indiana legislature simply unseated several Populists, even though it admitted that they had won a majority of the votes in their districts.

Again, both parties engaged in these tactics, though the financial edge of the Republicans probably meant that they came out ahead in the competitive corruption of politics at the time. More generally electoral fraud reinforced the advantages that money and organization carried: Elections were often decided not by who had the more popular platform, but by who was better prepared to rig the polls. At the same time, it greatly reduced the chances for electoral success of a platform that truly reflected the interests of the majority of the population.

It would be wrong, however, to think of the Long Gilded Age as an era in which there were heated clashes, in which the egalitarian impulses of the populace were forcibly suppressed by the forces of the elite. The truth was that most of the time the system's inherent bias against any form of populism (with a small *p*—I'm not referring to the specific programs of the Populist Party, of which more below) was so strong and obvious that politicians didn't even try to challenge the inequalities of the economic order.

Ironically the extreme weakness of populism in Gilded Age America made politics a more relaxed affair in certain respects than it is today. Most of the time, the conservative forces that sustained the Long Gilded Age didn't require an equivalent to today's disciplined movement conservatism to triumph. There was no need for an interlocking set of special institutions, Mafia-like in their demand for loyalty, to promulgate conservative thought, reward the faithful, and intimidate the press and any dissenters. There was no need to form alliances with religious fundamentalists, no need to exploit morality and lifestyle issues. And there was no need to distort foreign policy or engage in convenient foreign wars to distract the public.

The election of 1896 was the striking exception to the long-standing pattern of relaxed oligarchy. For a moment, it seemed as if Populism with a capital *P* really did represent a serious challenge to plutocratic rule. Populism failed, however, and not just because of a political system tilted in favor of those with money and organization. Populism lacked the kind of leadership that could bridge the divisions among the various groups whose interests would have been served by change. It was shipwrecked on the shoals of ethnic and geographic diversity.

The Problems of Populism

Business interests and the wealthy had good reason to be terrified in 1896: Many Americans were very angry about their situation. Farmers, suffering from falling prices and the burden of debt, were in an uproar. So were many industrial workers, who either lost their jobs or faced wage cuts in the slump that followed the Panic of 1893. The brutality with which the Homestead strike and the Pullman strike were suppressed was unusual even in an age when the use of force against workers was common.

Yet in the end, William Jennings Bryan, a Democrat who also received the nomination of the Populist Party, was defeated. Lack of money and extensive voter fraud were significant factors in his defeat. It's also clear, however, that Bryan failed to assemble the nation's disgruntled groups into an effective coalition.

That's not surprising. The losers from the Gilded Age economic order—the groups that would eventually benefit enormously from the New Deal—were divided along three fault lines that may have been unbridgeable in 1896. Moreover, they certainly weren't bridgeable by someone like Bryan.

The first and most important of these divides was between city and country. Although the United States was an industrial powerhouse by 1896, the majority of the population still lived close to the land. In 1890, 64 percent of Americans lived in rural areas, and another 14 percent lived in towns of fewer than 25,000 people. The political influence of urban dwellers grew more important over time, but rural and small-town America still contained the great majority of voters as late as 1930.

Nonetheless an effective progressive coalition needed urban workers—a purely rural movement wasn't strong enough to win the White House. But the Populists came from rural and small-town America, and few knew how to reach out to potential urban allies. Bryan chose to base his campaign almost entirely on the issue of Free Silver, which was, in effect, a call for inflationary policies that would reduce the burden of debt on farmers. It was an issue that meant nothing to urban workers.

One reason that farmers and urban workers were unable to make common cause was the cultural and social gap that lay between immigrants and the native born. The immigrant share of the population peaked in 1910 at 14.7 percent, with the vast majority in urban areas and particularly concentrated in the biggest cities. In that year 41 percent of New Yorkers were foreign born.[7] And these immigrants were foreign indeed to the Americans of the heartland. The Irish were considered alien well into the twentieth century: The 1928 campaign of Al Smith, an Irish American Catholic, was greeted with burning crosses. And by then the Irish were an old, well-established part of the American ethnic mix—not like the Italians, Poles, Jews, and others who made up much of late-nineteenth- and early-twentieth-century immigration. These immigrants were treated with the same kind of horror, the same claims that they could never become real Americans, that now characterizes the most extreme reaction to Mexican immigrants.

In the 1920s the mutual incomprehension of rural America and the immigrants was made even worse by Prohibition. It's hard now to appreciate the depth of the fear of alcohol, so extreme that it provoked a constitutional amendment. (We should always remember that the big issues that we think *should* have dominated past American politics have often been crowded off the public stage by disputes that seem bizarre in retrospect.) And the temperance movement tended to flourish in the same places that bred agrarian revolt: Kansas was both the birthplace of Populism and the birthplace of Prohibition. You could say that Prohibition was the original "values" issue, one perfectly calculated to drive a wedge between poor Protestant farmers and poor urban workers, many of whom came from Catholic cultures in which alcohol was a normal, accepted part of life. To be fair, though, both major parties were divided over Prohibition.

Most deadly of all was the division between poor whites and blacks. As a practical matter this was a problem only for Southern populists, since blacks were a tiny minority outside the South before the 1920s. In the South, however, blacks—consisting overwhelmingly of impoverished farmers—were a third of the population. Was it possible for white farmers, who shared many of the same economic interests, to make common cause with those of a different color?

In the long run the answer was no. One of the themes of this book will be the extent to which racial antagonism has had a pervasive and malign effect on American politics, largely to conservative advantage. Yet it's possible to glimpse another path that could have been taken. In a remarkable 1892 article, "The Negro Question in the South," Tom Watson of Georgia, leader of the Southern Populists, called for an alliance between the races:

> Why should the colored man always be taught that the white
> man of his neighborhood hates him, while a Northern man,
> who taxes every rag on his back, loves him? Why should not
> my tenant come to regard me as his friend rather than the
> manufacturer who plunders us both? Why should we perpetu-
> ate a policy which drives the black man into the arms of the
> Northern politician? . . . There never was a day during the
> last twenty years when the South could not have flung the
> money power into the dust by patiently teaching the Negro
> that we could not be wretched under any system which would
> not afflict him likewise; that we could not prosper under any
> law which would not also bring its blessings to him. . . .
>
> The conclusion, then, seems to me to be this: The crushing
> burdens which now oppress both races in the South will cause
> each to make an effort to cast them off. They will see a simi-
> larity of cause and a similarity of remedy. They will recognize
> that each should help the other in the work of repealing bad
> laws and enacting good ones. They will become political allies,
> and neither can injure the other without weakening both. It
> will be to the interest of both that each should have justice.
> And on these broad lines of mutual interest, mutual forbear-
> ance, and mutual support the present will be made the
> stepping-stone to future peace and prosperity.[8]

But Watson's proposed alliance never materialized. When Bryan won the 1896 nomination as the candidate of both the Populist and the Democratic parties, allowing him to run on two party tickets simultaneously, Watson was the vice-presidential nominee only on Bryan's Populist ticket. For the Democratic ticket Bryan chose as his running mate a conservative Southerner. And any chance for a populist coalition that spanned the racial gap was put on hold for decades. Watson himself became a harsh racist, as well as anti-Catholic and anti-Semitic, in his later years.

The divisions that crippled Populism in the 1890s continued to cripple reformers right through the 1920s. For evidence one need look no further than the presidential elections of 1924 and 1928. In 1924 it took the Democratic convention no less than 103 ballots to settle on a nominee, because of the bitter division between city and country. Al Smith, the Irish Catholic governor of New York, represented the party's future. At the convention, however, he was opposed by William Gibbs McAdoo, Woodrow Wilson's son-in-law—a corporate lawyer who had reinvented himself, in a way all too familiar today, as a cultural populist. As Arthur M. Schlesinger, Jr., put it, he "[made] himself over in the image of William Jennings Bryan. . . . He deferred to the religious passions of the Bible belt. He even adopted a cautious agnosticism toward the Ku Klux Klan." Indeed the convention rejected—by one vote—a motion to include a denunciation of the Klan in its platform.[9] In the end neither Smith nor McAdoo won the nomination, which went instead to a compromise candidate, John W. Davis of West Virginia. The vice-presidential nomination went to William Jennings Bryan's younger brother. And the ticket, needless to say, went down to ignominious defeat.

Four years later Al Smith easily won the nomination on the first ballot—but the old antagonisms resurfaced almost immediately. One Tennessee Democrat wrote to McAdoo that Smith planned to appeal "to the aliens, who feel that the older America, the America of Anglo-Saxon stock, is a hateful thing which must be overturned and humiliated; to the northern negroes, who lust for social equality and racial dominance; to the Catholics who have been made to believe that they are entitled to the White House, and to the Jews who likewise are to be instilled with the feeling that this is the time for God's chosen people to chastise America yesteryear." During the campaign the Ku Klux Klan stirred up anti-Catholic sentiment—Smith could see crosses burning as his train crossed Oklahoma. In an era when the South was normally solidly Democratic, Smith lost all the border states and five states of the old Confederacy.[10]

In short, during the Long Gilded Age—as in today's America—cultural and racial divisions among those with shared common economic interests prevented the emergence of an effective political challenge to extreme economic inequality. The difference between then and now was that the divisions of the Long Gilded Age were significantly more extreme than they are today. At the same time there were fewer people, even among political leaders, with the vision to see beyond them. This, in turn, brings us to another feature of the Long Gilded Age: the intellectual dominance of conservative, antigovernment ideology.

Conservative Intellectual Dominance

The January 7, 1923, edition of the *New York Times* ran a special article under the banner headline GROWING NATIONAL TAX BURDENS AS MENACE TO NATIONAL WELFARE. The blurb continued, "Rates of Increase in Countries World Over Shown—Federal Taxes Per Capita in United States Six Times as High as Before War—Public Expenditures Big Jump." The article conceded that most of the spending increase of the previous decade had been the result of World War I, but it warned ominously that "when the roaring of the guns ceased public expenditure still continued on a high scale. The result has been that heavy tax burdens remain an enormous drain on the resources of nations." Notably, the piece was presented not as opinion but as news; it presented the results of a study by the National Industrial Conference Board on the evils of excessive taxation, with no suggestion that anyone might disagree with the study's conclusion.

The reality behind the headline, by the way, was a rise in federal spending from 2 percent of GNP before the war to 4.7 percent afterward. Most of this increase was war related: even after the "roaring of the guns ceased," there was wartime debt to be serviced and veterans' benefits to be paid. Non-war-related spending had indeed risen, but only from 0.6 percent of GNP before the war to 0.9 percent afterward. And by the late 1920s, after a decade of renewed Republican political dominance, non-war-related spending as a percentage of GNP was back down almost to prewar levels.[11]

Today liberals complain about the success of movement conservatives in turning antigovernment ideology into conventional wisdom. This book will contain a fair amount of that kind of complaining in later chapters. In the Long Gilded Age, however, the tyranny of antigovernment ideology was far worse, and closer to the desired results of today's conservative propagandists. It was an era in which respectable opinion simply assumed, as a matter of course, that taxation had devastating economic effects, that any effort to mitigate poverty and inequality was highly irresponsible, and that anyone who suggested that unmitigated capitalism was unjust and could be improved was a dangerous radical, contaminated by European ideas.

We shouldn't ignore the fact that there were a fair number of genuinely dangerous radicals around. In particular there were surely far more communists and anarchists in America during the Long Gilded Age, particularly after the Russian Revolution, than there are today. There weren't enough to make a revolution, but there were enough to give conservatives yet another stick with which to beat back reform. In 1919, after a bomb exploded in front of the home of A. Mitchell Palmer, the attorney general, the U.S. government began the infamous Palmer raids, arresting thousands suspected of radical activity. Like the paranoia that gripped the nation for a while after 9/11, the Red Scare after World War I had the incidental effect of discrediting or intimidating ordinary liberals, people who believed that capitalism could be made more just without being abolished. And there were few enough of those in any case.

This was a peculiarly American blind spot. As early as 1881 Bismarck described the rationale for what we would now call a welfare state, which he saw as a way to pacify the lower classes and secure the kaiser's rule. The government, he said, "should cultivate the view also among the propertyless classes of the population, those who are the most numerous and the least educated, that the state is not only an institution of necessity but also one of welfare. By recognizable and direct advantages they must be led to look upon the state not as an agency devised solely for the protection of the better-situated classes of society but also as one serving their needs and interests."[12] With Bismarck's Germany leading the way, Europeans had begun to develop New Deal–like policies well before the U.S. political system was prepared to contemplate anything of the sort. In particular, Britain introduced a limited old-age insurance system in 1908 and a health insurance system in 1911.[13] Before World War I, Britain, Germany, and France—which developed its own distinctive early welfare state—were spending more on social programs, as a share of GDP, than the United States would until the late 1930s.

But in the United States the gospel of free enterprise remained dominant, so much so that it was one more factor crippling the

Democratic Party. Al Smith's defeat in 1928 owed a lot to bigotry. But the populists in his party had another big reason to be disillusioned: Smith's first act after being nominated was, in effect, to declare his fealty to the ruling economic ideology. He chose as his campaign manager John J. Raskob, a Republican industrialist whose only apparent point of agreement with liberals was his opposition to Prohibition, and appointed four more millionaires to top campaign positions. During the campaign Smith actually tried to win business support by portraying Herbert Hoover as someone dangerously inclined to impose government regulations on business. In effect Smith ran as a Bourbon Democrat. Like earlier Bourbons he was financially competitive: The Democrats spent $5.3 million, compared with $6.3 million for the Republicans. But with nothing distinctive to offer, Smith suffered a crushing defeat.[14]

Smith receded further into conservative dogma as the years went by. In his doomed attempt to gain the 1932 Democratic nomination, he was the voice of business, the opponent of change and reform. H. L. Mencken, characteristically, summed it up most pithily: "His association with the rich has apparently wobbled him and changed him. He has become a golf player."[15]

The Roots of the New Deal

To a modern observer the political mood in America after the 1928 election, when conservatives seemed everywhere triumphant and liberalism a lost cause, evokes more recent memories: the mood after the 2004 election, when commentators rushed to declare the death of liberalism and the birth of a permanent Republican majority. Actually, the commentators of 1928 seemed to have much greater justification: Herbert Hoover beat Al Smith in the popular vote by 58 to 41 percent. Even New York went for Hoover, although Franklin Delano Roosevelt managed to eke out a paper-thin victory in the gubernatorial race, winning by only 25,000 out of 2.2 million votes. It seemed as if the Long Gilded Age would go on forever.

What changed everything, of course, was the Great Depression, which made the New Deal possible. In retrospect, however, we can see that modest moves toward a more equal society were already under way before the depression struck—not at the federal but at the state level. As early as 1901 Maryland passed a workers' compensation law, entitling workers injured on the job to payments financed by mandatory employer contributions, only to have it declared unconstitutional. New York's 1910 law was similarly thrown out by the courts. But between 1911 and 1913 thirteen states managed to create basic workers' compensation systems. Over the same period a number of states created basic aid programs for widowed mothers and children.

Old-age support followed. In 1923 Montana, Pennsylvania, and Nevada passed old-age-pension laws. In the latter two states the laws were swiftly struck down by the courts. Nonetheless, by 1928 eleven states had some kind of retirement program, that is, some form of precursor to Social Security. And at the end of the decade, as the depression began to be felt, there was a push for unemployment insurance, with Wisconsin creating the first program in 1932. These programs had modest funding and covered few people; nonetheless they did establish the principle of social insurance, and also generated experience on which the New Deal could draw.

What is remarkable, in a way, is how many years of depression it took before the federal government was prepared to take similar action. Herbert Hoover had made his name with postwar relief efforts in Europe, yet he dug in his heels against any major attempt to provide aid at home in the face of national crisis.

Eventually, however, there was both the political will and the leadership for a true liberal program. Where Bryan, whose last major career act was as denouncer of the theory of evolution at the Scopes trial, had been the wrong man to change Gilded Age America, Franklin Delano Roosevelt was very much the right man at the right time. And under his leadership the nature of American society changed vastly for the better.

3

THE GREAT COMPRESSION

I n 1953 *Time* magazine, declaring that "the real news of the nation's political future and its economic direction lies in people who seldom see a reporter," sent one of its contributing editors, Alvin Josephy, on a national tour. His mission was to get a sense of America.

The portrait he painted bore little resemblance to the America of 1929. Where the America of the twenties had been a land of extremes, of vast wealth for a few but hard times for many, America in the fifties was all of a piece. "Even in the smallest towns and most isolated areas," the *Time* report began, "the U.S. is wearing a very prosperous, middle-class suit of clothes. . . . People are not growing wealthy, but more of them than ever before are getting along." And where the America of the twenties had been a land of political polarization, of sharp divides between the dominant right and the embattled left, America in the fifties was a place of political compromise: "Republicans and Democrats have a surprising sameness of outlook and political thinking." Unions had become staid establishment institutions. Farmers cheerfully told the man from *Time* that if farm subsidies were socialism, then they were socialists.[1]

Though the *Time* editor's impression that America had become a middle-class, middle-of-the-road nation wasn't based on hard evidence, many others shared the same impression. When John Kenneth Galbraith called his critique of postwar American values *The Affluent Society*, he was being sardonic; yet its starting point was the assertion that most Americans could afford the necessities of life. A few years later Michael Harrington wrote *The Other America* to remind people that not all Americans were, in fact, members of the middle class—but a large part of the reason he felt such a book was needed was because poverty was no longer a majority condition, and hence tended to disappear from view.

As we'll see, the numbers bear out what all these observers thought they saw. America in the 1950s *was* a middle-class society, to a far greater extent than it had been in the 1920s—or than it is today. Social injustice remained pervasive: Segregation still ruled in the South, and both overt racism and overt discrimination against women were the norm throughout the country. Yet ordinary workers and their families had good reason to feel that they were sharing in the nation's prosperity as never before. And, on the other side, the rich were a lot less rich than they had been a generation earlier.

The economic historians Claudia Goldin and Robert Margo call the narrowing of income gaps that took place in the United States between the twenties and the fifties—the sharp reduction in the gap between the rich and the working class, and the reduction in wage differentials among workers—"the Great Compression." Their deliberate use of a phrase that echoes "the Great Depression" is appropriate: Like the depression, the narrowing of income gaps was a defining event in American history, something that transformed the nature of our society and politics. Yet where the Great Depression lives on in our memory, the Great Compression has been largely forgotten. The achievement of a middle-class society, which once seemed an impossible dream, came to be taken for granted.

Now we live in a second Gilded Age, as the middle-class society of the postwar era rapidly vanishes. The conventional wisdom of our time is that while this is a bad thing, it's the result of forces beyond our control. But the story of the Great Compression is a powerful antidote to fatalism, a demonstration that political reform can create a more equitable distribution of income—and, in the process, create a healthier climate for democracy.

Let me expand on that a bit. In the thirties, as today, a key line of conservative defense against demands to do something about inequality was the claim that nothing *can* be done—that is, the claim that no policies can appreciably raise the share of national income going to working families, or at least that none can do so without wrecking the economy. Yet somehow Franklin Delano Roosevelt and Harry Truman managed to preside over a dramatic downward redistribution of income and wealth that made Americans far more equal than before—and not only wasn't the economy wrecked by this redistribution, the Great Compression set the stage for a great generation-long economic boom. If they could do it then, we should be able to repeat their achievement.

But how did they do it? I'll turn to possible explanations in a little while. But first let's take a closer look at the American scene after the Great Compression, circa 1955.

Portrait of a Middle-Class Nation

By the mid-1950s, Long Island's Gold Coast—the North Shore domain of the wealthy during the Long Gilded Age, and the financial hub of the Republican Party—was no more. Some of the mansions had been sold for a pittance, then either torn down to make room for middle-class tract housing or adapted for institutional use (country clubs, nursing homes, and religious retreats still occupy many of the great estates.) Others had been given away to non-profit institutions or the government, to avoid estate tax.

"What killed the legendary estates?" asks *Newsday*, the Long Island newspaper, in its guide to the structures still standing. Its answer is more or less right: "A triple whammy dealt by the advent of a federal income tax, the financial losses of the Great Depression and changes in the U.S. economic structure that made domestic service a less attractive job for the legions of workers needed to keep this way of life humming."[2]

If the Gold Coast mansions symbolized Long Island in the Long Gilded Age, there was no question what took its place in the 1950s: Levittown, the quintessential postwar suburb, which broke ground in 1947.

William Levitt's houses were tiny by the standards of today's McMansions: the original two-bedroom model had only 750 square feet of living space and no basement. But they were private, stand-alone homes, pre-equipped with washing machines and other home appliances, offering their inhabitants a standard of living previously considered out of reach for working-class Americans. And their suburban location presumed that ordinary families had their own cars, something that hadn't been true in 1929 but was definitely true by the 1950s.

Levitt's achievement was partly based on the application to civilian housing of construction techniques that had been used during the war to build army barracks. But the reason Levitt thought, correctly, that he would find a mass market for his houses was that there had been a radical downward shift of the economy's center of gravity. The rich no longer had anything like the purchasing power they'd had in 1929; ordinary workers had far more purchasing power than ever before.

Making statistical comparisons between the twenties and the fifties is a bit tricky, because before the advent of the welfare state the U.S. government didn't feel the need to collect much data on who earned what, and how people made ends meet. When FDR spoke in his second inaugural address of "one third of a nation ill-housed, ill-clad, ill-nourished," he was making a guess, not reporting an official statistic. In fact the United States didn't have a formal official definition of poverty, let alone an official estimate of the number of people below the poverty line, until one was created in 1964 to help Lyndon Johnson formulate goals for the Great Society. But despite the limitations of the data, it's clear that between the twenties and the fifties America became, to an unprecedented extent, a middle-class nation.

Part of the great narrowing of income differentials that took place between the twenties and the fifties involved leveling downward: the rich were significantly poorer in the fifties than they had been in the twenties. And I literally mean poorer: We're not just talking about relative impoverishment, a failure to keep up with income growth further down the scale, but about a large absolute decline in purchasing power. By the mid-fifties the real after-tax incomes of the richest 1 percent of Americans were probably 20 or 30 percent lower than they had been a generation earlier. And the real incomes of the really rich—say, those in the top tenth of one percent—were less than half what they had been in the twenties. (The real *pre*tax income of the top 1 percent was about the same in the mid-fifties as it was in 1929, while the pretax income of the top 0.1 percent had fallen about 40 percent. At the same time, income tax rates on the rich had risen sharply.[3])

Meanwhile the real income of the median family had more or less doubled since 1929.[4] And most families didn't just have higher income, they had more security too. Employers offered new benefits, like health insurance and retirement plans: Before the war only a small minority of Americans had health insurance, but by 1955 more than 60 percent had at least the most basic form of health insurance, coverage for the expenses of hospitalization.[5] And the federal government backed up the new security of private employment with crucial benefits such as unemployment insurance for laid-off workers and Social Security for retirees.

So working Americans were far better off in the fifties than they had been in the twenties, while the economic elite was worse off. And even among working Americans economic differences had narrowed. The available data show that by the 1950s unskilled and semiskilled workers, like the people manning assembly lines, had closed much of the pay gap with more skilled workers, like machinists. And employees with formal education, like lawyers and engineers, were paid much less of a premium over manual laborers than they had received in the twenties—or than they receive today.

Economic statistics are useful, of course, only to the extent that they shed light on the human condition. But these statistics do tell a human tale, that of a vast economic democratization of American society.

On one side the majority of Americans were able, for the first time, to afford a decent standard of living. I know that "decent" isn't a well-defined term, but here's what I mean: In the twenties the technology to provide the major comforts and conveniences of modern life already existed. A modern American transported back to, say, the time of Abraham Lincoln would be horrified at the roughness of life, no matter how much money he had. But a modern American transported back to the late 1920s and given a high enough income would find life by and large tolerable. The problem was that most Americans in the twenties couldn't afford to live that tolerable life. To take the most basic comfort: Most rural Americans still didn't have indoor plumbing, and many urban Americans had to share facilities with other families. Washing machines existed, but weren't standard in the home. Private automobiles and private telephones existed, but most families didn't have them. In 1936 the Gallup organization predicted a landslide victory for Alf Landon, the Republican presidential candidate. How did Gallup get it so wrong? Well, the poll was based on a telephone survey, but at the time only about a third of U.S. residences had a home phone—and those people who didn't have phones tended to be Roosevelt supporters. And so on down the line.

But by the fifties, although there were still rural Americans who relied on outhouses, and urban families living in tenements with toilets down the hall, they were a distinct minority. By 1955 a majority of American families owned a car. And 70 percent of residences had telephones.

On the other side F. Scott Fitzgerald's remark that the rich "are different from you and me" has never, before or since, been less true than it was in the generation that followed World War II. By the fifties, very few Americans were able to afford a lifestyle that put them in a different material universe from that occupied by the middle class. The rich might have had bigger houses than most people, but they could no longer afford to live in vast mansions—in particular, they couldn't afford the servants necessary to maintain those mansions. The traditional differences in dress between the rich and everyone else had largely vanished, partly because ordinary workers could now afford to wear (and clean) good clothes, partly because the rich could no longer afford to dress in a style that required legions of servants to help them get into and out of their wardrobes. Even the traditional rich man's advantage in mobility—to this day high-end stores are said to cater to the "carriage trade"—had vanished now that most people had cars.

I don't think it's romanticizing to say that all this contributed to a new sense of dignity among ordinary Americans. Everything we know about America during the Long Gilded Age makes it clear that it was, despite the nation's democratic ideology, a very class-conscious society—a place where the rich considered themselves the workers' "betters," and where workers lived in fear (and resentment) of the "bosses." But in postwar America—and here I can speak from my personal memory of the society in which I grew up, as well as what we can learn from what people said and wrote—much of that class consciousness was gone. Postwar American society had its poor, but the truly rich were rare and made little impact on society. A worker protected by a good union, as many were, had as secure a job and often nearly as high an income as a highly trained professional. And we all lived material lives that were no more different from one another than a Cadillac was from a Chevy: One life might be more luxurious than another, but there were no big differences in where people could go and what they could do.

But how did that democratic society come into being?

What Happened to the Rich?

Simon Kuznets, a Russian immigrant to the United States who won the Nobel Prize in Economics in 1971, more or less invented modern economic statistics. During the 1930s he created America's National Income Accounts, the system of numbers—including gross domestic product—that lets us keep track of the nation's income. By the 1950s Kuznets had turned his attention from the overall size of national income to its distribution. And in spite of the limitations of the data, he was able to show that the distribution of income in postwar America was much more equal than it had been before the Great Depression. But was this change the result of politics or of impersonal market forces?

In general economists, schooled in the importance of the invisible hand, tend to be skeptical about the ability of governments to shape the economy. As a result economists tend to look, in the first instance, to market forces as the cause of large changes in the distribution of income. And Kuznets's name is often associated (rather unfairly) with the view that there is a natural cycle of inequality driven by market forces. This natural cycle has come to be known as the "Kuznets curve."

Here's how the Kuznets curve is supposed to work: In the early stages of development, the story goes, investment opportunities for those who have money multiply, while wages are held down by an influx of cheap rural labor to the cities. The result is that as a country industrializes, inequality rises: An elite of wealthy industrialists emerges, while ordinary workers remain mired in poverty. In other words a period of vast inequality, like America's Long Gilded Age, is the natural product of development.

But eventually capital becomes more abundant, the flow of workers from the farms dries up, wages begin to rise, and profits level off or fall. Prosperity becomes widespread, and the economy becomes broadly middle class.

Until the 1980s most American economists, to the extent that they thought about the issue at all, believed that this was America's story over the course of the nineteenth and twentieth centuries. The Long Gilded Age, they thought, was a stage through which the country had to pass; the middle-class society that followed, they believed, was the natural, inevitable happy end state of the process of economic development.

But by the mid-1980s it became clear that the story wasn't over, that inequality was rising again. While many economists believe that this, too, is the inexorable result of market forces, such as technological changes that place a growing premium on skill, new concerns about inequality led to a look back at the equalization that took place during an earlier generation. And guess what: The more carefully one looks at that equalization, the less it looks like a gradual response to impersonal market forces, and the more it looks like a sudden change, brought on in large part by a change in the political balance of power.

The easiest place to see both the suddenness of the change and the probable importance of political factors is to look at the incomes of the wealthy—the top 1 percent or less of the income distribution.

We know more about the historical incomes of the wealthy than we know about the rest of the population, because the wealthy have been paying income taxes—and, in the process, providing the federal government with information about their financial status— since 1913. What tax data suggest is that there was no trend toward declining inequality until the mid-1930s or even later: When FDR delivered his second inaugural address in 1937, the one that spoke of one-third of a nation still in poverty, there was little evidence that the rich had any less dominant an economic position than they had had before World War I. But a mere decade later the rich had clearly been demoted: The sharp decline in incomes at the top, which we have documented for the 1950s, had already happened by 1946 or 1947. The relative impoverishment of the economic elite didn't happen gradually—it happened quite suddenly,

This sudden decline in the fortunes of the wealthy can be explained in large part with just one word: taxes.

Here's how to think about what happened. In prewar America

the sources of high incomes were different from what they are now. Where today's wealthy receive much of their income from employment (think of CEOs and their stock-option grants), in the twenties matters were simpler: The rich were rich because of the returns on the capital they owned. And since most income from capital went to a small fraction of the population—in 1929, 70 percent of stock dividends went to only 1 percent of Americans—the division of income between the rich and everyone else was largely determined by the division of national income between wages and returns to capital.

So you might think that the sharp fall in the share of the wealthy in American national income must have reflected a big shift in the distribution of income away from capital and toward labor. But it turns out that this didn't happen. In 1955 labor received 69 percent of the pretax income earned in the corporate sector, versus 31 percent for capital; this was barely different from the 67–33 split in 1929.

But while the division of *pre*tax income between capital and labor barely changed between the twenties and the fifties, the division of *after*-tax income between those who derived their income mainly from capital and those who mainly relied on wages changed radically.

In the twenties, taxes had been a minor factor for the rich. The top income tax rate was only 24 percent, and because the inheritence tax on even the largest estates was only 20 percent, wealthy dynasties had little difficulty maintaining themselves. But with the coming of the New Deal, the rich started to face taxes that were not only vastly higher than those of the twenties, but high by today's standards. The top income tax rate (currently only 35 percent) rose to 63 percent during the first Roosevelt administration, and 79 percent in the second. By the mid-fifties, as the United States faced the expenses of the Cold War, it had risen to 91 percent.

Moreover, these higher personal taxes came on capital income that had been significantly reduced not by a fall in the profits corporations earned but in the profits they were allowed to keep: The average federal tax on corporate profits rose from less than 14 percent in 1929 to more than 45 percent in 1955.

And one more thing: Not only did those who depended on income from capital find much of that income taxed away, they found it increasingly difficult to pass their wealth on to their children. The top estate tax rate rose from 20 percent to 45, then 60, then 70, and finally 77 percent. Partly as a result the ownership of wealth became significantly less concentrated: The richest 0.1 percent of Americans owned more than 20 percent of the nation's wealth in 1929, but only around 10 percent in the mid-1950s.

So what happened to the rich? Basically the New Deal taxed away much, perhaps most, of their income. No wonder FDR was viewed as a traitor to his class.

Workers and Unions

While the rich were the biggest victims of the Great Compression, blue-collar workers—above all, industrial workers—were the biggest beneficiaries. The three decades that followed the Great Compression, from the mid-forties to the mid-seventies, were the golden age of manual labor.

In fact, by the end of the 1950s American men with a high school degree but no college were earning about as much, adjusted for inflation, as workers with similar qualifications make today. And their relative status was, of course, much higher: Blue-collar workers with especially good jobs often made as much or more than many college-educated professionals.

Why were times so good for blue-collar workers? To some extent they were helped by the state of the world economy: U.S. manufacturing companies were able to pay high wages in part because they faced little foreign competition. They were also helped by a scarcity of labor created by the severe immigration restrictions imposed by the Immigration Act of 1924.

But if there's a single reason blue-collar workers did so much better in the fifties than they had in the twenties, it was the rise of unions.

At the end of the twenties, the American union movement was in retreat. Major organizing attempts failed, partly because employers successfully broke strikes, partly because the government consistently came down on the side of employers, arresting union organizers and deporting them if, as was often the case, they were foreign born. Union membership, which had surged during World War I, fell sharply thereafter. By 1930 only a bit more than 10 percent of nonagricultural workers were unionized, a number roughly comparable to the unionized share of private-sector workers today. Union membership continued to decline for the first few years of the depression, reaching a low point in 1933.

But under the New Deal unions surged in both membership and power. Union membership tripled from 1933 to 1938, then nearly doubled again by 1947. At the end of World War II more than a third of nonfarm workers were members of unions—and many others were paid wages that, explicitly or implicitly, were set either to match union wages or to keep workers happy enough to forestall union organizers.

Why did union membership surge? That's the subject of a serious debate among economists and historians.

One story about the surge in union membership gives most of

the credit (or blame, depending on your perspective) to the New Deal. Until the New Deal the federal government was a reliable ally of employers seeking to suppress union organizers or crush existing unions. Under FDR it became, instead, a protector of workers' right to organize. Roosevelt's statement on signing the Fair Labor Relations Act in 1935, which established the National Labor Relations Board, couldn't have been clearer: "This act defines, as a part of our substantive law, the right of self-organization of employees in industry for the purpose of collective bargaining, and provides methods by which the government can safeguard that legal right." Not surprisingly many historians argue that this reversal in public policy toward unions caused the great union surge.

An alternative story, however, places less emphasis on the role of government policy and more on the internal dynamic of the union movement itself. Richard Freeman, a prominent labor economist at Harvard, points out that the surge in unionization in the thirties mirrored an earlier surge between 1910 and 1920, and that there were similar surges in other Western countries in the thirties; this suggests that FDR and the New Deal may not have played a crucial role. Freeman argues that what really happened in the thirties was a two-stage process that was largely independent of government action. First the Great Depression, which led many employers to reduce wages, gave new strength to the union movement as angry workers organized to fight pay cuts. Then the rising strength of the union movement became self-reinforcing, as workers who had already joined unions provided crucial support in the form of financial aid, picketers, and so on to other workers seeking to organize.

It's not clear that we have to decide between these stories. The same factors that mobilized workers also helped provide the New Deal with the political power it needed to change federal policy. Meanwhile, even if FDR didn't single-handedly create the conditions for a powerful union movement, the government's shift from agent of the bosses to protector of the workers surely must have helped the union drive.

Whatever the relative weight of politics, the depression, and the dynamics of organizing in the union surge, everything we know about unions says that their new power was a major factor in the creation of a middle-class society. According to a wide range of scholarly research, unions have two main effects relevant to the Great Compression. First, unions raise average wages for their membership; they also, indirectly and to a lesser extent, raise wages for similar workers, even if they aren't represented by unions, as nonunionized employers try to diminish the appeal of union drives to their workers. As a result unions tend to reduce the gap in earnings between blue-collar workers and higher-paid occupations, such as managers. Second, unions tend to narrow income gaps among blue-collar workers, by negotiating bigger wage increases for their worst-paid members than for their best-paid members. And nonunion employers, seeking to forestall union organizers, tend to echo this effect. In other words the known effects of unions on wages are exactly what we see in the Great Compression: a rise in the wages of blue-collar workers compared with managers and professionals, and a narrowing of wage differentials among blue-collar workers themselves.

Still, unionization by itself wasn't enough to bring about the full extent of the compression. The full transformation needed the special circumstances of World War II.

The Wages of War

Under ordinary circumstances the government in a market economy like the United States can, at most, influence wages; it doesn't set them directly. But for almost four years in the 1940s important parts of the U.S. economy were more or less directly controlled by the government, as part of the war effort. And the government used its influence to produce a major equalization of income.

The National War Labor Board was actually created by Woodrow Wilson in 1918. Its mandate was to arbitrate disputes between labor and capital, in order to avoid strikes that might disrupt the war effort. In practice the board favored labor's interests—protecting the right of workers to organize and bargain collectively, pushing for a living wage. Union membership almost doubled over a short period.

After World War I the war labor board was abolished, and the federal government returned to its traditional pro-employer stance. As already noted, labor soon found itself in retreat, and the wartime gains were rolled back.

But FDR reestablished the National War Labor Board little more than a month after Pearl Harbor, this time with more power. The war created huge inflationary pressures, leading to government price controls on many key commodities. These controls would have been unsustainable if the labor shortages created by the war's demands led to huge wage increases, so wages in many key national industries were also placed under federal controls. Any increase in those wages had to be approved by the NWLB. In effect the government found itself not just arbitrating disputes but dictating wage rates to the private sector.

Not surprisingly, given the Roosevelt administration's values, the rules established by the NWLB tended to raise the wages of low-paid workers more than those of highly paid employees. Following a directive by Roosevelt that substandard wages should be raised, employers were given the freedom to raise any wage to forty cents an hour (the equivalent of about five dollars an hour today) without approval, or to fifty cents an hour with approval from the local office of the NWLB. By contrast increases above that level had to be approved by Washington, so the system had an inherent tendency to raise wages for low-paid workers faster than for the highly paid. The NWLB also set pay brackets for each occupation, and employers were free to raise any worker's wage to the bottom of the pay bracket for the worker's occupation. Again this favored wage increases for the low paid, but not for those with higher wage rates. Finally the NWLB allowed increases that eliminated differences in wages across plants—again raising the wages of those who were paid least.

As Goldin and Margo say, "Most of the criteria for wage increases used by the NWLB served to compress wages across and within industries." So during the brief period when the U.S. government was in a position to determine many workers' wages more or less directly, it used that power to make America a more equal society.

And the amazing thing is that the changes stuck.

Equality and the Postwar Boom

Suppose that Democrats in today's Congress were to propose a rerun of the policies that produced the Great Compression: huge increases in taxes on the rich, support for a vast expansion of union power, a period of wage controls used to greatly narrow pay differentials, and so on. What would conventional wisdom say about the effects of such a program?

First, there would be general skepticism that these policies would have much effect on inequality, at least in the long run. Standard economic theory tells us that attempts to defy the law of supply and demand usually fail; even if the government were to use wartime powers to decree a more equal structure of wages, the old wage gaps would reassert themselves as soon as the controls were lifted.

Second, there would be widespread assertions—and not only from the hard right—that such radical equalizing policies would wreak destruction on the economy by destroying incentives. High taxes on profits would lead to a collapse of business investment; high taxes on high incomes would lead to a collapse of entrepreneurship and individual initiative; powerful unions would demand excessive wage increases, leading to mass unemployment, and prevent productivity increases. One way to summarize this is to say that the changes in U.S. policies during the Great Compression look like an extreme form of the policies that are widely blamed today for "Eurosclerosis," the relatively low employment and (to a lesser extent) economic growth in many Western European economies.

Now, maybe these dire predictions would come true if we tried to replicate the Great Compression today. But the fact is that none of the bad consequences one might have expected from a drastic equalization of incomes actually materialized after World War II. On the contrary, the Great Compression succeeded in equalizing incomes for a long period—more than thirty years. And the era of equality was also a time of unprecedented prosperity, which we have never been able to recapture.

To get a sense of just how well things went after the Great Compression, let me suggest dividing postwar U.S. economic history into three eras: the postwar boom, from 1947 to 1973; the time of troubles, when oil crises and stagflation wracked the U.S. economy, from 1973 to 1980; and the modern era of reasonable growth with rising inequality, from 1980 until the present. (Why start in 1947? For two reasons: The Great Compression had been largely accomplished by then, and good data mostly start from that year.)

During the postwar boom the real income of the typical family roughly doubled, from about $22,000 in today's prices to $44,000. That's a growth rate of 2.7 percent per year. And incomes all through the income distribution grew at about the same rate, preserving the relatively equal distribution created by the Great Compression.

The time of troubles temporarily brought growth in median income to a halt. Growth resumed once inflation had been brought under control—but for the typical family even good times have never come close to matching the postwar boom. Since 1980 median family income has risen only about 0.7 percent a year. Even during the best of times—the Reagan-era "morning in America" expansion from 1982 to 1989, the Clinton-era boom from 1993 to 2000—family income grew more slowly than it did for a full generation after the Great Compression.

As always these are just numbers, providing at best an indication of what really happened in peoples' lives. But is there any question that the postwar generation was a time when almost everyone in America felt that living standards were rising rapidly, a time in which ordinary working Americans felt that they were achieving a level of prosperity beyond their parents' wildest dreams? And is there any question that the way we feel about the economy today is, at best, far more cautious—that most Americans today feel better off in some ways, but worse off in others, than they were a couple of decades ago?

Some people find the reality of how well the U.S. economy did in the wake of the Great Compression so disturbing, so contrary to their beliefs about the way the world works, that they've actually rewritten history to eliminate the postwar boom. Thus Larry Kudlow, who preaches his supply-side doctrine every weekday night on CNBC, tells us that thanks to Ronald Reagan's tax cuts, "for the first time since the post–Civil War period (but for the brief

Coolidge-Mellon period in the 1920s), the American economic system became the envy of the world." I guess the prosperity reported by that *Time* editor, not to mention all the available economic data, was simply an illusion.

But it was no illusion; the boom was real. The Great Compression, far from destroying American prosperity, seems if anything to have invigorated the economy. If that tale runs counter to what textbook economics says should have happened, well, there's something wrong with textbook economics. But that's a subject for a later chapter.

For now let's simply accept that during the thirties and forties liberals managed to achieve a remarkable reduction in income inequality, with almost entirely positive effects on the economy as a whole. The men and women behind that achievement offer today's liberals an object lesson in the difference leadership can make.

But who were these men and women, and why were they in a position both to make such large changes in our society and to make those changes stick?

THE POLITICS OF THE
WELFARE STATE

lmost every American of a certain age knows the photo: A grinning Harry Truman holds up an early edition of the *Chicago Daily Tribune*, bearing the banner headline DEWEY DEFEATS TRUMAN. No, he didn't. Truman's 1948 election victory, in the face of polls that seemed to guarantee a landslide for Dewey, was the greatest political upset in U.S. history.

Truman's come-from-behind victory has become an iconic moment in American political history, along with stories of how Truman's supporters on the campaign trail yelled, "Give 'em hell, Harry!" But I'm sure that very few Americans could tell you whom Harry was being urged to give hell, and what the hell was about. To the extent that Truman is remembered today, it's mostly as a foreign policy leader: the man who oversaw the creation of the Marshall Plan and the strategy of containment, the man who stood up to Stalin in Berlin and in Korea, and set America on the path to eventual victory in the Cold War.

In 1948, however, foreign policy wasn't a key campaign issue, partly because the Cold War hadn't started in earnest, partly because Republicans—torn between fervent anticommunism and their traditional isolationism—hadn't settled on a foreign policy position. The issue that preoccupied the electorate in 1948 was the fear that Republicans would try to undo FDR's domestic achievements. Thomas Dewey tried to soothe the electorate by campaigning on Yogi Berra–like platitudes, including the declaration that "Your future still lies ahead of you." But Truman turned the election into a referendum on the New Deal by focusing his attacks on the Republican-controlled Congress.

In 1948 that Congress was engaged in an attempt to roll back FDR's New Deal. The de facto leader of the Republicans in Congress was Sen. Robert Taft, and Taft, sometimes referred to as "Mr. Republican," was deeply opposed to the New Deal, which he regarded as "socialistic." This was more than ideological posturing: After Republicans gained control of Congress in 1946, Taft pushed through the Taft-Hartley Act, significantly rolling back the National Labor Relations Act of 1935, which was a key ingredient in the surge in union membership and power under the New Deal. Thus in 1948 voters had good reason to believe that a Republican victory, which would give them control of both Congress and the White House, would lead to a significant U-turn in the policies that produced the Great Compression.

By 1952, when the Republicans finally did regain the White House, much less was at stake. By that time Republican leaders had, as a matter of political necessity, accepted the institutions created by the New Deal as permanent features of the American scene. "Should any political party attempt to abolish social security, unemployment insurance, and eliminate labor laws and farm programs," wrote Dwight Eisenhower in a 1954 letter to his brother Edgar, "you would not hear of that party again in our political history. There is a tiny splinter group, of course, that believes you can do these things. Among them are H. L. Hunt (you possibly know his background), a few other Texas oil millionaires, and an occasional politician or business man from other areas. Their number is negligible and they are stupid."[1]

How did ideas and programs that were considered dangerously radical in the 1930s become the essence of respectability in the 1950s, with only a "tiny splinter group" calling for their repeal? To answer that question we need to look both at how changes in American society altered the political environment and at how the political parties responded to the new environment.

From Radicalism to Respectability

In the 1930s the New Deal was considered very radical indeed—and the New Dealers themselves were willing to use the language of class warfare. To read, or, better yet, listen to Franklin Delano Roosevelt's Madison Square Garden speech (the recording is available on the Web), delivered on the eve of the 1936 election, is to be reminded how cautious, how timid and well-mannered latter-day liberalism has become. Today those who want to increase the minimum wage or raise taxes on the rich take pains to reassure the public that they have nothing against wealth, that they're not proposing class warfare. But FDR let the malefactors of great wealth have it with both barrels:

> We had to struggle with the old enemies of peace—business
> and financial monopoly, speculation, reckless banking, class
> antagonism, sectionalism, war profiteering.

They had begun to consider the Government of the United
States as a mere appendage to their own affairs. We know now
that Government by organized money is just as dangerous as
Government by organized mob.

Never before in all our history have these forces been so
united against one candidate as they stand today. They are
unanimous in their hate for me—and I welcome their hatred.

FDR wasn't exaggerating when he said that the plutocrats hated
him—and they had very good reasons for their hatred. As I documented in chapter 3, the New Deal imposed a heavy tax burden on
corporations and the wealthy, fostered the growth of unions, and
oversaw a narrowing in income inequality that included a substantial fall in after-tax incomes at the top.

But a funny thing happened over the twenty years that followed
the Madison Square Garden speech. Thanks in large part to Truman's 1948 victory, New Deal policies remained in place: unions
remained powerful for several more decades, and taxes on corporations and the rich were even higher during the Eisenhower years
than they had been under FDR. Yet by the mid-fifties support for
the continuing existence of the policies that inspired such hatred
from "organized money"—in the Madison Square Garden speech
FDR singled out Social Security and unemployment insurance in
particular as programs smeared by the plutocrats—had become
the very definition of political moderation.

This transformation partly reflected shifts in demography and
other factors that favored the continuation of the welfare state. I'll
get to those shifts in a moment. But first let me talk briefly about
an enduring aspect of political economy that made the New Deal
extremely hard to achieve but relatively easy to defend: the innate
and generally rational conservatism of voters—not conservatism in

the sense of right-wing views, but in the sense of reluctance to support big changes in government policies unless the existing policies are obviously failing. In modern times we've seen that type of status-quo conservatism bring projects of both Democrats and Republicans to grief: Clinton's attempt to reform health care and Bush's attempt to privatize Social Security both failed in large part because voters feared the unknown.

In the 1920s status-quo conservatism helped block liberal reforms. Any proposal for higher taxes on the rich and increased benefits for workers and the poor, any suggestion of changing labor law in a way that would make unionization easier, was attacked on the grounds that the would-be reformers were irresponsible people who just didn't understand how the world worked—that their proposals, if adopted, would destroy the economy. Even FDR was to some extent a prisoner of the conventional wisdom, writing, "Too good to be true—you can't get something for nothing" in the margin of a book that, anticipating Keynes, called for deficit spending to support the economy during recessions.[2]

Once in power—and less inclined to dismiss radical ideas—FDR was faced with the task of persuading the public to reject conventional wisdom and accept radically new policies. He was able to overcome voters' natural conservatism thanks largely to accidents of history. First, the economic catastrophe of 1929–33 shattered the credibility of the old elite and its ideology, and the recovery that began in 1933, incomplete though it was, lent credibility to New Deal reforms. "We have always known that heedless self-interest was bad morals; now we know that it is bad economics," declared FDR in his second inaugural address. Second, World War II created conditions under which large-scale government intervention in the economy was clearly necessary, sweeping aside skepticism about radical measures. So by the time Eisenhower wrote that letter to his brother, the New Deal institutions were no longer considered radical innovations; they were part of the normal fabric of American life.

Of course it wouldn't have played out that way if the pre–New Deal conventional wisdom had been right—if taxing the rich, providing Social Security and unemployment benefits, and enhancing worker bargaining power had been disastrous for the economy. But the Great Compression was, in fact, followed by the greatest sustained economic boom in U.S. history. Moreover the Roosevelt administration demonstrated that one of the standard arguments against large-scale intervention in the economy—that it would inevitably lead to equally large-scale corruption—wasn't true. In retrospect it's startling just how clean the New Deal's record was. FDR presided over a huge expansion of federal spending, including highly discretionary spending by the Works Progress Administration. Yet the popular image of public relief, widely regarded as corrupt before the New Deal, actually improved markedly.

The New Deal's probity wasn't an accident. New Deal officials made almost a fetish out of policing their programs against potential corruption. In particular FDR created a powerful "division of progress investigation" to investigate complaints of malfeasance in the WPA. This division proved so effective that a later congressional investigation couldn't find a single serious irregularity it had overlooked.[3]

This dedication to honest government wasn't a sign of Roosevelt's personal virtue; rather it reflected a political imperative. FDR's mission in office was to show that government activism works. To maintain that mission's credibility he needed to keep his administration's record clean. And he did.

One more thing: although the U.S. entry into World War II wasn't planned as a gigantic demonstration of government effectiveness, it nonetheless had that effect. It became very difficult for conservatives to claim that government can't do anything well after the U.S. government demonstrated its ability not just to fight a global war but also to oversee a vast mobilization of national resources.

By 1948, then, the idea of an active government role in the economy—a role that, in practice, had the effect of greatly reducing inequality—had become respectable. Meanwhile the old view that the government should keep its hands off, which FDR ridiculed in his 1936 Madison Square Garden speech as "the doctrine that that Government is best which is most indifferent," had been relegated to crank status.

Winning the battle of ideas isn't enough, however, if that victory isn't supported by an effective political coalition. As it happened, though, the political landscape had changed in a way that shifted the center of political gravity downward, empowering those who gained from the Great Compression and had a stake in maintaining a relatively equal distribution of income.

An Enfranchised Nation

During the Long Gilded Age one major barrier to an effective political movement on behalf of working Americans was the simple fact that many workers, especially low-wage workers, were denied the vote, either by law or in practice.

The biggest group of disenfranchised workers was the African American population of the South—a group that continued to be denied the vote for a generation after the Great Compression, and is still partly disenfranchised today. For reasons we'll get to shortly, however, the South was a partner, albeit a troublesome one, in the coalition that supported economic equality until the 1970s.

But there was another disenfranchised population during the

Long Gilded Age that had effectively disappeared by the 1950s—nonnaturalized immigrants. In 1920, 20 percent of American adults were foreign born, and half of them weren't citizens. So only about 90 percent of adult residents of the United States were citizens, with the legal right to vote. Once the disenfranchised African Americans of the South are taken into account, in 1920 only about 80 percent of adults residing in the United States had the de facto right to vote. This disenfranchisement wasn't politically neutral: those who lacked the right to vote were generally poor compared with the average. As we'll see shortly relatively poor voters today tend to support Democrats in general and a strong welfare state in particular. The same would presumably have been true in the 1920s. So disenfranchisement removed part of the left side of the political spectrum, pushing American politics to the right of where they would have been if all adult residents had been able to vote.

After severe immigration restrictions were imposed in 1924, however, the fraction of adults without the right to vote steadily dropped. By 1940 immigrants were only 13 percent of the adult population, and more than 60 percent of those immigrants had been naturalized, so by 1940 some 95 percent of adult residents of the United States were citizens. By 1950 the immigrant share was down to 10 percent, three-quarters of whom had been nationalized; noncitizen adult residents of the country were down to a trivial 3 percent of the adult population.

Between 1924 and the 1950s, then, immigrants without citizenship basically disappeared from the American scene. The result was a country in which the vast majority of white blue-collar workers were enfranchised. Moreover by the fifties relatively poor whites were much more likely to actually avail themselves of their right to vote than they had been in the twenties, because they were union members or had friends or family members in unions, which raised their political awareness and motivation. The result was an electorate considerably more disposed to support the welfare state, broadly defined, than the electorate of 1920—or the electorate today.

The Peculiar Role of the South

The South is still different in many ways from the rest of the United States. But in the 1950s it was truly another country—a place of overt segregation and discrimination, with the inferior status of blacks enshrined in law and public policy and enforced with violence. *Brown v. Board of Education*, the Supreme Court decision that required an end to segregated school systems, didn't come until 1954. Rosa Parks refused to move to the back of a Montgomery bus in 1955, and the Supreme Court decision ending segregation on public transportation wasn't handed down until late 1956. Voting rights for blacks were an even longer time coming: The Voting Rights Act was enacted in 1964, the year in which three civil rights workers were murdered in Philadelphia, Mississippi, the place where Ronald Reagan would later choose to start his 1980 presidential campaign—with a speech on states' rights.

The brutal racial politics of the South, together with its general backwardness, made it in many ways a deeply conservative region—even more so than it is today. Yet the South was also, for a long time, a key part of the New Deal coalition.

Electoral maps tell the story. On today's maps the South is solid red. Aside from Maryland and Delaware, John Kerry carried not a single state south of the Mason-Dixon line. But in 1948 not a single Southern state went for Dewey, although several did back the segregationist candidacy of Strom Thurmond.

Why did the South support the Democrats? There's an obvious, ugly reason why Southern whites *could* support Democrats in the 1950s: Although the Democratic Party had become the party of economic equality, it tacitly accepted Jim Crow. It was only when Democrats became the party of racial equality as well that the Republicans, who began as opponents of slavery but became the defenders of wealth, moved into the gap. I'll have more to say about that exchange of places later in the book, especially when I look at how Ronald Reagan triumphed in 1980.

But why was the South Democratic in the first place? The enduring bitterness left by the Civil War was part of the story; you could say that for generations Southern Democrats won by running against Abraham Lincoln.

But the fact that the South was much poorer than the rest of the country meant that it also received a disproportionate share of benefits generated by the New Deal. Southern states are still somewhat poorer than the national average, but in the fifties the South was desperately poor. As late as 1959 per capita income in Mississippi was less than one thousand dollars a year (about five thousand dollars in today's prices), giving it an average standard of living barely 40 percent as high as that of wealthy states like Connecticut, New York, and New Jersey. The South was also still a rural, farming region, long after the rest of America had become an urban nation. By 1950 the United States outside the South had three urban residents for every rural inhabitant—but the South was still more rural than urban.

As a result the New Deal was almost pure gain for the South. On one side, the high taxes FDR levied on the wealthy and on corporations placed little burden on the South, where there were few rich people and the corporations were mainly owned by Northerners. On the other side New Deal programs, from Social Security to unemployment insurance to rural power, were especially important for the low-wage workers who made up most of the South's population. Even now, the fact that the South depends a lot on the welfare state makes an occasional impact on our politics: When George W. Bush tried to privatize Social Security in 2005, his handlers discovered that opposition was, if anything, more intense in the "red states" that supported him in 2004, especially in the South, than in the rest of the country.

Here's one way to put it: Although the racial divide in the South went along with reactionary local politics, the region had so much to gain from the welfare state thanks to its poverty that at the national level it was willing to support Northern liberals—up to a point. There were, however, sharp limits to the kinds of policies the Southern whites would support. This became all too clear when Harry Truman tried to complete the New Deal, adding the element that would have created a full-fledged welfare state comparable to that of Canada or Western European nations: national health insurance.

In 1946 Truman proposed a system of national health insurance that would have created a single-payer system comparable to the Canadian system today. His chances of pushing the plan through initially looked good. Indeed, it would have been much easier to establish national health insurance in the 1940s than it would be today. Total spending on health care in 1946 was only 4.1 percent of GDP, compared with more than 16 percent of GDP now. Also, since private health insurance was still a relatively undeveloped industry in the forties, insurance companies weren't the powerful interest group they are now. The pharmaceutical lobby wouldn't become a major force until the 1980s. Meanwhile public opinion in 1946 was strongly in favor of guaranteed health insurance.

But Truman's effort failed. Much of the responsibility for that failure lies with the American Medical Association, which spent $5 million opposing Truman's plan; adjusting for the size of the economy, that's equivalent to $200 million today. In a blatant abuse of the doctor-patient relationship, the AMA enlisted family doctors to speak to their patients in its effort to block national insurance. It ostracized doctors who supported Truman's plan, even to the extent of urging that they be denied hospital privileges. It's shocking even now to read how doctors were told to lecture their patients on the evils of "socialized medicine."

But the AMA didn't defeat Truman's plan alone. There was also crucial opposition to national health insurance from Southern Democrats, despite the fact that the impoverished South, where many people couldn't afford adequate medical care, would have gained a financial windfall. But Southern politicians believed that a national health insurance system would force the region to racially integrate its hospitals. (They were probably right. Medicare, a program for seniors equivalent in many ways to the system Truman wanted for everyone, was introduced in 1966—and one result was the desegregation of hospitals across the United States.) Keeping black people out of white hospitals was more important to Southern politicians than providing poor whites with the means to get medical treatment.

Truman's failure on health care presaged the eventual collapse of the New Deal coalition. The support of Southern whites for economic equality was always ambivalent, and became more so over time. The familiar story says that the South bolted the coalition when the Democratic Party got serious about civil rights—and that's certainly a large part of what happened. It's also true, however, that as the South as a whole grew richer, the region had less to gain from redistributionist policies, and was set free to indulge the reactionary instincts that came from the disenfranchisement of blacks. But in the 1950s all this was far in the future.

Unions

Between 1935 and 1945 the percentage of American workers in unions rose from 12 to 35 percent; as late as 1970, 27 percent of workers were union members. And unions generally, though not always, supported Democrats. In the 1948 election, roughly three-quarters of the members of the two big union organizations, the American Federation of Labor and the Congress of Industrial Organizations, voted for Truman.

The role of unions in making the Democrats the nation's dominant party went well beyond the tendency of union members to vote for Democratic candidates. Consider Will Rogers's famous quip, "I am not a member of any organized political party. I'm a Democrat." This was a fair characterization of the Democratic Party before the New Deal, as it is today. But it was much less true when organized labor was a powerful force: Unions provided the party with a ready-made organizational structure. Not only did unions provide a reliable source of campaign finance; even more important in an age before campaigns were largely conducted on TV, they provided Democrats with a standing army of campaign workers who distributed lawn signs, bumper stickers, and campaign literature, engaged in door-to-door canvassing, and mobilized for get-out-the-vote efforts on election day.

A more subtle but probably equally crucial consequence of a powerful union movement was its effect on the political awareness and voter participation rates of lower- and middle-income Americans. Those of us who follow politics closely often find it difficult to appreciate how little attention most Americans pay to the whole thing. But this apathy is understandable: Although the outcomes of elections can have large impacts on peoples' lives, it's very unlikely that an individual voter's decision will affect those outcomes. Therefore people with jobs to do and children to raise have little incentive to pay close attention to political horseraces. In practice this rational lack of interest imparts an upward class bias to the political process: higher-income people are more likely to pay attention to politics, and more likely to vote, than are lower- and middle-class Americans. As a result, the typical *voter* has a substantially higher income than the typical *person*, which is one reason politicians tend to design their policies with the relatively affluent in mind.

But unions have the effect of reducing this class bias. Unions explicitly urge their members to vote; maybe more important, the discussion of politics that takes place at union meetings, the political messages in mailings to union members, and so on, tend to raise political awareness not just among union workers but among those they talk to, including spouses, friends, and family. Since people tend to associate with others of similar income, this means more political participation among lower-income Americans. One recent statistical analysis[4] estimated that if the share of unionized workers in the labor force had been as high in 2000 as it was in 1964, an additional 10 percent of adults in the lower two-thirds of the income distribution would have voted, compared with only an additional 3 percent of the top third. So the strength of the union movement lowered the economic center of gravity of U.S. politics, which greatly benefited the Democrats.

In sum, then, the political economy of the United States in the 1950s and into the 1960s was far more favorable to income-equalizing economic policies than it had been during the Long Gilded Age. The welfare state was no longer considered radical; instead, those who wanted to dismantle it were regarded as cranks. There was no longer a large class of disenfranchised immigrant workers. The South was, conditionally and temporarily, on the side of economic equality, as long as that didn't translate into racial equality. And a powerful union movement had the effect of mobilizing lower-income voters.

The Political Parties in the Age of Equality

Ellis G. Arnal, the former governor of Georgia, wrote a contrarian but, it turned out, highly accurate article in the October 1948 issue of the *Atlantic Monthly* called "The Democrats Can Win." In it he emphasized the underlying strength of a Democratic coalition that "is described by its critics as a combination of the South, the labor unions, the city machines, and the intellectual Left. Not a wholly accurate description, it will serve." I've already talked about the South and the unions. Let's briefly consider his other two elements.

Urban political machines, based largely on the support of immigrants, predated the Roosevelt years. In fact, they had been a major source of Democratic support since the nineteenth century. And the New Deal's policies had the effect, if anything, of undermining their power. The key to the machines' appeal to urban voters was their ability to provide aid to families in trouble and patronage jobs; the New Deal's expansion of the government social safety net and the rise in wages as a result of the Great Compression made these services less crucial. Nonetheless these urban machines were still powerful well into the 1960s, and their persistence helped Democrats win elections.

What about the "intellectual Left"? Obviously there have never been enough intellectuals to make them an important voting bloc for either party. But to focus on the mechanical side of things gives too little credit to the importance of message and ideas. In the 1930s the left had ideas about what to do; the right didn't, except to preach that the economy would eventually heal itself. FDR's success gave liberal intellectuals credibility and prestige that persisted long after the momentum of the New Deal had been largely exhausted—just as, in our own day, it remained common to assert that all the new ideas were on the right long after any real sense of innovation on the right was gone. In 1958 John Kenneth Galbraith wryly remarked that among liberals, "To proclaim the need for new ideas has served, in some measure, as a substitute for them." But the sense that new ideas came from the left remained an advantage of the Democrats.

Meanwhile, by the 1950s the Republican Party was in many ways a shadow of its former self. Before the Great Depression and the Great Compression, Republicans had two great political advantages: money, and the perception of competence. Contributions from a wealthy elite normally gave the Republicans a large financial advantage; and people tended to assume that the GOP, the party of business, the party of take-charge men like Herbert Hoover, knew how to run the country.

But the Great Compression greatly reduced the resources of the elite, while the Great Depression shattered the nation's belief that business knows best. Herbert Hoover became the very symbol of incompetence. And after the triumph in World War II and the great postwar boom, who could credibly claim that Democrats didn't know how to run things?

Still, the Republican party survived—but it did so by moving toward the new political center. Eisenhower won the White House partly because of his reputation from World War II, partly because the public was fed up with the Korean War. But he was also acceptable because he preached "moderation," and considered those who wanted to roll back the New Deal "stupid." The Republican Party became, for several decades, a true big tent, with room both for some unrepentant small-government conservatives and for big spending, big-government types like Nelson Rockefeller of New York. To get a sense of just how un-ideological the Republicans became, it's helpful to turn to quantitative studies of voting behavior in Congress.

The seminal work here, already mentioned in chapter 1, is that of Keith Poole of the University of California, San Diego, and Howard Rosenthal of the Russell Sage Foundation, who have developed a systematic way of locating members of Congress along a left-right spectrum. (They also identify a second dimension of politics—race—which has been crucial in the rise of movement conservatism. But let's leave that aside for now.) The method, roughly speaking, works like this: Start with roll-call votes on a number of bills that bear on economic issues. First, make a preliminary ranking of these bills on a left-to-right political spectrum. Second, rank members of Congress from left to right based on how they voted on these bills. Third, use the ranking of legislators to refine the left-right ranking of the legislation, and repeat the process all over again. After a few rounds you've arrived at a consistent ranking of both bills and politicians along the left-right spectrum.[5] Poole, Rosenthal, and Nolan McCarty of Princeton University have applied this method to each Congress since the nineteenth century. What stands out from their results is just how modest the differences between Republicans and Democrats were in the fifties and sixties, compared with a huge gulf before the New Deal, and an even larger gap today.

Poole and Rosenthal measure the gap between the parties with an index of political polarization that, while highly informative, is difficult to summarize in an intuitive way. For my purposes it's sufficient to look at two descriptive measures that behave very similarly to their index over time. One measure is what I'll call "minority-party overlap": the number of Democrats to the right of the leftmost Republican, when Republicans controlled Congress, or the number of Republicans to the left of the rightmost Democrat, when Democrats controlled Congress. The other measure is what I'll call "minority-party crossover": the number of members of the minority party who are actually on the other side of the political divide from their party—Democrats who are to the right of the median member of Congress, or Republicans to the left. In each measure more overlap indicates a less polarized political system, while the absence of overlap suggests that there isn't a strong political center.

Table 2 shows these numbers for three Congresses: the 70th Congress, which sat in 1927–28 and 1928–29; the 85th Congress, which sat in 1957 and 1958; and the 108th Congress, which sat in 2003 and 2004. The table shows that congressional partisanship was much less intense in the 1950s than it had been before the New Deal—or than it is today. In the 70th Congress, in which Republicans controlled the House of Representatives, there was hardly any minority party overlap: only two Democrats were to the right of the leftmost Republican. And there was no minority party crossover: all Democrats were left of center. The situation was even more extreme in the 108th Congress, which was also controlled by Republicans: Every Democrat was to the left of the leftmost Republican, and needless to say there was no crossover. In the 85th Congress, however, which was controlled by Democrats, there were many Republicans to the left of the rightmost Democrat (largely because there were a number of quite conservative Southern Democrats.) More amazingly, nine Republican members of the House were literally left of center—that is, voted to the left of the median Congressman. That's a situation that would be inconceivable today. For one thing, a twenty-first century Republican who took a genuinely left-of-center position would never get through the primary process, because movement conservatives would make sure that he faced a lavishly funded challenger, and because Republican primary voters, skewed sharply to the right, would surely support that challenger. In the fifties, however, Republicans couldn't afford to enforce ideological purity if they wanted to win elections. As a result, actual liberals like Nelson Rockefeller and Jacob Javits, who would have been summarily excommunicated today, remained party members in good standing.

Table 2. Measures of Similarity Between the Parties

	Minority Party Overlap	Minority Party Crossover
70th Congress, 1927–29	2	0
85th Congress, 1957–58	112	9
108th Congress, 2003–4	0	0

Source: www.library.unt.edu/govinfo/usfed/years.html.

The relative absence of difference between the parties' positions on economic policy meant that voting behavior on the part of the public was very different from what it is today. In recent elections partisan voting has been very strongly correlated with income: The higher a voter's income, the more likely he or she is to vote Republican. This presumably reflects voters' understanding that a vote for a Republican is a vote for policies that favor the affluent as opposed to the poor and working class. But the relatively nonideological nature of the Republican Party in the fifties, reflected in the way its members voted in Congress, was also reflected in public perceptions. During the postwar boom, voters evidently saw very little difference between the parties on economic policy, at least when voting in presidential elections. Table 3 compares the average voting patterns of white voters grouped by income level in presidential elections between 1952 and 1972 on one side and 1976 and 2004 on the other. In the more recent period there was a strong relationship between higher income levels and voting Republican. During the period from 1952 to 1972, the era of bipartisan acceptance of the welfare state, however, there was hardly any relationship between income level and voting preference. The one presidential election in which there was a large voting difference by income level was 1964, the year in which Barry Goldwater—a true movement conservative, and the harbinger of things to come—seized the Republican nomination. Other surveys show that in the fifties and sixties there was remarkably little relationship between a voter's income and his or her party registration: The upper third of the income distribution was only slightly more Republican than the middle or lower thirds.

Table 3. Percentage of Whites Voting Democratic in Presidential Elections, by Income group

	Percentage Voting Democratic in 1952–1972	Percentage Voting Democratic in 1976–2004
Poorest Third	46	51
Middle Third	47	44
Richest Third	42	37

Source: Larry Bartels, "What's the Matter with *What's the Matter with Kansas?*" p. 13 (photocopy, Princeton University, 2005).

If the Republican Party of the fifties and sixties didn't stand for economic conservatism, what did it stand for? Or maybe the question is better phrased as follows: What did voters who voted Republican think they were voting for?

To some extent they were voting for the traditional ethnic order. The Republican Party of the 1950s was, above all, the WASP party—the party of non-Southern white Anglo-Saxon Protestants, with the Anglo-Saxon bit somewhat optional. (Eisenhower came from German stock, but that didn't matter.) During the 1950s, 51 percent of those who considered themselves Republicans were WASPs, even though the group made up only 30 percent of the electorate.[6] White Protestants had been the dominant ethnic group in the United States for most of its history, but the rise of the New Deal, with many Catholic union members in its base and with a large role for Jewish intellectuals, undermined that dominance. And much of the rest of the country was suspicious of the change. It's hard now to recapture that state of mind, but as late as the 1960 election a significant number of Americans voted against Kennedy simply because he was Catholic.

More creditably, many Americans voted Republican as a check on the power of the dominant Democratic coalition. From the thirties through the seventies, Democrats commanded a much larger share of registered voters than the Republicans. Although this didn't translate into a Democratic advantage in capturing the White House—between the 1948 election and the election of Ronald Reagan the Republicans held the presidency for four terms, the Democrats for three—it did translate into consistent Democratic control of Congress from 1952 on. This consistent control led to abuses—not gross corruption, for the most part, but petty corruption and, perhaps more important, complacency and lack of attention to popular concerns. Republicans became the alternative for those who valued some accountability. In particular, Republicans in the Northeast often presented themselves as reformers who would clean up the system rather than change it in any fundamental way.

In sum, between 1948 and sometime in the 1970s both parties accepted the changes that had taken place during the Great Compression. To a large extent the New Deal had created the political conditions that sustained this consensus. A highly progressive tax system limited wealth at the top, and the rich were too weak politically to protest. Social Security and unemployment insurance were untouchable programs, and Medicare eventually achieved the same status. Strong unions were an accepted part of the national scene.

This equilibrium would collapse in the 1970s. But the forces that would destroy the politics of equality began building in the 1960s, a decade in which everything went right for the economy, but everything seemed to go wrong for American democracy.

5

THE SIXTIES:

A TROUBLED PROSPERITY

It was the best of times, it was the worst of times.

In economic terms the sixties were as good as it gets. In *The Pump House Gang*, published in 1968, Tom Wolfe wrote of a "magic economy" in which everything seemed easy. And by just about any standard, that's the kind of economy America had in the sixties. The chaos and upheaval of that decade took place against the backdrop of the best economy America has ever had.

It was an economy that seemingly provided jobs for everyone. What's more those abundant jobs came with wages that were higher than ever, and rising every year. At the bottom end, workers were much better off than they would ever be again: The minimum wage in 1966, at $1.25 an hour, was the equivalent of more than $8.00 in today's dollars, far higher than today's minimum wage of $5.15. By 1966 the typical man in his thirties was earning as much as his modern equivalent; by the time the great boom ended, in the early seventies, men would be earning about 14 percent *more* than they do now.[1] It's true that family incomes were a bit less than they are today, because fewer women worked and the gap between women's and men's wages was larger. And because incomes were a bit lower than they are now, middle-class families lived in smaller houses, were less likely to have two cars, and in general had a somewhat lower material standard of living than their counterparts today. Yet the standard of living felt high to most Americans, both because it was far higher than it had been for the previous genera-tion, and because a more equal society offered fewer occasions to feel left out. As MIT economists Frank Levy and Peter Temin have pointed out, the broad-based rise in income meant that a blue-col-lar machine operator earned more, in real terms, than most man-agers had earned a generation earlier. As a result more Americans than ever before considered themselves middle class.[2]

Economic security was also unprecedented. By 1966, 80 percent of the population had health insurance, up from only 30 percent at the end of World War II, and by 1970 the fraction of the population with health insurance surpassed today's 85 percent level. Workers who lost their jobs despite the low unemployment rate were much more likely to receive unemployment insurance than laid-off work-ers are today, and that insurance covered a larger fraction of their lost wages than does today's. And as Levy and Temin point out, ris-ing wages across the board meant that even laid-off workers whose next job paid less than the one they lost found that within a few years they had recovered their previous standard of living.

If the slogan "It's the economy, stupid," had been valid, Amer-ica would have been a country of mass political contentment. Yet in August 1966, when an AP/Ipsos Poll asked people, "Generally speaking, would you say things in this country are heading in the right direction, or are they off on the wrong track?" only 26 percent said "right direction," while 71 percent said "wrong track."

It's no mystery why. For many, perhaps most, Americans any satisfaction over continuing material progress was outweighed by the overwhelming sense that American society was falling apart. Crime was soaring; cities were devastated by riots; privileged youth were growing their hair, taking drugs, and having premarital sex; demonstrators were out in the streets denouncing the Vietnam War. Historians today may look back at the upheavals of the sixties and see them as representing separate trends—the motivations of muggers and those of student radicals, the motivations of hippies and those of middle-aged war opponents were by no means the same. Yet the public sense of chaos unleashed had a real foundation.

In the 1966 elections voters would express their dismay at the polls, giving Republicans major gains in Congress. In California, an actor-turned-politician named Ronald Reagan became governor by campaigning against welfare cheats, urban rioters, long-haired college students—and the state's fair housing act.

Now, the Republican Party of 1966 was a much more moderate institution than the Republican party we know today. Movement conservatism—the subject of my next chapter—existed, and had managed to nominate Barry Goldwater in 1964, but it hadn't yet secured control of the party. Ronald Reagan wasn't yet an enthusiastic tax cutter and Richard Nixon actually governed as a liberal in many ways: He indexed Social Security for inflation, created Supplemental Security Income (a major program for the disabled elderly), expanded government regulation of workplace safety and the environment, and even tried to introduce universal health insurance.

Yet the seeds of movement conservatism's eventual dominance were sown in the 1960s—or, to be more accurate, between 1964, the year of Lyndon Johnson's landslide victory over Barry Goldwater, and 1972, the year of Richard Nixon's even bigger landslide victory over George McGovern.

Those years were, of course, the years of escalation and mass casualties in Vietnam, an era in which America was torn apart by questions of war and peace. Vietnam was certainly *the* issue of the time. Without Vietnam, Lyndon Johnson would almost certainly have run for a second full term, demonstrators and police wouldn't have fought pitched battles outside the Democratic Convention in Chicago, and Nixon would never have made it to the White House.

The long-term effects of Vietnam on American politics, however, were less than you might think. According to conventional wisdom the struggle over Vietnam crippled the Democratic Party, condemning it to a permanent position of weakness on national security. As we'll see in this and later chapters, that conventional wisdom overstates the case. The war did little to shake the Democrats' hold on Congress. As for the image of Democrats as weak on national security: Nixon was highly successful in portraying *George McGovern* as weak on national security, but it's much less clear that the Democratic Party as a whole came to be viewed the same way until much later. The image of weak Democrats didn't really sink in until the 1980s, and was projected back in a rewriting of history.

What really happened in the sixties was that Republicans learned how to exploit emerging cultural resentments and fears to win elections. Above all, Republicans learned how to exploit white backlash against the civil rights movement and its consequences. That discovery would eventually make it possible for movement conservatives to win the White House and take control of Congress.

So let's start with the event that mattered most in the long run: Lyndon Johnson's decision to champion civil rights.

Civil Rights and the Defection of the South

As a man whose roots go deeply into Southern soil, I know how agonizing racial feelings are. I know how difficult it is to reshape the attitudes and the structure of our society. But a century has passed—more than 100 years—since the Negro was freed. And he is not fully free tonight. It was more than 100 years ago that Abraham Lincoln—a great President of another party—signed the Emancipation Proclamation. But emancipation is a proclamation and not a fact.

A century has passed—more than 100 years—since equality was promised, and yet the Negro is not equal. A century has passed since the day of promise, and the promise is unkept. The time of justice has now come.

So spoke Lyndon Johnson in March 1965, declaring his determination to pass what eventually became the Voting Rights Act, a week after police violently attacked a voting rights march in Selma, Alabama.

Johnson's decision to end the de facto disenfranchisement of African Americans culminated a nearly twenty-year evolution within the Democratic Party. It began in 1947, when Harry Truman created a committee on civil rights, with instructions to recommend legislation protecting Negroes from discrimination. Like most good deeds in politics, Truman's move contained an element of calculation: He believed that by winning black votes in Northern cities he could pull out a victory in the 1948 election. And so it proved, even though the inclusion of civil rights in the Democratic platform led to a walkout of Southern delegates and the third-party presidential candidacy of the segregationist governor of South Carolina, Strom Thurmond.

Political calculation aside, it was inevitable that the party that created the New Deal would eventually become the party of civil rights. The New Deal was a populist movement—and like the populist movement of the nineteenth century, it found itself reaching out for support to blacks, who had the most to gain from a more equal distribution of income. Later, World War II forced the pace: not only did blacks fight for America, but the legacy of Nazism helped make overt racism unacceptable. After the 1948 Democratic Convention, Truman ordered the army integrated. World War II was followed by the Cold War, in which the Soviet Union tried to portray itself as the true champion of the proposition that all men are created equal. Truman and many others believed that America needed to end its long history of segregation and discrimination in order to reclaim the moral high ground.

Today hardly any politician, from North or South, would dare quarrel publicly with the sentiments Johnson expressed when he introduced the Voting Rights Act. (Though in their hearts some surely believe, as Trent Lott blurted out in his 2002 eulogy of Strom Thurmond, that if the ardent segregationist had been elected in 1948 we wouldn't have had "all these problems.") Forty years on the freedom riders are regarded as heroes and Martin Luther King has become a national icon, a symbol of the better angels of America's nature. In the sixties, however, many white Americans found the push for civil rights deeply disturbing and threatening.

In part that's because a fairly large fraction of Americans were still unreconstructed segregationists. Between 1964 and 1978 the American National Election Studies survey asked people whether they favored "desegregation, strict segregation, or something in between." In 1964 a full 23 percent still answered "strict segregation," compared with 32 percent wanting desegregation.

Most of the outright segregationists were Southerners. But even in the North, where there was less sympathy for strict segregation, there was palpable fear of the changes the civil rights movement was bringing. Throughout the sixties, more than 60 percent of voters agreed that "the civil rights people have been trying to push too fast." This reaction partly reflected the way the goals of the civil rights movement widened over time. At first it was simply a matter of undoing Jim Crow—the explicit, blatant disenfranchisement and sometimes violently enforced second-class status of blacks in the South. The crudity and brutality of Jim Crow made it, in the end, a relatively easy target for reform: The nation's sympathies were engaged by the civil rights marchers; its sense of itself was outraged by the viciousness of the resistance by Southern racists. And undoing Jim Crow required no more than declaring the formal, government-enforced institutions of Southern segregation illegal.

Once the formal institutions of Southern apartheid were gone, however, there still remained the reality of less formal but de facto discrimination and segregation—which, unlike formal segregation, existed all over the country. And as civil rights activists tried to take on this reality, the nature of the confrontation changed. In the eyes of many nonSouthern whites, it was one thing to tell school districts that they couldn't explicitly maintain separate schools for white and black children, but it was something quite different to redraw school district boundaries and put children on buses in an attempt to end de facto segregation. Similarly, many non-Southern whites viewed laws telling state governments that they couldn't refuse services to black people as legitimate, but viewed as illegitimate laws outlawing racial discrimination by private landlords or by homeowners selling their homes. Civil rights advocates were right to believe that de facto segregation and discrimination—which despite claims that they represented voluntary choice were often in practice supported by threats of violence—represented barriers to progress every bit as important as Jim Crow. In attempting to remedy these wrongs, however, the civil rights movement inevitably brought itself a much wider range of enemies.

Enterprising politicians took notice. Ronald Reagan, who had opposed the Civil Rights Act and the Voting Act—calling the latter "humiliating to the South"—ran for governor of California in part on a promise to repeal the state's fair housing act. "If an individual wants to discriminate against Negroes or others in selling or renting his house," Reagan said, "he has a right to do so."

Above all, public perception of the civil rights movement became entangled with the rising tide of urban disorder—a linkage that served to legitimate and harden resistance to further civil rights progress.

Urban Disorder

In October 1967 Richard Nixon published a now-famous article in *Reader's Digest* titled "What Has Happened to America?" The article, which was actually written by Pat Buchanan, wrapped up all the nation's turmoil in one package: Liberal permissiveness, Nixon/Buchanan claimed, was the root of all evil.[3]

"Just three years ago," the article began, "this nation seemed to be completing its greatest decade of racial progress." But now the nation was "among the most lawless and violent in the history of free peoples." Urban riots were "the most virulent symptoms to date of another, and in some ways graver, national disorder— the decline in respect for public authority and the rule of law in America."

And it was all the fault of the liberals.

> The shocking crime and disorder in American life today, flow
> in large measure from two fundamental changes that have
> occurred in the attitudes of many Americans. First, there

is the permissiveness toward violation of the law and public order by those who agree with the cause in question. Second, there is the indulgence of crime because of sympathy for the past grievances of those who have become criminals. Our judges have gone too far in weakening the peace forces as against the criminal forces. Our opinion-makers have gone too far in promoting the doctrine that when a law is broken, society, not the criminal is to blame.

Nixon and Buchanan knew what they were doing. A conservative, went a line that became popular in the 1960s, is a liberal who has been mugged. These days crime has faded as a political issue: Crime rates plunged in the nineties, and they plunged most in New York City, once seen as the epitome of all that was wrong with American society. But in the sixties, "law and order" was arguably the single most effective rallying cry of conservatives.

There was a reason Americans felt that law and order were breaking down: They were. The crime rate more than tripled between 1957 and 1970. The rate of robbery, which *Historical Statistics of the United States* defines as "stealing or taking anything of value from the care, custody, or control of a person by force or violence or by putting in fear"—in other words, mugging—more than quadrupled.

Why did crime surge? The short answer is that we don't really know much about what causes crime to rise or fall, as demonstrated by the inability of experts to predict major changes in crime rates. The crime surge of the sixties, which confounded the expectations of liberals who expected growing social justice to be rewarded with better behavior, came as a complete surprise. So did the plunging crime rates of the nineties, which confounded conservatives who believed that no improvement in crime would be possible without a return to traditional social values. As Steven Levitt of the University of Chicago has pointed out, in the nineties "the crime decline was so unanticipated that it was widely dismissed as temporary or illusory long after it had begun."[4]

Perhaps the most plausible explanation for the great crime wave rests on demography. After World War II millions of blacks left the rural South for Northern cities—and along with their white fellow citizens, they also had a lot of children. As the baby boom reached adolescence, there was a large increase in the number of young males, and young urban black males in particular. It's true that the actual increase in crime was much larger than the increase in the number of people in crime-prone demographic groups, but there may have been a "multiplier effect" because the demographic changes overwhelmed the forces of social control. The proliferation of crime-prone young males created new, dangerous norms for behavior. And the increase in the number of people likely to commit crimes wasn't matched by any corresponding increase in the number of police officers to arrest them or jail cells to hold them. During the sixties the number of people in prison remained essentially flat even as crime soared—a sharp contrast with what happened in the nineties, when the number of people in prison continued to rise even as crime plunged.

Other factors were at work, too. One was a lack of inner-city jobs. Millions of Southern blacks had moved to Northern cities in search of manufacturing jobs—jobs that were abundant in the forties and fifties, thanks to the wartime boom and the peacetime consumer boom that followed. In the 1960s, however, those same cities began turning into an economic trap. Thanks to changing technologies of production and transportation, manufacturing began moving out of crowded urban industrial districts to sprawling plants in the suburbs; as a result jobs became scarce in the inner-city areas where blacks lived. Yet the black population remained penned in those inner cities due both to segregation and the inability to afford cars. The result was high unemployment among urban blacks even in the face of a booming economy.[5]

And the lack of jobs in the inner city, as famously argued by the sociologist William Julius Wilson, probably helped foster a destructive culture. Wilson also argued that the beginnings of desegregation perversely worsened the problem, because middle-class blacks took advantage of reduced housing discrimination to flee the ghetto, leaving behind a population segregated by class as well as race.

Whatever the reasons for rising crime in the sixties, what people saw was that law and order were breaking down. Many of them were more than willing to follow Nixon's lead and place the blame on purported liberal permissiveness. There's no evidence that permissiveness—as opposed to, say, lack of prison capacity or sufficient employment opportunities for blacks—was a significant factor in the crime wave. But the public, confronted by rising crime at the same time the nation was attempting to correct past injustices, was all too willing to make the connection.

And in the public mind concerns about crime were inextricably mixed with fear of large-scale urban violence.

The era of urban riots that began with the Harlem riot of 1964 lasted only four years—that is, although there would be riots after 1968, like the 1992 Los Angeles riot that followed the police beating of Rodney King, they would never feel like a national wave. In the riot years, however, it seemed as if all of urban America was going up in flames.

The causes of the rise and fall of urban riots remain as obscure as the causes of the rise and fall of crime. Many, probably most, riots began with acts of police brutality. The 1964 Harlem riot, for example, began when a police officer shot a fifteen-year-old black youth. And during the riots the police often ran amok. Still, police brutality against blacks was nothing new. So why, for four years in the 1960s, did such acts provoke large-scale riots?

Social scientists have found that riots were most likely to happen in cities outside the South that had large black populations. The absence of Southern riots presumably reflected the tight level of social control. Or to put it less euphemistically, in the South blacks were too terrorized to riot. Repression was less total in Northern cities, and the great postwar migration ensured that by the sixties many of these cities had huge black populations, including an increasing number of younger blacks who had never lived in the South. These demographic trends, which were essentially the same demographic trends that helped cause rising crime, combined with the terrible living conditions in urban ghettos, probably set the stage for violent reactions against acts of brutality that would once simply have been endured.

Did the civil rights movement have anything to do with urban riots? The 1968 report of the National Advisory Commission on Civil Disorders, generally referred to as the Kerner Commission, suggested that it did. "White racism," it declared, "is essentially responsible for the explosive mixture which has been accumulating in our cities since the end of World War II." While placing the ultimate blame on white racism, however, the report suggested that the proximate causes of the riots lay in the expectations created by the civil rights movement:

Frustrated hopes are the residue of the unfulfilled expectations aroused by the great judicial and legislative victories of the Civil Rights Movement and the dramatic struggle for equal rights in the South.

A climate that tends toward approval and encouragement of violence as a form of protest has been created by white terrorism directed against nonviolent protest; by the open defiance of law and federal authority by state and local officials resisting desegregation; and by some protest groups engaging in civil disobedience who turn their backs on nonviolence, go beyond the constitutionally protected rights of petition and free assembly, and resort to violence to attempt to compel alteration of laws and policies with which they disagree.

The frustrations of powerlessness have led some Negroes to the conviction that there is no effective alternative to violence as a means of achieving redress of grievances, and of "moving the system." These frustrations are reflected in alienation and hostility toward the institutions of law and government and the white society which controls them, and in the reach toward racial consciousness and solidarity reflected in the slogan "Black Power."

A new mood has sprung up among Negroes, particularly among the young, in which self-esteem and enhanced racial pride are replacing apathy and submission to "the system.

Lyndon Johnson was deeply dismayed by the Kerner Commission report, which he felt played right into the hands of conservatives. Blaming white racism for urban disorder, no matter how true the accusation might have been, was no way to win white votes. Suggesting that attempts to diminish the heavy hand of racism might have catalyzed violence wasn't likely to encourage further reform so much as to empower those who didn't want a civil rights movement in the first place. And it certainly helped Nixon.

And in the minds of white voters, crime and riots merged with another widely publicized indicator of America's breakdown: rising welfare dependency.

The Welfare Explosion

After his death in 2004 Ronald Reagan was eulogized as a lovable, avuncular fellow, devoted to the cause of freedom, defined by his victory over the Soviet evil empire and, maybe, by his devotion to tax cuts. But the Ronald Reagan who became California's governor in 1966 was something quite different: the representative of and vehicle for white voters angry at the bums on welfare. In his auto-biography Reagan described the groups who urged him to run for governor of California in 1966:

> People were tired of wasteful government programs and wel-
> fare chiselers; and they were angry about the constant spiral
> of taxes and government regulations, arrogant bureaucrats,
> and public officials who thought all of mankind's problems
> could be solved by throwing the taxpayers' dollars at them.[6]

The image is clear: Welfare chiselers were driving up decent peoples' taxes. Never mind that it wasn't true, at least not to any significant extent—that Aid to Families with Dependent Children, the program most people meant when they said "welfare," never was a major cost of government,[7] and that cheating was never a significant problem. (In later years Reagan would refer again and again to the grossly exaggerated story of a Chicago welfare queen driving her welfare Cadillac.) The fact was that welfare rolls were indeed rising. By 1966 twice as many Americans were on welfare as there had been a decade earlier. That was just the beginning: The welfare rolls more than doubled again in the "welfare explosion" of the late 1960s and early 1970s.[8] And Reagan didn't need to point out that a substantial fraction of those who entered the welfare rolls were black.

What caused the welfare explosion? A change in attitude, according to the mainstream media: "In Washington," wrote *Time* in 1970,

> they call it the "welfare syndrome." Largely because of the work of groups like the National Welfare Rights Organization, which now has chapters in all 50 states, the poor no longer feel that any stigma is attached to applying for welfare. Tens of thousands of persons who were once too timid or too ashamed to go on the dole are now rapping on the doors of their local welfare offices and demanding the payments they consider to be their right.[9]

The author and pundit Mickey Kaus, writing thirty years later, was blunter about what really changed: "Before the 'welfare explosion' of the late 1960s many poor blacks were blocked or discouraged from receiving welfare."[10]

The welfare explosion, then, was probably in part a byproduct of the civil rights movement. Like the rise in crime it was probably also in part a result of the shift of manufacturing out of central cities, leaving black urban populations with few ways to earn a living. It's clear that whatever the reasons for growing welfare rolls, they played all too easily into the growing sense of many Americans that, as Reagan would have it, "arrogant bureaucrats" were taking their hard-earned dollars and giving them away to people who didn't deserve them. And while Reagan may have defined those undeserving people by the presumed content of their character—they were "welfare chiselers"—many of his supporters surely defined the undeserving by the color of their skin.

Although race was a primary motivator, was the backlash only about race?

Sex and Drugs and Rock and Roll

Ah, the Summer of Love! For Americans of a certain age—baby boomers looking back at their youth, or maybe at the youth they wish they'd had—the sixties have taken on a nostalgic glow. But at the time the reaction of most Americans to the emergence of the counterculture was horror and anger, not admiration.

Why did the counterculture arise? Again nobody really knows, but there were some obvious factors. That magic economy was surely part of the story: Because making a living seemed easy, the cost of experimenting with an alternative lifestyle seemed low— you could always go back and get a regular job. In fact, you have to wonder whether the Nixon recession of 1969–71—which saw the unemployment rate rise from 3.5 to 6 percent—didn't do more to end the hippie movement than the killings at Altamont.

Also, familiarity with prosperity may have bred contempt. While the older generation was gratified and amazed at its ability to live a middle-class lifestyle, the young saw only the limits of what money can buy. In the 1967 film *The Graduate*, Dustin Hoffman's character, Benjamin, is dismayed when his father's friend, demanding that he pay attention, tells him, "Just one word—plastics." Benjamin, trying to explain his unease to his father, explains that he wants his future to be "different."

As with so much of what happened in the sixties, demography surely played a role. The counterculture emerged circa 1964—the year in which the leading edge of the baby boom reached college age. Sheer numbers made it easier for young people to break with the cultural conventions of their elders. There were also techno-logical changes—the Pill made sexual experimentation easier than in any previous historical era. And the youth of the sixties may have had different values in part because they were the first generation to have grown up watching TV, exposed to a barrage of images (and advertisements) that, though designed to sell products, also had the effect of undermining traditional values.

The youth rebellion frightened and infuriated many Americans—Ronald Reagan in particular. During his campaign for governor of California he promised to "investigate the charges of communism and blatant sexual misbehavior on the Berkeley campus." He spoke of "sexual orgies so vile I cannot describe them to you," and at one point claimed to have proof that the Alameda county district attor-ney had investigated a student dance which had turned into "an orgy," where they had displayed on a giant screen "pictures of men and women, nude, in sensuous poses, provocative, fondling." In fact there was no such investigation—like the welfare queen with her Cadillac, the dance-turned-orgy was a figment of Reagan's imagination.

It all sounds comical now. Communism and sexual misbehav-ior—the sum of all fears! It's almost impossible to avoid engaging in armchair psychoanalysis: Why was the future president so obsessed with what those Berkeley students were doing? For middle-class Americans, however, the changing social norms of the 1960s cre-ated real anxiety. On one side Americans feared being mugged—which really did happen to a lot of people in the newly dangerous cities. On the other side they were afraid that their children would tune in, turn on, and drop out. And that really happened, too.

Since my concern in this book is with political economy, how-ever, the question is whether the cultural rebellion of youth had a major, lasting political impact. And there's not much evidence that it swayed many voters. Most people disapproved of what the kids were up to, but only a minority viewed their actions as a serious threat. Thus a 1971 Harris Poll asked, "Do you feel that hippies are a real danger to society, more harmful to themselves than to society, or do you feel they are not particularly harmful to anyone?" Only 22 percent said that hippies were a real danger; the same percentage said they weren't particularly harmful; 53 percent said they were mainly harmful to themselves.[11] Perhaps even more telling than the polls was the behavior of politicians keen to exploit public dismay over what was happening in America. To read the speeches of Richard Nixon and Spiro Agnew, his attack-dog vice president, is to be struck at how little, when all is said and done, they talked about cultural anxieties. Even Nixon's 1969 "silent majority" speech, often described as pitting regular Americans against hippies and the counterculture, actually focused not on broader cultural conflicts but specifically on demonstrations against the Vietnam war.[12]

Yet as the example of Reagan suggests, some people were intensely dismayed by the youth rebellion, for reasons they may not have admitted even to themselves. And an obsession with other peoples' sexual lives has been an enduring factor in movement conservatism—a key source of the movement's, um, passion.

Vietnam

Lyndon Johnson didn't want a war. His 1967 State of the Union address is remarkable for its mournful tone, its lack of bombast. "No better words could describe our present course," he declared, "than those once spoken by the great Thomas Jefferson: 'It is the melancholy law of human societies to be compelled sometimes to choose a great evil in order to ward off a greater.' . . . I wish I could report to you that the conflict is almost over. This I cannot do. We face more cost, more loss, and more agony. For the end is not yet."

Nonetheless Johnson and the nation got sucked into war. That war divided the nation bitterly, in ways that have become familiar once again in recent years. There were huge demonstrations, sometimes met with violent responses. A few young Americans became so radicalized that they turned to fantasies of violent revolution. Meanwhile Richard Nixon exploited the war to win the White House, a victory made possible because Johnson, trapped by the war, chose not to run for reelection. Four years later Nixon was able to pull off a political feat, turning an unpopular war to his advantage, that was echoed by George W. Bush's victory in 2004. Even though the public had turned overwhelmingly against the war, Nixon succeeded in making George McGovern's call for withdrawal from Vietnam sound irresponsible and weak.

Surely, then, Vietnam must have transformed American politics—or so you might think. When one looks closely at the evidence, however, the case for Vietnam as a turning point is surprisingly hard to make. For Vietnam to have been decisive, either the antiwar movement or the backlash against that movement—or both—would have had to grow into a sustained force in American politics, continuing to shape policies and elections even after the war was over. In fact none of this happened.

The antiwar movement, which loomed so large in the sixties and early seventies, faded away with remarkable speed once the draft ended in 1973 and most U.S. forces were withdrawn from Vietnam. The antiwar activists went on to other things; radical leftism never took hold as a significant political force.

On the other side Nixon was never able to convert the backlash against the antiwar movement into major congressional victories.

There's a persistent myth that Vietnam "destroyed the Democrats."
But that myth is contradicted by the history of congressional control during the war years, shown in table 4. Even in 1972, the year
of Nixon's landslide victory over McGovern, the Democrats easily held on to their majority in the House and actually widened
their lead in the Senate. And the dirty tricks Nixon used to assure
himself of victory in 1972 produced, in the Watergate scandal, the
mother of all blowbacks—and a sharp jump in Democratic electoral fortunes.

What's more the available evidence just doesn't show a broad
public perception in the early post-Vietnam years of Democrats as
weak on national security. Polls taken after the fall of Saigon but
before the Iranian hostage crisis suggest a rough parity between
the parties on national security, not the overwhelming GOP advantage of legend. For example, a search of the Roper Center's iPOLL
for "Republican and Military" between 1975 and 1979 turns up
two Harris Polls from 1978 and one Republican National Committee Poll from 1979. None of the three shows a large Republican
advantage on the question of which party can be trusted on military security.

Table 4. The Persistence of the Democratic Majority

| | | Democratic Seats In: | |
Congress	Years	Senate	House
90th	1967–1968	64	248
91st	1969–1970	58	243
92nd	1971–1972	54	255
93rd	1973–1974	56	242
94th	1975–1976	61	291

Source: www.library.unt.edu/govinfo/usfed/years.html.

Eventually, the Democrats did find themselves in trouble, and there would come a time when Republicans would effectively use the claim that American troops in Vietnam were stabbed in the back to portray Democrats as weak on national security. But the realities of Vietnam had very little to do with all that.

What the Sixties Wrought

The sixties were the time of hippies and student radicals, of hardhats beating up longhairs, of war and protest. It would be foolish to say that none of this mattered. Yet all these things played at best a minor direct role in laying the foundations for the changes that would take place in American political economy over the next thirty years. In an indirect sense they may have mattered more: The lessons learned by Republicans about how to exploit cultural backlash would serve movement conservatives well in future decades, even as the sources of backlash shifted from hippies and crime to abortion and gay marriage.

What really mattered most for the long run, however, was the fracturing of the New Deal coalition over race. After the passage of the Civil Rights Act, Johnson told Bill Moyers, then a presidential aide, "I think we've just delivered the South to the Republican Party for the rest of my life, and yours." He was right: In their decisive victory in the 2006 congressional elections, Democrats won the Northeast by 28 percentage points, the West by 11 percentage points, the Midwest by 5 percentage points—but trailed Republicans by 6 points in the South.[13]

That fracture opened the door to a new kind of politics. The changing politics of race made it possible for a revived conservative movement, whose ultimate goal was to reverse the achievements of the New Deal, to win national elections—even though it supported

policies that favored the interests of a narrow elite over those of
middle- and lower-income Americans.

Before this movement—movement conservatism—could win
elections, however, it first had to establish an institutional base,
and take over the Republican Party. How it did that is the subject
of the next chapter.

6

MOVEMENT CONSERVATISM

Even as Dwight Eisenhower was preaching the virtues of a toned-down, "modern" Republicanism, a new kind of conservative was beginning to emerge. Unlike the McKinley-type conservatives who fought first FDR and then Eisenhower—men who were traditional, stuffy, and above all old—these "new conservatives," as they came to be known, were young, brash, and media savvy. They saw themselves as outsiders challenging the establishment. They were, however, well-financed from the start.

William F. Buckley blazed the trail. His 1951 book, *God and Man at Yale*, which condemned the university for harboring faculty hostile to or at least skeptical of Christianity, not to mention teaching Keynesian economics, made him a national figure. In 1955 he founded the *National Review*.

It's worth looking at early issues of the *National Review*, to get a sense of what movement conservatives sounded like before they learned to speak in code. Today leading figures on the American right are masters of what the British call "dog-whistle politics": They say things that appeal to certain groups in a way that only the targeted groups can hear—and thereby avoid having the extremism of their positions become generally obvious. As we'll see later in this chapter, Ronald Reagan was able to signal sympathy for racism without ever saying anything overtly racist. As we'll see later in this book, George W. Bush consistently uses language that sounds at worst slightly stilted to most Americans, but is fraught with meaning to the most extreme, end-of-days religious extremists. But in the early days of the *National Review* positions were stated more openly.

Thus in 1957 the magazine published an editorial celebrating a Senate vote that, it believed, would help the South continue the disenfranchisement of blacks.

The central question that emerges—and it is not a parliamentary question or a question that is answered by merely consulting a catalog of the rights of American citizens, born Equal—is whether the White community in the South is entitled to take such measures as are necessary to prevail, politically and culturally, in areas in which it does not predominate numerically? The sobering answer is Yes—the White community is so entitled because, for the time being, it is the advanced race. . . .

National Review believes that the South's premises are correct. If the majority wills what is socially atavistic, then to thwart the majority may be, though undemocratic, enlightened. It is more important for any community, anywhere in the world, to affirm and live by civilized standards, than to bow to the demands of the numerical majority. Sometimes it becomes impossible to assert the will of a minority, in which case it must give way, and the society will regress; sometimes the numerical minority cannot prevail except by violence: then it must determine whether the prevalence of its will is worth the terrible price of violence.[1]

The "catalog of the rights of American citizens, born Equal" dismissed by the editorial would, presumably, be the document known as the Constitution of the United States. And what was the editorial referring to when it talked of the "terrible price of violence" that might sometimes be worth paying if society is not to regress? William F. Buckley cleared that up later in 1957, in his "Letter from Spain":

> General Franco is an authentic national hero. It is generally conceded that he above others had the combination of talents, the perseverance, and the sense of the righteousness of his cause, that were required to wrest Spain from the hands of the visionaries, ideologues, Marxists and nihilists that were imposing on her, in the thirties, a regime so grotesque as to do violence to the Spanish soul, to deny, even, Spain's historical identity.[2]

The "regime so grotesque" overthrown by Generalissimo Francisco Franco—with crucial aid from Mussolini and Hitler—was in fact Spain's democratically elected government. The methods Franco used to protect Spain's "soul" included mass murder and the consignment of political opponents and anyone suspected of being a political opponent to concentration camps. Nor was this all in the past when Buckley praised the dictator: As the historian Paul Preston notes, Franco's opponents were "still subject to police terror and execution" as late as the 1970s.[3]

In the half-century since those articles were published, movement conservatives have learned to be more circumspect. These
days they claim to be champions of freedom and personal choice.
From the beginning, however, the movement was profoundly
undemocratic, concerned, above all, with defending religion and
property. Chapter 1 of *God and Man at Yale* denounced the school
for not being "pro-Christian," and Chapter 2, although titled "Indi-
vidualism at Yale," was mainly an attack on professors who taught
Keynesian economics and had kind words for progressive taxation
and the welfare state. And if democracy wouldn't produce an environment sufficiently protective of religion and property, so much
the worse for democracy.

The fact, however, was that there was no Franco in America, and
no real prospect of one arising. To gain power in this country, the
new conservatives would have to take control of a political party
and win elections.

Finding a Popular Base

In 1964 a coalition of conservative activists seized control of the
Republican National Convention and nominated Barry Goldwater
for president. It was, however, a false dawn for the right. The fledg-
ling conservative movement was able to nominate Goldwater only
because the Republican establishment was caught by surprise, and
the movement still had no way to win national elections: Goldwater went down to humiliating defeat. To achieve its goals movement conservatism needed a broader base. And Ronald Reagan,
more than anyone else, showed the way.

On October 27, 1964, Reagan gave a TV speech on behalf of
Goldwater's doomed campaign that the reporters David Broder
and Stephen Hess would later call "the most successful national

political debut since William Jennings Bryan electrified the 1896 Democratic Convention with the 'Cross of Gold' speech." In later years Reagan's address—formally called "A Time for Choosing"—would come to be known simply as "the speech."

Lincoln's speech at Cooper Union it wasn't. Reagan's speech might best be described as a rant—a rant against the evils of big government, based not on logical argument but on a mix of gee-whiz statistics and anecdotes.

The statistics were misleading at best, and the anecdotes suspect. "Federal employees number 2.5 million, and federal, state, and local, one out of six of the nation's work force is employed by the government" declared Reagan, conveying the impression of a vast, useless bureaucracy. It would have spoiled his point if people had known what those useless bureaucrats were actually doing: In 1964 almost two-thirds of federal employees worked either in the Defense department or in the postal service, while most state and local employees were schoolteachers, policemen, or firemen. He attacked Aid to Families with Dependent Children with a story about a woman with seven children who wanted a divorce because her welfare check would be larger than her husband's paycheck—a story he claimed to have heard from an unnamed judge in Los Angeles.

Reagan also displayed a remarkable callousness. "We were told four years ago that 17 million people went to bed hungry each night," he said, referring to one of John F. Kennedy's campaign lines. "Well that was probably true. They were all on a diet."

At the end, seemingly out of nowhere, came a sudden transition to what sounded like a demand for military confrontation with communism:

Those who would trade our freedom for the soup kitchen of the welfare state have told us they have a utopian solution

of peace without victory. They call their policy "accommodation." And they say if we'll only avoid any direct confrontation
with the enemy, he'll forget his evil ways and learn to love us.
All who oppose them are indicted as warmongers.

It wasn't a great speech by any normal standard. Yet Broder and
Hess were right: it made a huge impact. The *National Review*, with
its arch High Tory rhetoric, spoke only to a tiny if wealthy, self-con-
sciously elitist minority. Reagan had found a way to espouse more
or less the same policies but in language that played to the perceptions—and prejudices—of the common man. His speeches resonated with people who wouldn't have been able to follow Buckley's
convoluted sentences and neither knew nor cared about how Generalissimo Franco saved Spain's soul. What Reagan had discovered
was a way to give movement conservatism a true popular base.

In part Reagan did this by using small-government rhetoric to tap
into white backlash without being explicitly racist. Even when he
wasn't railing against welfare cheats—and everyone knew whom he
was referring to—his diatribes against armies of bureaucrats wast-
ing taxpayers' money were clearly aimed at voters who thought their
money was being taken away for the benefit of you-know-who.

Reagan also, however, tapped into genuine grassroots paranoia
over the Communist threat.

It's no accident that George Clooney chose to make *Good Night,
and Good Luck*, a dramatization of Edward R. Murrow's confrontation with Joe McCarthy, in 2005: Communism was the terrorism of the 1950s. The realities of the enemy were very different: A
nuclear-armed Soviet Union posed a true existential threat to the
United States in a way Islamic terrorists don't, and the Warsaw

Pact, unlike the "axis of evil," really existed. Psychologically, however, the response to the Communist threat of the 1950s seems familiar and understandable today.

Ironically, one problem with being a superpower is that it's hard to explain to its citizens the limits of that power. Canadians don't wonder why their government is unable to impose its will on the world. Americans, however, are all too easily convinced that those who threaten the nation can simply be eliminated by force—and that anyone who urges restraint is weak at best, treasonous at worst.

In reality there was no sane alternative to a restrained approach. Like modern terrorism, communism in the fifties and sixties was a threat that could be contained but not eliminated. Moreover, in the end, the strategy of containment—of refraining from any direct attempt to overthrow Communist regimes by force, fighting only defensive wars, and combating Soviet influence with aid and diplomacy—was completely successful: World War III never happened, and the United States won the Cold War decisively. But it was a strategy that, like a rational response to terrorism, seemed cowardly to people who saw only weakness and degeneracy in restraint. Reagan's caricature of containment as the belief that "if we'll only avoid any direct confrontation with the enemy, he'll forget his evil ways and learn to love us" was echoed forty years later by Dick Cheney's ridicule of John Kerry for saying that the "war on terror" should best be seen as a policing problem.

Reagan thought that those advocating containment were weak fools, who advocated a "utopian solution of peace without victory." Others on the right, notably Joseph McCarthy, thought they were traitors—and many maintained that belief even after McCarthy's downfall. For McCarthyites the frustrations of a superpower, in particular America's inability to prevent Communist victory in China, could only be explained by treason at the highest levels:

> How can we account for our present situation unless we
> believe that men high in this government are concerting to
> deliver us to disaster? This must be the product of a great con-
> spiracy on a scale so immense as to dwarf any previous such
> venture in the history of man. A conspiracy of infamy so black
> that, when it is finally exposed, its principals shall be forever
> deserving of the maledictions of all honest men.[4]

Another great irony of the situation was that anticommunism
was far more virulent and extreme in America, where there were
hardly any Communists, than in Western Europe, where Communist parties remained a potent political force until the collapse of
the Soviet Union. Not that Western European anticommunism was
weak: European parties of the right were, in many cases, defined
by their opposition to communism. And European anticommunism, even—or perhaps especially—if it came at the expense of
democracy, had its American admirers: As we've seen the staff at
the *National Review*, the original house organ of movement conservatism, were ardent admirers of Generalissimo Francisco Franco.

Outside Spain, however, European anticommunists were traditional conservatives, defenders of the existing democratic order.
In the United States, anticommunism—directed against shadowy
enemies who supposedly controlled the nation's policy—became
a radical, even revolutionary movement. As the historian Richard
Hofstadter put it in his famous 1964 essay "The Paranoid Style in
American Politics," the modern American right wing

> feels dispossessed: America has been largely taken away from
> them and their kind, though they are determined to try to
> repossess it and to prevent the final destructive act of sub-
> version. The old American virtues have already been eaten

away by cosmopolitans and intellectuals; the old competitive capitalism has been gradually undermined by socialistic and communistic schemers; the old national security and independence have been destroyed by treasonous plots, having as their most powerful agents not merely outsiders and foreigners as of old but major statesmen who are at the very centers of American power.[5]

Oddly, this feeling of dispossession and victimization found special resonance in America's rapidly growing suburbs—above all in Orange County, California, the home of Disneyland and at the time the embodiment of the new American dream. There was, it seemed, something about being a new homeowner, someone who moved both west and out to get away from it all—from the Midwest to the coast, from the city to the suburbs—that made people especially anxious about threats that it would all be taken away, especially willing to believe in dark conspiracies against their way of life. (It also didn't hurt that Orange Country was at the heart of the military-industrial complex: As the home of many defense contractors, it was a place where many people had a personal financial stake in high tension between the West and the Soviet Union.) In recent years the Bush administration has carefully stoked the anxieties of "security moms," but in the fifties and sixties the rebellion of the "suburban warriors" was a true grassroots movement, ready to rally behind politicians who seemed to share its concerns.[6]

The founders of movement conservatism, however high-minded their rhetoric may have been, showed little hesitation about riding the wave of paranoia. The political philosopher Peter Viereck was one of the few "new conservatives" to break with the movement as it evolved into movement conservatism proper. In a 1962 article in the *New Republic*, "The New Conservatism: One of Its Founders

Asks What Went Wrong," he pointed out that many of the most prominent new conservatives "failed the acid test of the McCarthy temptation of the 1950s in the same way that the fellow-traveler failed the acid test of the Communist temptation of the 1930s." Indeed, as Viereck pointed out, Goldwater—who, like Reagan, has been reinvented by popular history as a much less extreme and threatening figure than he really was—"ardently defended the McCarthy tyranny to the very end."[7] And while movement conservatives eventually dissociated themselves from Robert Welch, the founder of the John Birch Society, they were careful not to condemn the society itself, or its conspiracy-theory beliefs.

Movement conservatism, then, found a mass popular base by finding ways to appeal to two grassroots sentiments: white backlash and paranoia about communism. The emergence of this popular base went a long way toward turning the politically marginal "new conservatives" of the 1950s into a force to be reckoned with. And the rise of the popular base was supplemented by the creation of a different kind of base, which couldn't deliver votes but could deliver cash: fervent support on the part of the business community.

Building a Business Base

Today we take it for granted that most of the business community is solidly behind the hard right. The drug industry wants its monopoly power left undisturbed; the insurance industry wants to fend off national health care; the power companies want freedom from environmental regulations; and everyone wants tax breaks. In the fifties and sixties, however, with memories of the New Deal's triumphs still fresh, large corporations were politically cautious. The initial business base of movement conservatism was mainly among smaller, often privately owned businesses. And the focus of their ire was, above all, unions.

It's hard now to grasp how important that issue was. *Time*'s readers were probably a bit puzzled in 1998, when the magazine named Walter Reuther, who was president of the United Automobile Workers from 1946 until his death in 1970, one of the one hundred most influential people of the twentieth century. By the century's end, American unionism was a shadow of its former self, and Reuther had been all but forgotten. But once upon a time Reuther was a towering—and, to some people, terrifying—figure. In 1958 Barry Goldwater declared Reuther a "more dangerous menace than the Sputnik or anything Soviet Russia might do to America."

In the 1950s America was a nation in which organized labor played a powerful, visible role. More than 30 percent of nonagricultural workers were union members, compared with less than 12 percent today. America's unionization rate was higher than that of Canada, Italy, or France, and not far short of that in West Germany. Aside from their economic effects, unions played a central political role, providing the backbone of the Democratic Party's strength outside the South. Unions were not, however, accepted by everyone as a fact of life.

It might have seemed that the issue of the political and economic legitimacy of unions had been settled by the extraordinary labor victories of the 1930s and 1940s. Those victories were, however, incomplete, in two important ways. First, the New Deal created a welfare state, but one that fell short of those achieved in other wealthy countries, especially when it came to health care. Unions had to push for private-sector benefits to fill the gaps. As they did, they ran into renewed opposition. Second, despite the relatively high rate of unionization, there were big regional disparities: Large parts of the country remained hostile territory for unions, and fertile ground for antiunion politicians.

Let's start with the incomplete welfare state. All Western democracies emerged from the stresses of the Great Depression and World War II with some kind of welfare state. The extent of these welfare states varied, however. In Social Security the United States created a relatively generous public guarantee of retirement income, comparable to or better than that of other wealthy countries. On other matters, however, the U.S. welfare state was much less comprehensive than those of other countries. In particular, we've never had guaranteed health insurance.

Yet by the 1960s most Americans did have health insurance, many workers had disability insurance, a substantial number had generous unemployment benefits and retirement benefits—with none of these things provided by the government. Instead they were provided by private employers. As the political scientist Jacob Hacker has pointed out, postwar America evolved a welfare state that, measured in terms of social welfare spending as a share of the economy, was almost as big as those of Western Europe. But in the United States much of that spending came from private employers rather than the state.[8]

Why did the private employers provide all these benefits? In part because insurance was a good way to attract employees, especially during World War II, when wage controls prevented companies from competing for scarce labor by raising wages. Also, compensation that takes the form of benefits has the advantage of not being subject to income tax, so that a dollar given to an employee in the form of health benefits is worth more to the recipient than a dollar paid in straight salary. But after the war benefits became a prime target of union negotiations. In its explanation of why Reuther belonged in the top one hundred, *Time* wrote that

Reuther kept pressing for new and better benefits, and over time, the union won the things that employees today take for granted. Year by year, workers gained, among others, comprehensive health-care programs, tuition-refund programs, life insurance, profit sharing, severance pay, prepaid legal-service plans, bereavement pay, jury-duty pay—plus improvements in vacations, holidays and rest time.[9]

These demands didn't place an unacceptable burden on auto companies and other large employers: In an age before widespread foreign competition they could pass on the higher costs to consumers. After all, each auto maker, each steel company, knew that its domestic competitors were negotiating the same deal.

However, from the point of view of the owner of a medium-size business—say, a department store—union demands didn't look so tolerable. Such a business might not face international competition, but it faced competition from other businesses that might not be unionized, including ultrasmall businesses, mom-and-pop operations, that were too small to become union targets. For owners of medium-size businesses the growing demands of unions were infuriating, even threatening.

Barry Goldwater's family owned a department store in Phoenix. As Rick Perlstein puts it in his remarkable book *Before the Storm: Barry Goldwater and the Unmaking of the American Consensus*, Goldwater was a "merchant prince"—a member of the class most likely to push back against the growing demands of the union movement. Perlstein points out that owners of medium-size, family-run businesses were the core constituency of the "Manionite" movement, one of the founding sources of movement conservatism. (Clarence Manion, the dean of the Notre Dame law school, was a pioneering direct-mailer who crusaded against the "Internationalists, One-Worlders, Socialists, and Communists" he believed infested the government.[10])

Goldwater also came from Arizona—a state where the "right to work," a legal prohibition on contracts requiring that a company's workers be union members, is embodied in the state constitution. This illustrates the second reason labor victories of the New Deal era hadn't settled the role of unions in the American polity: Although unionization was securely established in the nation's industrial heartland, unions were much less prevalent and powerful in what would eventually be known as the Sunbelt. In the fifties manufacturing workers in the South were only about half as likely to be unionized as those in the Midwest. As the nation's industrial base and population shifted south and west, many influential people—particularly much of the existing power structure in the Sunbelt—wanted to make sure that the labor movement didn't follow.

Strident antiunionism was what initially gave Goldwater national prominence. His remark about the menace of Walther Reuther was made during a Senate investigation of alleged union corruption. Despite the best efforts of the investigators, they couldn't find any malfeasance on Reuther's part: He was so scrupulous that he even paid his own dry-cleaning bills when traveling on union business. For real corruption, you had to look at Jimmy Hoffa's Teamsters, one of the few unions that supported Republican candidates. Nonetheless Goldwater's role in the investigation solidified his position as a leader of the emerging right wing of the Republican Party.

Antiunionism gave movement conservatism its first solid base in the business community. From the 1960s on, business owners who hated unions were a solid source of financial support. And this support was rewarded. As I'll explain in chapter 8, in the seventies and eighties America's political shift to the right empowered businesses to confront and, to a large extent, crush the union movement, with huge consequences for both wage inequality and the political balance of power.

Building an Intelligentsia

As movement conservatism was acquiring a popular base and a solid base in the business community, it was also acquiring what amounted to a party intelligentsia. To be sure, the original "new conservatives," exemplified by Buckley and the *National Review*, were intellectuals—but they didn't provide the kind of steady drumbeat of studies and articles, combining seemingly serious scholarship with relentless support for the right's position, that nowadays always accompanies any debate on public policy. Movement conservatism's intelligentsia didn't really take shape until the "new conservatives" were joined by the neoconservatives, a quite different group, and both were given regular employment by a powerful institutional infrastructure.

The origins of neoconservatism can be traced largely to two groups: Chicago economists led by Milton Friedman, who led the pushback against Keynesian economics, and sociologists led by Irving Kristol and associated with the magazine *The Public Interest*, who rebelled against the Great Society.

The conservative economic intelligentsia emerged first, because the real truths of economics create a natural propensity in economists to go all the way to free-market fundamentalism. As Adam Smith saw, and many generations of economists have elaborated, markets often have a way of getting self-interest to serve the common good. Individuals seeking only gain for themselves are led, "as by an invisible hand," to produce goods that other people need, when they need them. It's a powerful and true insight. Even liberal economists have a healthy respect for the effectiveness of markets as a way of organizing economic activity.

On the other hand, sometimes markets don't work. This point was driven home to economists, as well as everyone else, by the searing experience of the Great Depression. In the early years after World War II, with the memory of the depression still fresh, most economists believed that keeping the economy on track required an extensive role for the government. Mainstream economics rejected calls for a planned economy, but it did accept the need for government intervention to fight recessions, as well as a generally increased role of government in the economy as a whole.

Once the crisis had passed, however, it was inevitable that some economists would return to the old faith. By the late 1940s Friedman and his colleague George Stigler were already inveighing (with considerable justification) against the evils of rent control. Over the course of the 1950s this expanded into a broad attack on government intervention and regulation in general. By the early 1960s Friedman had made almost a complete return to free-market fundamentalism, arguing that even the Great Depression was caused not by market failure but by government failure. His argument was slippery and, I'd argue, bordered on intellectual dishonesty.[11] But the fact that a great economist felt compelled to engage in intellectual sleight of hand is, itself, an indication of the powerful allure of free-market fundamentalism. Free-market economists began rejecting not just the New Deal, but the reforms of the Progressive Era, suggesting that even such government actions as policing food and drug safety were unjustified. And Friedman associated himself with the Goldwater campaign.

The revolt of the sociologists came later than the return of free-market fundamentalism, and had a darker tone. Where Friedman and his associates radiated Panglossian optimism, the group that coalesced around Kristol and *The Public Interest*, founded in 1965, were skeptics, even cynics. They were rebelling against Lyndon Johnson's Great Society, which they saw—with some justice—as a foolish, doomed exercise in social engineering. "We were especially provoked," Kristol would later write, "by the widespread acceptance of left-wing sociological ideas that were incorporated in the War on Poverty."[12]

And so you had Daniel Patrick Moynihan rejecting liberal pieties by arguing that the roots of much black poverty lay not so much in discrimination as in the rise of female-headed families, Edward Banfield rejecting the claim that urban riots were about racism by arguing that most rioters were not so much protesting injustice as simply engaging in looting.

The Friedmanites and the neoconservatives saw themselves as outsiders, alienated from the liberal establishment. To a remarkable extent the heirs of these movements still manage to feel this way. Yet by the 1970s the intelligentsia of movement conservatism had an establishment of its own, with financial backing on a scale beyond the wildest dreams of its liberal opponents. To put it bluntly, becoming a conservative intellectual became a good career move.

In a 1996 report, "Buying a Movement," People for the American Way described the career of Dinesh d'Souza, who rose to prominence with his 1991 best seller *Illiberal Education*, an attack on affirmative action and political correctness on campus. Leaving aside the merits of his work, the interesting point is the way D'Souza's career differed from those of a previous generation of conservatives.

The original modern conservative intellectuals were, for the most part, scholars who happened to be or become conservative. Milton Friedman, to take the most spectacular example, was in the first instance a professional economist, whose work on consumer behavior, monetary forces, and inflation is accepted and honored by the vast majority of economists, whatever their political persuasion. He would have won the Nobel Memorial Prize in Economics whatever his politics. Similarly most of the "dozen or so scholars and intellectuals" who Kristol says formed the "nucleus" of *The Public Interest* were academic sociologists who built their careers on more or less nonpolitical work, and came to conservatism only later.

D'Souza, however, has had a very different kind of career. He moved from editing a conservative college publication, the *Dartmouth Review*, to editing a conservative alumni publication, *Prospect*. After writing a complimentary biography of the evangelist Jerry Falwell, he became a senior domestic policy analyst in the Reagan administration. He then moved to a position at a conservative think tank, the American Enterprise Institute, where he wrote *Illiberal Education* and a later book, *The End of Racism* (in which he declared that "for many whites the criminal and irresponsible black underclass represents a revival of barbarism in the midst of Western civilization"), with support from the conservative Olin Foundation. His books have been promoted by conservative magazines, especially the *National Review*.

D'Souza, in other words, is something that didn't exist forty years ago: a professional conservative intellectual, who has made his entire career inside an interlocking set of essentially partisan institutions.

Where did these institutions come from? The story, in brief, is that in the late 1960s and early 1970s members of the new conservative intelligentsia persuaded both wealthy individuals and some corporate leaders to funnel cash into a conservative intellectual infrastructure. To a large extent this infrastructure consists of think tanks that are set up to resemble academic institutions, but only publish studies that play into a preconceived point of view. The American Enterprise Institute, although it was founded in 1943, expanded dramatically beginning in 1971, when it began receiving substantial amounts of corporate money and grants from conservative family foundations. The Heritage Foundation was created in 1973 with cash from Joseph Coors and Richard Mellon Scaife. The libertarian Cato Institute relied heavily on funds from the Koch family foundations.

Media organizations are also part of the infrastructure. The same set of foundations that have funded conservative think tanks also gave substantial support to *The Public Interest*, as well as publications like *The American Spectator*, which obsessively pursued alleged scandals during the Clinton years.

In seeking the support of foundations and business groups, neoconservatives cheerfully accepted a coarsening of their ideas. "We say, repeatedly," Kristol wrote in 1995, "that ideas have consequences, which is true but what we have in mind are complex, thoughtful, and well-articulated ideas. What we so easily overlook is the fact that simple ideas, allied to passion and organization, also have consequences." You might think that this was a lament—but Kristol was actually congratulating himself and his comrades-in-arms for going along with crude formulations of conservatism in order to achieve political success.

This was especially true in economics, where *The Public Interest*, along with the editorial page of the *Wall Street Journal*, became the principal advocate of supply-side economics. Supply-side doctrine, which claimed without evidence that tax cuts would pay for themselves, never got any traction in the world of professional economic research, even among conservatives. N. Gregory Mankiw, the Harvard economist who was the chairman of Bush's Council of Economic Advisers between 2003 and 2005, famously described the supply-siders as "cranks and charlatans" in the first edition of his textbook on the principles of economics. (The phrase vanished from later editions.) Why, then, was Kristol convinced that the supply-siders were right? The answer is that he wasn't—he didn't care whether they were wrong or right. Kristol's only concern was that the supply-siders' ideas were politically useful. Here's how he put it in his 1995 essay:

> Among the core social scientists around The Public Interest there were no economists. (They came later, as we "matured.") This explains my own rather cavalier attitude toward the budget deficit and other monetary or fiscal problems. The task, as I saw it, was to create a new majority, which evidently would mean a conservative majority, which came to mean, in turn, a Republican majority—so political effectiveness was the priority, not the accounting deficiencies of government.[13]

Remarkably this statement comes just a few paragraphs after Kristol's declaration that The Public Interest was effective in its early days because "most of us were social scientists, and as Pat Moynihan put it, the best use of social science is to refute false social science." One guesses that it all depends on the use to which false social science is put.

Nixon and the Great Transition

Ronald Reagan's 1966 California campaign marked the first great electoral success for movement conservatism. Reagan's achievement was, however, overshadowed by the rise of Richard Nixon to the presidency, and his landslide victory in 1972. Nixon's success, however, can't be regarded as a triumph for movement conservatism, because Nixon was a transitional figure. He used the movement's political strategy—indeed, to a large extent he invented it. But he didn't share the movement's goals. For Nixon it was all personal.

It's almost impossible to overstate Nixon's impact on the way American politics is conducted. Nixon, after all, showed how you could exploit racial divisions, anxiety about social change, and paranoia about foreign threats to peel working-class whites away from the New Deal coalition. He introduced the art of media manipulation: Roger Ailes, the president of Fox News, was Nixon's media consultant, and is a central figure in Joe McGinniss's 1969 book *The Selling of the President*. Later, Nixon pioneered the media intimidation that so successfully suppressed dissent for much of the Bush administration, as well as the tactic of blaming the news media for reporting bad news.

It was during the Nixon years that the successful execution of dirty tricks became a passport to advancement in the Republican Party. In 1970 a young Karl Rove printed fake leaflets advertising free beer on campaign stationery stolen from a Democratic candidate, disrupting a campaign rally; the next year Rove dropped out of college to become the paid executive director of the College Republican National Committee.[14] Two years later, when Rove ran for chairman of the College Republicans, he cheated his way to victory—with the blessing of the then chairman of the Republican National Committee, one George H. W. Bush.[15]

Movement conservatives applauded these tactics. What they didn't like were Nixon's policies. When Rick Perlstein, the author of *Before the Storm*, gave a talk (to a group of conservatives) about the conservative role in the Nixon administration's dirty tricks, one of the other panelists protested that Nixon hadn't been a conservative, adding, "I didn't like Nixon until Watergate."[16]

Indeed Nixon's actual policies, as opposed to his political tactics, were not at all what movement conservatives wanted. In domestic affairs he governed as a moderate, even a liberal, raising taxes, expanding environmental regulation, even seeking to introduce national health insurance. In foreign affairs he showed equal pragmatism, opening a dialogue with Communist China while simultaneously continuing to fight the Communist China–allied North Vietnamese. Nixon, it became clear, hated many things, but he did not share the conservative movement's hatred for government intervention and the welfare state. In any case the times weren't yet right.

By the mid-1970s movement conservatism was, in a sense, in a position similar to that of the movement that eventually became the New Deal in the late 1920s. The ideas were there; the organization was there; the intellectual cadres were in place. To achieve power, however, the movement needed a crisis.

What it got was a double crisis, both foreign and domestic.

In foreign affairs the fall of Vietnam was followed by what looked at the time like a wave of Communist victories in Southeast Asia and in Africa, then by the Soviet invasion of Afghanistan and—unrelated, but feeding the sense of anxiety—the Islamic revolution in Iran and the humiliation of the hostage crisis. On the domestic front a combination of bad policy and the energy crisis created the nightmare of stagflation, of high unemployment combined with double-digit inflation.

In retrospect the hand-wringing over Communist advances looks ludicrous; the Soviet invasion of Afghanistan, in particular, turned out to be the beginning of communism's collapse. The Islamic revolution in Iran was a real setback, but it's hard to see how an aggressive foreign policy could have done anything except worsen the situation. As for the economic crisis, it was caused by a combination of bad luck and bad monetary policy, neither of which had anything to do with liberalism.

Nonetheless the dire mood of the 1970s made it possible for movement conservatives to claim that liberal policies had been discredited. And the newly empowered movement soon achieved a remarkable reversal of the New Deal's achievements.

7

THE GREAT DIVERGENCE

Medieval theologians debated how many angels could fit on the head of a pin. Modern economists debate whether American median income has risen or fallen since the early 1970s. What's really telling is the fact that we're even having this debate. America is a far more productive and hence far richer country than it was a generation ago. The value of the output an average worker produces in an hour, even after you adjust for inflation, has risen almost 50 percent since 1973. Yet the growing concentration of income in the hands of a small minority has proceeded so rapidly that we're not sure whether the typical American has gained *anything* from rising productivity.

The great postwar boom, a boom whose benefits were shared by almost everyone in America, came to an end with the economic crisis of the 1970s—a crisis brought on by rising oil prices, out-of-control inflation, and sagging productivity. The crisis abated in the 1980s, but the sense of broadly shared economic gains never returned. It's true that there have been periods of optimism—Reagan's "Morning in America," as the economy recovered from the severe slump of the early eighties, the feverish get-rich-quick era of the late nineties. Since the end of the postwar boom, however, economic progress has always felt tentative and temporary.

Yet *average* income—the total income of the nation, divided by the number of people—has gone up substantially since 1973, the last year of the great boom. We are, after all, a much more productive nation than we were when the boom ended, and hence a richer nation as well. Think of all the technological advances in our lives since 1973: personal computers and fax machines, cell phones and bar-code scanners. Other major productivity-enhancing technologies, like freight containers that can be lifted directly from ship decks onto trucks and trains, existed in 1973 but weren't yet in widespread use. All these changes have greatly increased the amount the average worker produces in a normal working day, and correspondingly raised U.S. average income substantially.

Average income, however, doesn't necessarily tell you how most people are doing. If Bill Gates walks into a bar, the average wealth of the bar's clientele soars, but the men already there when he walked in are no wealthier than before. That's why economists trying to describe the fortunes of the typical member of a group, not the few people doing extremely well or extremely badly, usually talk not about *average* income but about *median* income—the income of a person richer than half the population but poorer than the other half. The median income in the bar, unlike the average income, doesn't soar when Bill Gates walks in.

As it turns out, Bill Gates walking into a bar is a pretty good metaphor for what has actually happened in the United States over the past generation: Average income has risen substantially, but that's mainly because a few people have gotten much, much richer. Median income, depending on which definition you use, has either risen modestly or actually declined.

About the complications: You might think that median income would be a straightforward thing to calculate: find the American richer than half the population but poorer than the other half, and calculate his or her income. In fact, however, there are two areas of dispute, not easily resolved: how to define the relevant population, and how to measure changes in the cost of living. Before we get to the complications, however, let me repeat the punch line: The fact that we're even arguing about whether the typical American has gotten ahead tells you most of what you need to know. In 1973 there wasn't a debate about whether typical Americans were better or worse off than they had been in the 1940s. Every measure showed that living standards had more or less doubled since the end of World War II. Nobody was nostalgic for the jobs and wages of a generation earlier. Today the American economy as a whole is clearly much richer than it was in 1973, the year generally taken to mark the end of the postwar boom, but economists are arguing about whether typical Americans have benefited at all from the gains of the nation as a whole.

Now for the complications: It turns out that we can't just line up all 300 million people in America in order of income and calculate the income of American number 150,000,000. After all, children don't belong in the lineup, because they only have income to the extent that the households they live in do. So perhaps we should be looking at households rather than individuals. If we do that we find that median household income, adjusted for inflation, grew modestly from 1973 to 2005, the most recent year for which we have data: The total gain was about 16 percent.

Even this modest gain may, however, overstate how well American families were doing, because it was achieved in part through longer working hours. In 1973 many wives still didn't work outside the home, and many who did worked only part-time. I don't mean to imply that there's something wrong with more women working, but a gain in family income that occurs because a spouse goes to work isn't the same thing as a wage increase. In particular it may carry hidden costs that offset some of the gains in money income, such as reduced time to spend on housework, greater dependence on prepared food, day-care expenses, and so on.

We get a considerably more pessimistic take on the data if we ask how easy it is for American families today to live the way many of them did a generation ago, with a single male breadwinner. According to the available data, it has gotten harder: The median inflation-adjusted earnings of men working full-time in 2005 were slightly lower than they had been in 1973. And even that statistic is deceptively favorable. Thanks to the maturing of the baby boomers today's work force is older and more experienced than the work force of 1973—and more experienced workers should, other things being equal, command higher wages. If we look at the earnings of men aged thirty-five to forty-four— men who would, a generation ago, often have been supporting stay-at-home wives—we find that inflation-adjusted wages were 12 percent *higher* in 1973 than they are now.

Controversies over defining the relevant population are only part of the reason economists manage to argue about whether typical Americans have gotten ahead since 1973. There is also a different set of questions, involving the measurement of prices. I keep referring to "inflation-adjusted" income—which means that income a generation ago is converted into today's dollars by adjusting for changes in the consumer price index. Now some economists argue that the CPI overstates true inflation, because it doesn't fully take account of new products and services that have improved our lives. As a result, they say, the standard of living has risen more than the official numbers suggest. Call it the "but they didn't have Netflix" argument. Seriously, there are many goods and services available today that either hadn't been invented or weren't on the market in 1973, from cell phones to the Internet. Most important, surely, are drugs and medical techniques that not only save lives but improve the quality of life for tens of millions of people. On the other hand, in some ways life has gotten harder for working families in ways the official numbers don't capture: there's more intense competition to live in a good school district, traffic congestion is worse, and so on.

Maybe the last word should be given to the public. According to a 2006 survey taken by the Pew Research Center, most working Americans believe that the average worker "has to work harder to earn a decent living" today than he did twenty or thirty years earlier.[1] Is this just nostalgia for a remembered golden age? Maybe, but there was no such nostalgia a generation ago about the way America was a generation before *that*. The point is that the typical American family hasn't made clear progress in the last thirtysome-thing years. And that's not normal.

Winners and Losers

As I've suggested with my Bill-Gates-in-a-bar analogy, ordinary American workers have failed to reap the gains from rising produc-tivity because of rising inequality. But who were the winners and losers from this upward redistribution of income? It wasn't just Bill Gates—but it was a surprisingly narrow group.

If gains in productivity had been evenly shared across the work-force, the typical worker's income would be about 35 percent higher now than it was in the early seventies.[2] But the upward redistribution of income meant that the typical worker saw a far smaller gain. Indeed, everyone below roughly the 90th percentile of the wage distribution—the bottom of the top 10 percent—saw his or her income grow more slowly than average, while only those above the 90th percentile saw above-average gains. So the limited gains of the typical American worker were the flip side of above-average gains for the top 10 percent.

And the really big gains went to the really, really rich. In Oliver Stone's 1987 movie *Wall Street*, Gordon Gekko—the corporate raider modeled in part on Ivan Boesky, played by Michael Douglas—mocks the limited ambition of his protégé, played by Charlie Sheen. "Do you want to be just another $400,000 a year working Wall Street stiff, flying first class and being *comfortable*?"

At the time an income of $400,000 a year would have put someone at about the 99.9th percentile of the wage distribution—pretty good, you might think. But as Stone realized, by the late 1980s something astonishing was happening in the upper reaches of the income distribution: The rich were pulling away from the merely affluent, and the super-rich were pulling away from the merely rich. People in the bottom half of the top 10 percent, corresponding roughly to incomes in the $100,000 to $150,000 range, though they did better than Americans further down the scale, didn't do all that well—in fact, in the period after 1973 they didn't gain nearly as much, in percentage terms, as they did during the postwar boom. Only the top 1 percent has done better since the 1970s than it did in the generation after World War II. Once you get way up the scale, however, the gains have been spectacular—the top tenth of a percent saw its income rise fivefold, and the top .01 percent of Americans is seven times richer than they were in 1973.

Who are these people, and why are they doing so much better than everyone else? In the original Gilded Age, people with very high incomes generally received those incomes due to the assets they owned: The economic elite owned valuable land and mineral resources or highly profitable companies. Even now capital income—income from assets such as stocks, bonds, and property—is much more concentrated in the hands of a few than earned income. So is "entrepreneurial income"—income from ownership of companies. But ownership is no longer the main source of elite status. These days even multimillionaires get most of their income in the form of paid compensation for their labor.

Needless to say we're not talking about wage slaves toiling for an hourly rate. If the quintessential high-income American circa 1905 was an industrial baron who owned factories, his counterpart a hundred years later is a top executive, lavishly rewarded for his labors with bonuses and stock options. Even at the very top, the highest-income 0.01 percent of the population—the richest one in ten thousand—almost half of income comes in the form of compensation. A rough estimate is that about half of the wage income of this superelite comes from the earnings of top executives—not just CEOs but those a few ranks below—at major companies. Much of the rest of the wage income of the top 0.01 percent appears to represent the incomes of sports and entertainment celebrities.

So a large part of the overall increase in inequality is, in a direct sense, the result of a change in the way society pays its allegedly best and brightest. They were always paid well, but now they're paid incredibly well.

The question, of course, is what caused that to happen. Broadly speaking there are two competing explanations for the great divergence in incomes that has taken place since the 1970s. The first explanation, favored by people who want to sound reasonable and judicious, is that a rising demand for skill, due mainly to technological change with an assist from globalization, is responsible. The alternative explanation stresses changes in institutions, norms, and political power.

The Demand for Skill

The standard explanation of rising inequality—I'm tempted to call it the safe explanation, since it's favored by people who don't want to make waves— says that rising inequality is mainly caused by a rising demand for skilled labor, which in turn is driven largely by technological change. For example, Edward Lazear, chairman of the Council of Economic Advisers in 2006, had this to say:

> Most of the inequality reflects an increase in returns to "investing in skills"—workers completing more school, getting more training, and acquiring new capabilities. . . . What accounts for this divergence of earnings for the skilled and earnings for the unskilled? Most economists believe that fundamentally this is traceable to technological change that has occurred over the past two or three decades. In our technologically-advanced society, skill has higher value than it does in a less technologically-advanced society . . . with the growing importance of computers, the types of skills that are required in school and through investment in learning on the job become almost essential in making a worker productive. The typical job that individuals do today requires a much higher level of technical skills than the kinds of jobs that workers did in 1900 or in 1970.[3]

To enlarge on Lazear's remarks: Information technology, in the form of personal computers, cell phones, local area networks, the Internet, and so on, increases the demand for people with enough formal training to build, program, operate, and repair the new gadgets. At the same time it reduces the need for workers who do routine tasks. For example, there are far fewer secretaries in modern offices than there were in 1970, because word processing has largely eliminated the need for typists, and networks have greatly reduced the need for physical filing and retrieval; but there are as many managers as ever. Bar-code scanners tied to local networks have reduced the number of people needed to man cash registers and the number required to keep track of inventory, but there are more marketing consultants than ever. And so on throughout the economy.

The hypothesis that technological change, by raising the demand for skill, has led to growing inequality is so widespread that at conferences economists often use the abbreviation SBTC—skill-biased technical change—without explanation, assuming that their listeners know what they're talking about. It's an appealing hypothesis for three main reasons. First, the timing works: The upward trend in inequality began about the same time that computing power and its applications began their great explosion. True, mainframe computers—large machines that sat in a room by themselves, crunching payrolls and other business data—were in widespread use in the sixties. But they had little impact on how most workers did their jobs. Modern information technology didn't come into its own until Intel introduced the first integrated circuit—the first computer chip—in 1971. Only then could the technology become pervasive. Second, SBTC is the kind of hypothesis economists feel comfortable with: it's just supply and demand, with no need to bring in the kinds of things sociologists talk about but economists find hard to incorporate in their models, things like institutions, norms, and political power. Finally, SBTC says that the rise in inequality isn't anybody's fault: It's just technology, working through the invisible hand.

That said, there's remarkably little direct evidence for the proposition that technological change has caused rising inequality. The truth is that there's no easy way to measure the effect of technology on markets; on this issue and others, economists mainly invoke technology to explain things they can't explain by other measurable forces. The procedure goes something like this: First, assume that rising inequality is caused by technology, growing international trade, and immigration. Then, estimate the effects of trade and immigration—a tendentious procedure in itself, but we do at least have data on the volume of imports and the number of immigrants. Finally, attribute whatever isn't explained by these measurable factors to technology. That is, economists who assert that technological change is the main cause of rising inequality arrive at that conclusion by a process of exclusion: They've concluded that trade and immigration aren't big enough to explain what has happened, so technology must be the culprit.

As I've just suggested, the main factors economists have considered as alternative explanations for rising inequality are immigration and international trade, both of which should, in principle, also have acted to raise the wages of the skilled while reducing those of less-skilled Americans.

Immigration is, of course, a very hot political issue in its own right. In 1970, almost half a century after the Immigration Act of 1924 closed the door on mass immigration from low-wage countries, less than 5 percent of U.S. adults were foreign born. But for reasons that remain somewhat unclear,* immigration began to pick up in the late 1960s, and soared after 1980. Today, immigrants

* Changes in immigration law in 1965 made family reunification the central goal of immigration policy, shifting the focus away from the attempt to restrict immigration mainly to Western Europe. But economists studying Mexican immigration find that there were relatively few barriers even before 1965.

make up about 15 percent of the workforce. In itself this should have exerted some depressing effect on overall wages: there are considerably more workers competing for U.S. jobs than there would have been without immigration.

Furthermore, a majority of immigrants over the past generation have come from Latin America, and many of the rest from other Third World countries; this means that immigrants, both legal and illegal, are on average considerably less educated than are native-born workers. A third of immigrants have the equivalent of less than a high-school diploma. As a result the arrival of large numbers of immigrants has made less-educated labor more abundant in the United States, while making highly educated workers relatively scarcer. Supply and demand then predicts that immigration should have depressed the wages of less-skilled workers, while raising those of highly skilled workers.

The effects, however, are at most medium-size. Even the most pessimistic mainstream estimates, by George Borjas and Larry Katz of Harvard, suggest that immigration has reduced the wages of high-school dropouts by about 5 percent, with a much smaller effect on workers with a high school degree, and a small positive effect on highly educated workers. Moreover, other economists think the Borjas-Katz numbers are too high.

In chapter 8 I'll argue that immigration may have promoted inequality in a more indirect way, by shifting the balance of *political* power up the economic scale. But the direct economic effect has been modest.

What about international trade? Much international trade probably has little or no effect on the distribution of income. For example, trade in automobiles and parts between the United States and Canada—two high-wage countries occupying different niches of the same industry, shipping each other goods produced with roughly the same mix of skilled and unskilled labor—isn't likely to have much effect on wage inequality in either country. But U.S. trade with, say, Bangladesh is a different story. Bangladesh mainly exports clothing—the classic labor-intensive good, produced by workers who need little formal education and no more capital equipment than a sewing machine. In return Bangladesh buys sophisticated goods—airplanes, chemicals, computers.

There's no question that U.S. trade with Bangladesh and other Third World countries, including China, widens inequality. Suppose that you buy a pair of pants made in Bangladesh that could have been made domestically. By buying the foreign pants you are in effect forcing the workers who would have been employed producing a made-in-America pair of pants to look for other jobs. Of course the converse is also true when the United States exports something: When Bangladesh buys a Boeing airplane, the American workers employed in producing that plane don't have to look for other jobs. But the labor embodied in U.S. exports is very different from the labor employed in U.S. industries that compete with imports. We tend to export "skill-intensive" products like aircraft, supercomputers, and Hollywood movies; we tend to import "labor-intensive" goods like pants and toys. So U.S. trade with Third World countries reduces job opportunities for less-skilled American workers, while increasing demand for more-skilled workers. There's no question that this widens the wage gap between the less-skilled and the more-skilled, contributing to increased inequality. And the rapid growth of trade with low-wage countries, especially Mexico and China, suggests that this effect has been increasing over the past fifteen years.

What's really important to understand, however, is that skill-

biased technological change, immigration, and growing international trade are, at best, explanations of a rising gap between
less-educated and more-educated workers. And despite the claims
of Lazear and many others, that's only part of the tale of rising
inequality. It's true that the payoff to education has risen—but
even the college educated have for the most part seen their wage
gains lag behind rising productivity. For example, the median
college-educated man has seen his real income rise only 17 percent
since 1973.

That's because the big gains in income have gone not to a broad
group of well-paid workers but to a narrow group of extremely well-
paid people. In general those who receive enormous incomes are
also well educated, but their gains aren't representative of the gains
of educated workers as a whole. CEOs and schoolteachers both
typically have master's degrees, but schoolteachers have seen only
modest gains since 1973, while CEOs have seen their income rise
from about thirty times that of the average worker in 1970 to more
than three hundred times as much today.

The observation that even highly educated Americans have, for
the most part, seen their incomes fall behind the average, while a
handful of people have done incredibly well, undercuts the case for
skill-biased technological change as an explanation of inequality
and supports the argument that it's largely due to changes in institutions, such as the strength of labor unions, and norms, such as
the once powerful but now weak belief that having the boss make
vastly more than the workers is bad for morale.

Institutions: The End of the Treaty of Detroit

The idea that changes in institutions and changes in norms,
rather than anonymous skill-biased technical change, explain rising

inequality has been gaining growing support among economists, for two main reasons. First, an institutions-and-norms explanation of rising inequality today links current events to the dramatic *fall* in inequality—the Great Compression—that took place in the 1930s and 1940s. Second, an institutions-and-norms story helps explain American exceptionalism: No other advanced country has seen the same kind of surge in inequality that has taken place here.

The Great Compression in itself—or more accurately, its persistence—makes a good case for the crucial role of social forces as opposed to the invisible hand in determining income distribution. As I discussed in chapter 3, the middle-class America baby boomers grew up in didn't evolve gradually. It was constructed in a very short period by New Deal legislation, union activity, and wage controls during World War II. Yet the relatively flat income distribution imposed during the war lasted for decades after wartime control of the economy ended. This persistence makes a strong case that anonymous market forces are less decisive than Economics 101 teaches. As Piketty and Saez put it:

> The compression of wages during the war can be explained by the wage controls of the war economy, but how can we explain the fact that high wage earners did not recover after the wage controls were removed? This evidence cannot be immediately reconciled with explanations of the reduction of inequality based solely on technical change. . . . We think that this pattern or evolution of inequality is additional indirect evidence that nonmarket mechanisms such as labor market institutions and social norms regarding inequality may play a role in setting compensation.[4]

The MIT economists Frank Levy and Peter Temin have led the way in explaining how those "labor market institutions and social norms" worked.[5] They point to a set of institutional arrangements they call the Treaty of Detroit—the name given by *Fortune* magazine to a landmark 1949 bargain struck between the United Auto Workers and General Motors. Under that agreement, UAW members were guaranteed wages that rose with productivity, as well as health and retirement benefits; what GM got in return was labor peace.

Levy and Temin appropriate the term to refer not only to the formal arrangement between the auto companies and their workers but also to the way that arrangement was emulated throughout the U.S. economy. Other unions based their bargaining demands on the standard set by the UAW, leading to the spread of wage-and-benefit packages that, while usually not as plush as what Walter Reuther managed to get, ensured that workers shared in the fruits of progress. And even nonunion workers were strongly affected, because the threat of union activity often led nonunionized employers to offer their workers more or less what their unionized counterparts were getting: The economy of the fifties and sixties was characterized by "pattern wages," in which wage settlements of major unions and corporations established norms for the economy as a whole.

At the same time the existence of powerful unions acted as a restraint on the incomes of both management and stockholders. Top executives knew that if they paid themselves huge salaries, they would be inviting trouble with their workers; similarly corporations that made high profits while failing to raise wages were putting labor relations at risk.

The federal government was also an informal party to the Treaty of Detroit: It intervened, in various ways, to support workers' bargaining positions and restrain perceived excess at the top. Workers' productivity was substantially lower in the 1960s than it is today, but the minimum wage, adjusted for inflation, was considerably higher. Labor laws were interpreted and enforced in a way that favored unions. And there was often direct political pressure on large companies and top executives who were seen as stepping over the line. John F. Kennedy famously demanded that steel companies, which had just negotiated a modest wage settlement, rescind a price increase.

To see how different labor relations were under the Treaty of Detroit from their state today, compare two iconic corporations, one of the past, one of the present.

In the final years of the postwar boom General Motors was America's largest private employer aside from the regulated telephone monopoly. Its CEO was, correspondingly, among America's highest paid executives: Charles Johnson's 1969 salary was $795,000, about $4.3 million in today's dollars—and that salary excited considerable comment. But ordinary GM workers were also paid well. In 1969 auto industry production workers earned on average almost $9,000, the equivalent of more than $40,000 today. GM workers, who also received excellent health and retirement benefits, were considered solidly in the middle class.

Today Wal-Mart is America's largest corporation, with 800,000 employees. In 2005 Lee Scott, its chairman, was paid almost $23 million. That's more than five times Charles Johnson's inflation-adjusted salary, but Mr. Scott's compensation excited relatively little comment, since wasn't exceptional for the CEO of a large corporation these days. The wages paid to Wal-Mart's workers, on the other hand, do attract attention, because they are low even by current standards. On average Wal-Mart's nonsupervisory employees are paid about $18,000 a year, less than half what GM workers were paid thirty-five years ago, adjusted for inflation. Wal-Mart is also notorious both for the low percentage of its workers who receive health benefits, and the stinginess of those scarce benefits.[6]

What Piketty and Saez, Levy and Temin, and a growing number of other economists argue is that the contrast between GM then and Wal-Mart now is representative of what has happened in the economy at large—that in the 1970s and after, the Treaty of Detroit was rescinded, the institutions and norms that had limited inequality after World War II went away, and inequality surged back to Gilded Age levels. In other words, the great divergence of incomes since the seventies is basically the Great Compression in reverse. In the 1930s and 1940s institutions were created and norms established that limited inequality; starting in the 1970s those institutions and norms were torn down, leading to rising inequality. The institutions-and-norms explanation integrates the rise and fall of middle-class America into a single story.

The institutions-and-norms explanation also correctly predicts how trends in inequality should differ among countries. Bear in mind that the forces of technological change and globalization have affected every advanced country: Europe has applied information technology almost as rapidly as we have, cheap clothing in Europe is just as likely to be made in China as is cheap clothing in America. If technology and globalization are the driving forces behind rising inequality, then Europe should be experiencing the same rise in inequality as the United States. In terms of institutions and norms, however, things are very different among advanced nations: In Europe, for example, unions remain strong, and old norms condemning very high pay and emphasizing the entitlements of workers haven't faded away. So if institutions are the story, we'd expect the U.S. experience of rising inequality to be exceptional, not echoed in Europe.

And on that comparison, an institutions-and-norms explanation wins: America is unique. The clearest evidence comes from income tax data, which allow a comparison of the share of income accruing to the economic elite. These data show that during World War II and its aftermath all advanced countries experienced a Great Compression, a sharp drop in inequality. In the United States this leveling was reversed beginning in the 1970s, and the effects of the Great Compression have now been fully eliminated. In Canada, which is closely linked to the U.S. economy, and in Britain, which had its own period of conservative dominance under Margaret Thatcher, there has been a more limited trend toward renewed inequality. But in Japan and France there has been very little change in inequality since 1980.[7]

There's also spottier and less consistent information from surveys of household incomes. The picture there is fuzzier, but again the United States and, to a lesser extent, Britain stand out as countries where inequality sharply increased, while other advanced countries experienced either minor increases or no change at all.[8]

There is, in short, a strong circumstantial case for believing that institutions and norms, rather than technology or globalization, are the big sources of rising inequality in the United States. The obvious example of changing institutions is the collapse of the U.S. union movement. But what do I mean when I talk about changing norms?

Norms and Inequality:
The Case of the Runaway CEOs

When economists talk about how changing norms have led to rising inequality, they often have one concrete example in mind: the runaway growth of executive pay. Although executives at major corporations aren't the only big winners from rising inequality, their visibility makes them a good illustration of what is happening more broadly throughout the economy.

According to a Federal Reserve study, in the 1970s the chief executives at 102 major companies (those that were in the top 50 as measured by sales at some point over the period 1940–1990) were paid on average about $1.2 million in today's dollars. That wasn't hardship pay, to say the least. But it was only a bit more than CEOs were paid in the 1930s, and "only" 40 times what the average full-time worker in the U.S. economy as a whole was paid at the time. By the early years of this decade, however, CEO pay averaged more than $9 million a year, 367 times the pay of the average worker. Other top executives also saw huge increases in pay, though not as large as that of CEOs: The next two highest officers in major companies made 31 times the average worker's salary in the seventies, but 169 times as much by the early 2000s.[9]

To make some sense of this extraordinary development, let's start with an idealized story about the determinants of executive pay.[10] Imagine that the profitability of each company depends on the quality of its CEO, and that the bigger the company, the larger the CEO's impact on profit. Imagine also that the quality of potential CEOs is observable: everyone knows who is the 100th best executive in America, the 99th best, and so on. In that case, there will be a competition for executives that ends up assigning the best executives to the biggest companies, where their contribution matters the most. And as a result of that competition, each executive's pay will reflect his or her quality.

An immediate implication of this story is that at the top, even small differences in perceived executive quality will translate into big differences in salaries. The reason is competition: For a giant company the difference in profitability between having the 10th best executive and the 11th best executive may easily be tens of millions of dollars each year. In that sense the idealized model suggests that top executives might be earning their pay. And the idealized model also says that if executives are paid far more today than they were a generation ago, it must be because for some reason—more intense competition, higher stock prices, whatever—it matters more than it used to to have the best man running a company.

But once we relax the idealized premises of the story, it's not hard to see why executive pay is a lot less tied down by fundamental forces of supply and demand, and a lot more subject to changes in social norms and political power, than this story implies.

First, neither the quality of executives nor the extent to which that quality matters are hard numbers. Assessing the productivity of corporate leaders isn't like measuring how many bricks a worker can lay in a hour. You can't even reliably evaluate managers by looking at the profitability of the companies they run, because profits depend on a lot of factors outside the chief executive's control. Moreover profitability can, for extended periods, be in the eye of the beholder: Enron looked like a fabulously successful company to most of the world; Toll Brothers, the McMansion king, looked like a great success as long as the housing bubble was still inflating. So the question of how much to pay a top executive has a strong element of subjectivity, even fashion, to it. In the fifties and sixties big companies didn't think it was important to have a famous, charismatic leader: CEOs rarely made the covers of business magazines, and companies tended to promote from within, stressing the virtues of being a team player. By contrast, in the eighties and thereafter CEOs became rock stars—they defined their companies as much as their companies defined them. Are corporate boards wiser now than they were when they chose solid insiders to run companies, or have they just been caught up in the culture of celebrity?

Second, even to the extent that corporate boards correctly judge both the quality of executives and the extent to which quality matters for profitability, the actual amount they end up paying their top executives depends a lot on what *other* companies do. Thus, in the corporate world of the 1960s and 1970s, companies rarely paid eye-popping salaries to perceived management superstars. In fact companies tended to see huge paychecks at the top as a possible source of reduced team spirit, as well as a potential source of labor problems. In that environment even a corporate board that *did* believe that hiring star executives was the way to go didn't have to offer exorbitant pay to attract those stars. But today executive pay in the millions or tens of millions is the norm. And even corporate boards that aren't smitten with the notion of superstar leadership end up paying high salaries, partly to attract executives whom they consider adequate, partly because the financial markets will be suspicious of a company whose CEO isn't lavishly paid.

Finally, to the extent that there is a market for corporate talent, who, exactly, are the buyers? Who determines how good a CEO is, and how much he has to be paid to keep another company from poaching his entrepreneurial know-how? The answer, of course, is that corporate boards, largely selected by the CEO, hire compensation experts, almost always chosen by the CEO, to determine how much the CEO is worth. It is, shall we say, a situation conducive to overstatement both of the executive's personal qualities and of how much those supposed personal qualities matter for the company's bottom line.

What all this suggests is that incomes at the top—the paychecks of top executives and, by analogy, the incomes of many other income superstars—may depend a lot on "soft" factors such as social attitudes and the political background. Perhaps the strongest statement of this view comes from Lucian Bebchuk and

Jesse Fried, authors of the 2004 book *Pay Without Performance*. Bebchuk and Fried argue that top executives in effect set their own paychecks, that neither the quality of the executives nor the marketplace for talent has any real bearing. The only thing that limits executive pay, they argue, is the "outrage constraint": the concern that very high executive compensation will create a backlash from usually quiescent shareholders, workers, politicians, or the general public.[11]

To the extent that this view is correct, soaring incomes at the top can be seen as a social and political, rather than narrowly economic phenomenon: high incomes shot up not because of an increased demand for talent but because a variety of factors caused the death of outrage. News organizations that might once have condemned lavishly paid executives lauded their business genius instead; politicians who might once have led populist denunciations of corporate fat cats sought to flatter the people who provide campaign contributions; unions that might once have walked out to protest giant executive bonuses had been crushed by years of union busting. Oh, and one more thing. Because the top marginal tax rate has declined from 70 percent in the early 1970s to 35 percent today, there's more incentive for a top executive to take advantage of his position: He gets to keep much more of his excess pay. And the result is an explosion of income inequality at the top of the scale.

The idea that rising pay at the top of the scale mainly reflects social and political change, rather than the invisible hand of the market, strikes some people as implausible—too much at odds with Economics 101. But it's an idea that has some surprising supporters: Some of the most ardent defenders of the way modern executives are paid say almost the same thing.

Before I get to those defenders, let me give you a few words from someone who listened to what they said. From Gordon Gekko's

famous speech to the shareholders of Teldar Paper in the movie
Wall Street:

> Now, in the days of the free market, when our country was
> a top industrial power, there was accountability to the stock-
> holder. The Carnegies, the Mellons, the men that built this
> great industrial empire, made sure of it because it was their
> money at stake. Today, management has no stake in the com-
> pany! . . . The point is, ladies and gentlemen, that greed—for
> lack of a better word—is good. Greed is right. Greed works.

What those who watch the movie today may not realize is that
the words Oliver Stone put in Gordon Gekko's mouth were strik-
ingly similar to what the leading theorists on executive pay were
saying at the time. In 1990 Michael Jensen of the Harvard Business School and Kevin Murphy of the University of Rochester
published an article in the *Harvard Business Review*, summariz-
ing their already influential views on executive pay. The trouble
with American business, they declared, is that "the compensation
of top executives is virtually independent of performance. On
average corporate America pays its most important leaders like
bureaucrats. Is it any wonder then that so many CEOs act like
bureaucrats rather than the value-maximizing entrepreneurs companies need to enhance their standing in world markets?" In other
words, greed is good.[12]

Why, then, weren't companies linking pay to performance?
Because of social and political pressure:

> Why don't boards of directors link pay more closely to perfor-
> mance? Commentators offer many explanations, but nearly
> every analysis we've seen overlooks one powerful ingredient—

the costs imposed by making executive salaries public. Government disclosure rules ensure that executive pay remains a visible and controversial topic. The benefits of disclosure are obvious; it provides safeguards against "looting" by managers in collusion with "captive" directors.

The costs of disclosure are less well appreciated but may well exceed the benefits. Managerial labor contracts are not a private matter between employers and employees. Third parties play an important role in the contracting process, and strong political forces operate inside and outside companies to shape executive pay. Moreover, authority over compensation decisions rests not with the shareholders but with compensation committees generally composed of outside directors. These committees are elected by shareholders but are not perfect agents for them. Public disclosure of "what the boss makes" gives ammunition to outside constituencies with their own special-interest agendas. Compensation committees typically react to the agitation over pay levels by capping—explicitly or implicitly—the amount of money the CEO earns.[13]

In other words Jensen and Murphy, writing at a time when executive pay was still low by today's standards, believed that social norms, in the form of the outrage constraint, were holding executive paychecks down. Of course they saw this as a bad thing, not a good thing. They dismissed concerns about executive self-dealing, placing "looting" and "captive" in scare quotes. But their implicit explanation of trends in executive pay was the same as that of critics of high pay. Executive pay, they pointed out, had actually fallen in real terms between the late 1930s and the early 1980s, even as companies grew much bigger. The reason, they asserted, was public pressure. So they were arguing that social and political considerations, not narrowly economic forces, led to the sharp reduction in income differences between workers and bosses in the postwar era.

Today the idea that huge paychecks are part of a beneficial system in which executives are given an incentive to perform well has become something of a sick joke. A 2001 article in *Fortune*, "The Great CEO Pay Heist,"[14] encapsulated the cynicism: "You might have expected it to go like this: The stock isn't moving, so the CEO shouldn't be rewarded. But it was actually the opposite: The stock isn't moving, so we've got to find some other basis for rewarding the CEO." And the article quoted a somewhat repentant Michael Jensen: "I've generally worried these guys weren't getting paid enough. But now even I'm troubled."[15] But no matter: The doctrine that greed is good did its work, by helping to change social and political norms. Paychecks that would have made front-page news and created a furor a generation ago hardly rate mention today.

Not surprisingly, executive pay in European countries—which haven't experienced the same change in norms and institutions—has lagged far behind. The CEO of BP, based in the United Kingdom, is paid less than half as much as the CEO of Chevron, a company half BP's size, but based in America. As a European pay consultant put it, "There is no shame factor in the U.S. In Europe, there is more of a concern about the social impact."[16]

To be fair, CEOs aren't the only members of the economic elite who have seen their incomes soar since the 1970s. Some economists have long argued that certain kinds of technological change, such as the rise of the mass media, may be producing large salary gaps between people who seem, on the surface, to have similar qualifications.[17] Indeed the rise of the mass media may help explain why celebrities of various types make so much more than they used to. And it's possible to argue that in a vague way technology may help explain why income gaps have widened among lawyers and other professionals: Maybe fax machines and the Internet let the top guns take on more of the work requiring that extra something, while less talented professionals are left with the routine drudge work. Still, the example of CEO pay shows how changes in institutions and norms can lead to rising inequality—and as we've already seen, international comparisons suggest that institutions, not technology, are at the heart of the changes over the past thirty years.

The Reason Why

Since the 1970s norms and institutions in the United States have changed in ways that either encouraged or permitted sharply higher inequality. Where, however, did the change in norms and institutions come from? The answer appears to be politics.

Consider, for example, the fate of the unions. Unions were once an important factor limiting income inequality, both because of their direct effect in raising their members' wages and because the union pattern of wage settlements—which consistently raised the wages of less-well-paid workers more—was, in the fifties and sixties, reflected in the labor market as a whole. The decline of the unions has removed that moderating influence. But why did unions decline?

The conventional answer is that the decline of unions is a result of the changing structure of the workforce. According to this view, the American economy used to be dominated by manufacturing, which was also where the most powerful unions were—think of the UAW and the Steelworkers. Now we're mostly a service economy, partly because of technological change, partly because we're

importing so many manufactured goods. Surely, then, deindustrial-
ization must explain the decline of unions.

Except that it turns out that it doesn't. Manufacturing has
declined in importance, but most of the decline in union membership comes from a collapse of unionization *within* manufacturing, from 39 percent of workers in 1973 to 13 percent in 2005.
Also, there's no economic law saying that unionization has to be
restricted to manufacturing. On the contrary, a company like Wal-
Mart, which doesn't face foreign competition, should be an even
better target for unionization than are manufacturing companies.
Think how that would change the shape of the U.S. economy:
If Wal-Mart employees were part of a union that could demand
higher wages and better benefits, retail prices might be slightly
higher, but the retail giant wouldn't go out of business—and the
American middle class would have several hundred thousand additional members. Imagine extending that story to other retail giants,
or better yet to the service sector as a whole, and you can get a
sense of how the Great Compression happened under FDR.

Why, then, isn't Wal-Mart unionized? Why, in general, did the
union movement lose ground in manufacturing while failing to
gain members in the rising service industries? The answer is simple
and brutal: Business interests, which seemed to have reached an
accommodation with the labor movement in the 1960s, went on
the offensive against unions beginning in the 1970s. And we're
not talking about gentle persuasion, we're talking about hardball
tactics, often including the illegal firing of workers who tried to
organize or supported union activity. During the late seventies and
early eighties at least one in every twenty workers who voted for a
union was illegally fired; some estimates put the number as high as
one in eight.

The collapse of the U.S. union movement that took place beginning in the 1970s has no counterpart in any other Western nation.
Table 5 shows a stark comparison between the United States and
Canada. In the 1960s the U.S. workforce was, if anything, slightly
more unionized than Canada's workforce. By the end of the 1990s,
however, U.S. unions had been all but driven out of the private sector, while Canada's union movement was essentially intact. The difference, of course, was politics: America's political climate turned
favorable to union busting, while Canada's didn't.

I described in chapter 6 the centrality of antiunionism to Barry
Goldwater's rise, and the way opposition to unions played a key role
in the consolidation of movement conservatism's business base. By
the second half of the 1970s, movement conservatives had enough
political clout that businesses felt empowered to take on unions.

And once Ronald Reagan took office the campaign against
unions was aided and abetted by political support at the highest
levels. In particular, Reagan's suppression of the air traffic control-
lers' union was the signal for a broad assault on unions throughout
the economy. The rollback of unions, which were once a powerful
constraint on inequality, was political in the broadest sense. It was

Table 5. Percentage of Unionized Wage and Salary Workers

	United States	Canada
1960	30.4	32.3
1999	13.5	32.6

Source: David Card, Thomas Lemieux, and W. Craig Riddell, *Unionization
and Wage Inequality: A Comparitive Study of the U.S., the U.K., and Canada*
(National Bureau of Economic Research working paper no. 9473, Jan.
2003).

an exercise in the use of power, both within the government and in our society at large.

To understand the Great Divergence, then, we need to understand how it was that movement conservatism became such a powerful factor in American political life.

8

THE POLITICS OF INEQUALITY

For six years, from 1994 to the end of the Clinton administration, a Republican Congress and a Democratic president waged a bitter power struggle. The impeachment
drama of 1998 is the event most people remember. But the government shutdown of 1995, which was about matters of state rather
than personal behavior, was more revealing. It was openly a fight
about different visions of government and society.

The shutdown occurred primarily because Newt Gingrich, the
Speaker of the House, was trying to impose a plan that would
sharply cut Medicare's funding[1] and, equally important, give
healthy seniors an incentive to drop out of Medicare, undermining both the program's universality and its financial base. In effect
Gingrich wanted to subject Medicare to slow death by strangula-
tion. Gingrich had enough votes to get his plan through Congress,
but he didn't have the votes to override a presidential veto. So he

tried to force Clinton's hand by denying the federal government the funds it needed to keep operating.

Now, a federal shutdown doesn't literally mean that all federal offices are locked up and closed. About half the federal workforce stayed on the job, and the most essential services were maintained. But the rawness of the event was still remarkable: Republicans were willing to play chicken with the government's ability to function in their drive to take down one of the pillars of the U.S. welfare state.

As it turned out, Gingrich had misjudged both Clinton and the voters. Clinton held firm. The public blamed Gingrich, not the Clinton administration, for the standoff, and the Republicans eventually backed down. Clinton's impeachment three years later, which seems otherwise a bizarre event, is best understood as Gingrich's attempt to take revenge. The 1995 shutdown demonstrated just how partisan American politics had become—and unlike the impeachment the 1995 confrontation showed what the partisanship was really about.

Many figures in both politics and the press suffer from a malady some liberals have taken to calling "Broderism,"[2] which causes them to mourn the passing of bipartisanship but to speak as if the inability of today's politicians to get along is the result of mysterious character flaws. There's no question that some of our leading politicians have character flaws in abundance—Clinton had his problems, and Gingrich, who was carrying on his own affair with a subordinate even as he denounced Clinton's immorality, displayed a combination of grandiosity and hypocrisy rare even among politicians. But policy, not personalities, is the reason politics has become so bitter and partisan.

The great age of bipartisanship wasn't a reflection of the gentlemanly character of an earlier generation of politicians. Rather, it reflected the subdued nature of political conflict in an era when the parties weren't that far apart on basic issues. After the 1948 election Republicans decided that the achievements of the New Deal couldn't be reversed, and stopped trying, while Democrats, who had made a revolution in the thirties and forties, settled down to a program of incremental reform. The result was a generation-long era of muted partisanship. That era ended, and bitter partisanship reemerged, when the Republicans changed their minds a second time. The reason there's so much hatred between the parties today is that beginning in the 1970s the GOP became, once again, a party defined by its opposition to taxes on the rich and benefits for the poor and middle class, and willing to do whatever it takes to promote that agenda.

Understanding the nature of the partisan divide is one thing; understanding its causes is another. In fact the rightward march of the Republican Party poses two great puzzles: First, why would one of America's two great political parties launch a crusade to dismantle the welfare state in an era of rapidly rising inequality, an era in which taxing the rich to pay for middle- and lower-class benefits should have become more popular, not less? Second, why has the Republican Party been able to win so many elections, despite its antipopulist economic agenda?

In this chapter I'll try to resolve the first of these puzzles, reserving the second question for the next chapter. Before I get there, however, let me deal with a common objection: the claim that whatever they may say, the parties aren't very different in what they do.

The Partisan Divide

During the 2000 campaign Ralph Nader mocked politicians from the two major parties as "Republicrats," indistinguishable representatives of moneyed interests. Even in that election, when George W. Bush somehow got the press to describe him as a moderate, most Americans disagreed, and at this point the vast majority of Americans view the parties as being very different indeed. Still, how the parties are perceived may not be a good guide to what they actually do. Are they really all that different?

When Nader first became prominent in the sixties, the parties really were as similar as he says. Up to the mid-1970s the parties were hard to distinguish in many ways: John F. Kennedy cut taxes, Richard Nixon raised them, and the votes on major pieces of legislation often involved significant crossing of party lines in both directions. For example, an important part of the support for the 1965 legislation that created Medicare and Medicaid came from Republicans, while significant opposition came from Democrats. In the final House vote, seventy Republicans voted yea, while forty-seven Democrats voted nay. But that was another political era.

To see how much things have changed, consider one easily measurable indicator of partisan differences: tax policy, especially tax policy toward the wealthy. Reagan, Clinton, and George W. Bush each started his administration with a major change in tax policy. Reagan and Bush reduced taxes on the rich; Clinton raised them.

Specifically, Reagan began his term with a sharp reduction in personal income tax rates, and a sharp cut in the effective tax rate on corporate profits. Both of these measures delivered disproportionately large benefits to upper-income households, which paid a much higher income tax rate to start with, and also owned most of the stocks that benefited from lower corporate taxes. By contrast Clinton raised the income tax rate on the highest bracket, while eliminating the upper limit on the Medicare payroll tax—mainly hitting the same elite group that was the prime beneficiary of the Reagan tax cuts. Bush cut taxes twice, in 2001 and 2003, exploiting the brief illusion of success in Iraq to push through the second round of cuts. The first cut sharply reduced the top income tax rate and phased out the estate tax, which falls only on the wealthy, while the second reduced taxes on dividends and capital gains, again mainly benefiting the highest-income Americans.

Table 6 shows the actual effective tax rate paid by the top 1 percent of the population—that is, the percentage of income people in that group (which currently corresponds to incomes of approximately $425,000 a year or more) actually paid in taxes—for selected years. Sure enough, the rich gained a lot under Reagan and Bush II, while losing a lot under Clinton. (In both the Reagan and Clinton years the initial changes in tax policy were eroded over time, as each president had to deal with a Congress controlled by the opposition party, but the point stands.)

For the most part these tax changes passed on near-party-line votes. The Clinton-Gore tax increase of 1993 passed the House without a single Republican vote; the Bush tax cut of 2003 passed the House with only one Republican voting against, and only seven Democrats voting in favor. The 2005 Gasoline for America's Security Act—basically a set of tax breaks for oil companies—passed by

Table 6. Average Federal Tax Rates on the Top 1 Percent

1980	34.6
1982	27.7
1992	30.6
1994	35.8
2000	33.0
2004	31.1

Source: Congressional Budget Office, "Historical Federal Effective Tax Rates," http://www.cbo.gov/ftpdoc.cfm?index=7718&type=1.

a one-vote margin, with only thirteen Republicans voting no and not a single Democrat in favor.

The record on spending can seem less clear-cut, but that's only because the parties have been less able to implement their agendas.

Reagan initially tried to make deep cuts in Social Security, only to abandon the attempt in the face of overwhelming congressional and public reaction. Reagan did, however, manage to push through new rules that reduced benefits under the food stamp program, Aid to Families with Dependent Children, and unemployment insurance. Clinton famously tried to introduce a form of universal health care—and completely failed. He did, however, preside over a substantial increase in the Earned Income Tax Credit, which raises the incomes of low-wage workers.

After the 1994 election gave Republicans control of Congress, they tried—as we have seen—to undermine the financing of Medicare. They failed, and Bush the younger actually pushed through a significant expansion in Medicare, to cover prescription drugs. But this was clearly intended to provide political cover, and the new program was designed in a way that favored drug company interests. Moreover, by introducing a large subsidy for Medicare Advantage plans, in which tax money is funneled through private-sector middlemen, Bush's Medicare bill took a major step toward Gingrich's goal of privatizing the program. In 2005 Bush sought to partially privatize Social Security, while cutting promised future benefits; if implemented, Bush's plan would have eliminated traditional Social Security within a few decades. Like Reagan's attempt to scale back Social Security, however, this attempt quickly failed.

So the difference between the parties is not an illusion. Republicans cut taxes on the rich and try to shrink government benefits and undermine the welfare state. Democrats raise taxes on the rich while trying to expand government benefits and strengthen the welfare state.

And the public has picked up on the change. In the sixties and seventies, voters tended to be more or less evenly divided on the question of whether there was a significant difference between the parties. By 2004, however, 76 percent of Americans saw significant differences between the parties, up from 46 percent in 1972.[3]

The Radicalization of the GOP

"Comprehensive health insurance," declared the president, "is an idea whose time has come in America. Let us act now to assure all Americans financial access to high quality medical care." Was that Bill Clinton speaking? No, it was Richard Nixon, whose Comprehensive Health Insurance Plan, proposed in 1974, broadly resembled plans being offered by liberal Democrats like John Edwards today. The legislation never got very far, however, because Nixon was soon enveloped in the Watergate affair.[4]

Modern movement conservatives sometimes say, contemptuously, that Nixon governed as a liberal. And in terms of economic and environmental policy, it's true, at least by today's standards. In addition to proposing universal health care, Nixon pushed for a guaranteed minimum income. On the revenue side, Nixon pushed through a tax increase in 1969, including creation of the alternative minimum tax, which was intended to crack down on wealthy Americans who managed to use tax shelters to avoid taxes. On another front he passed the Clean Air Act, and sent dozens of environmental measures to Congress. Veterans of the Environmental Protection Agency have told me that the Nixon years were a golden age.

Nixon, in short, was a transitional figure. Although he used many of the political tactics associated with movement conservatism, he was a pragmatist rather than an ideologue, as were many Republicans. The character of the Republican Party changed rapidly in the post-Nixon years. In 1984 Thomas Edsall of the *Washington Post* published *The New Politics of Inequality*, a remarkably insightful and prescient analysis of the changes already taking place in American politics. At the core of his analysis was the renewal and radicalization of the Republican Party that, in his view, took place in the mid-to-late 1970s:

> Such previously hostile and mutually suspicious groups as the corporate lobbying community; ideological right-wing organizations committed to a conservative set of social and cultural values; sunbelt entrepreneurial interests, particularly independent oil; a number of so-called neo-conservative or cold war intellectuals with hard-line views on defense and foreign policy who, although sometimes nominally Democratic, provide support for the politics and policies of the GOP; economists advocating radical alteration of the tax system, with tax preferences skewed toward corporations and the affluent—all of these groups found that the Republican Party offered enough common ground for the formation of an alliance.[5]

In other words, movement conservatism had taken over the GOP.

Ronald Reagan was the first movement conservative president. Within Ronald Reagan's inner circle, views that had once been confined to what Eisenhower described as a "tiny splinter group" reigned: David Stockman, Reagan's budget director, considered Social Security an example of "closet socialism," while fervent supply-siders, who believed that cutting taxes would increase revenue, were given key positions in the Treasury Department and elsewhere in the government. Reagan also did his best to reverse Nixon's environmental achievements, slashing the budget of the Environmental Protection Agency and gutting its enforcement activities. His first secretary of the interior, James Watt, was a fervent antienvironmentalist with strong ties to the religious right who quintupled the amount of public land open to coal mining. Watt was famously forced to resign after boasting that his staff included "a black, a woman, two Jews, and a cripple."[6]

Reagan's ability to impose a movement conservative agenda was, however, limited by political realities. Democrats controlled the House of Representatives throughout his administration. Republicans held a majority in the Senate until his last two years in office, but many Senate Republicans were still Eisenhower-style moderates. These political realities forced Reagan to moderate his policies. For example, although his inner circle wanted to slash Social Security benefits, he was eventually forced to secure Social Security's finances with a tax increase instead.

After Reagan, however, the GOP became thoroughly radicalized. Consider the 2004 platform of the Texas Republican Party, which gives an idea of what the party faithful really think: national platforms have to present at least an appearance of moderation, but in Texas Republicans can be Republicans. It calls for the elimination of federal agencies "including, but not limited to, the Bureau of Alcohol, Tobacco, and Firearms; the position of Surgeon General; the Environmental Protection Agency; the Departments of Energy, Housing and Urban Development, Health and Human Services, Education, Commerce, and Labor." The platform also calls for the privatization of Social Security and the abolition of the minimum wage. In effect Texas Republicans want to repeal the New Deal completely.

In fact movement conservatives want to go even further, as illustrated by the campaign to end taxes on inherited wealth. The estate tax is an ancient institution, introduced in its modern form in 1916. It is the most progressive of federal taxes—that is, it falls more disproportionately on the wealthy than any other tax. In the late 1990s, before the Bush tax cuts, a mere 2 percent of decedents had estates large enough to face any tax at all. In terms of income, the richest 1 percent of the population paid almost two-thirds of the estate tax, and the richest 10 percent paid 96 percent of the taxes.[7]

Since only a handful of voters pay estate taxes, while many voters benefit from government programs the estate tax helps pay for, any party seeking to cater to median or typical voters would, you might think, be inclined to leave the estate tax alone. In fact, that's what the Republican Party did for seventy years: Its last serious attempt to repeal the estate tax until recent years took place in 1925–26— and this attempt failed in large part because even some Republicans opposed repeal.[8] But in the 1990s the Republican Party once again began making estate tax repeal a priority. And the 2001 Bush tax cuts included a phaseout of the estate tax, with rates going down and exemptions going up, concluding with total elimination of the tax in 2010. In other words today's Republican party is willing to go further than the Republican Party of the 1920s, the last, golden years of the Long Gilded Age, in cutting taxes on the wealthy.

Some movement conservatives are open about their desire to turn back the clock. Grover Norquist, the antitax advocate who has been described as the "field marshal" of the tax-cut drive, is best known for saying, "My goal is to cut government in half in twenty-five years, to get it down to the size where we can drown it in the bathtub."[9] Even more revealing, however, is his statement that he wants to bring America back to "the McKinley era, absent the protectionism," to the way America was "up until Teddy Roosevelt, when the socialists took over. The income tax, the death tax, regulation, all that."[10]

The modern Republican Party, then, has been taken over by radicals, people who want to undo the twentieth century. There hasn't been any corresponding radicalization of the Democratic Party, so the right-wing takeover of the GOP is the underlying cause of today's bitter partisanship. There remains, however, the question of how movement conservatives managed to seize and keep control of one of America's two major political parties.

The Vast Conspiracy

The nature of the hold movement conservatism has on the Republican Party may be summed up very simply: Yes, Virginia, there is a vast right-wing conspiracy. That is, there is an interlocking set of institutions ultimately answering to a small group of people that collectively reward loyalists and punish dissenters. These institutions provide obedient politicians with the resources to win elections, safe havens in the event of defeat, and lucrative career opportunities after they leave office. They guarantee favorable news coverage to politicians who follow the party line, while harassing and undermining opponents. And they support a large standing army of party intellectuals and activists.

The world of right-wing think tanks, although it's far from being the most important component of the "vast conspiracy," offers a useful window into how the conspiracy works. Here are a few scenes from modern think tank life:

Item: Bruce Bartlett, a conservative economist and veteran of the Reagan administration, works at the National Center for Planning Analysis, a think tank that specializes in advocating privatization. NCPA's financial support includes funding from twelve foundations, including Castle Rock, Earhart, JM, Koch, Bradley, Scaife, and Olin.[11] Disillusioned with George W. Bush's policies, Bartlett writes *Impostor*, a book that accuses Bush of not being a true conservative. He is promptly fired from his think tank position.

Item: Sen. Rick Santorum, a hard-line conservative representing the relatively moderate state of Pennsylvania, is swept away in the 2006 midterm election. He promptly takes a job as director of the "America's Enemies" program at the Ethics and Public Policy Center, an organization whose self-proclaimed mission is "to clarify and reinforce the bond between the Judeo-Christian moral tradition and the public debate over domestic and foreign policy issues." EPPC is supported by grants from eight foundations: Castle Rock, Earhart, Koch, Bradley, Smith Richardson, Olin, and two of the Scaife foundations.[12]

Item: The National Center for Public Policy Research is a think tank devoted to "providing free market solutions to today's public policy problems"—an activity that in recent years has mainly involved casting doubt on global warming. It made the news in 2004 when it was learned that NCPPR was helping Jack Abramoff, the Republican lobbyist, launder funds: The think tank funneled $1 million to a fake direct-mail firm that shared Abramoff's address. Why NCPPR? Since its founding in 1982, the organization has been headed by Amy Moritz Ridenour, an associate of Abramoff's when he became president of the College Republicans in 1981. Ridenour's husband is also on the payroll, with both being paid six-figure salaries. NCPPR receives funding from Castle Rock, Earhart, Scaife, Bradley, and Olin.[13]

There's nothing on the left comparable to the right-wing think tank universe. The *Washington Post* has a regular feature called "Think Tank Town," which "publishes columns submitted by 11 prominent think tanks." Of the eleven institutions so honored, five are movement conservative organizations: the American Enterprise Institute, the Cato Institute, the Heritage Foundation, the Manhattan Institute, and the Hudson Institute. Only one, the Center for American Progress, can really be considered an arm of the progressive movement—and it wasn't founded until 2003. Other think tanks, like the Brookings Institution, although often described as "liberal," are in reality vaguely centrist organizations without a fixed policy line. There are a few progressive think tanks other than CAP that play a significant role in policy debate, such as the Center on Budget and Policy Priorities and the Economic Policy Institute. In terms of funding and manpower, however, these organizations are minnows compared with the movement conservative whales.

The proliferation of movement conservative think tanks since the 1970s means that it's possible for a movement intellectual to make quite a good living by espousing certain positions. There's a price to be paid—as Bruce Bartlett discovered, you're expected to be an apparatchik, not an independent thinker—but many consider it a good deal.

To a very large extent these think tanks were conjured into existence by a handful of foundations created by wealthy families. The bigger think tanks, Heritage and AEI in particular, also receive large amounts of corporate money.

The network of conservative think tanks has its counterpart in the world of journalism. Publications such as the *National Journal*, the *Public Interest*, and the *American Spectator* were, like the movement conservative think tanks, created with a lot of help from right-wing foundations—more or less the same foundations that helped create the think tanks. There are also a number of movement conservative newspapers: The editorial page of the *Wall Street Journal* has long played a key role, while the *Washington Times*, controlled by Sun Myung Moon's Unification Church, has become the de facto house organ of the Bush administration. And there is, of course, Fox News, with its Orwellian slogan, Fair and Balanced.

Last but certainly not least, there's the nexus among lobbyists and politicians. The apparent diversity of corporate lobbying groups, like the apparent diversity of conservative think tanks, conceals the movement's true centralization. Until his defeat in 2006 forced him to take a new job confronting America's enemies, Sen. Rick Santorum held a meeting every Tuesday with about two dozen top lobbyists. Here's how Nicholas Confessore described those meetings in 2003:

> Every week, the lobbyists present pass around a list of the jobs available and discuss whom to support. Santorum's responsibility is to make sure each one is filled by a loyal Republican— a senator's chief of staff, for instance, or a top White House aide, or another lobbyist whose reliability has been demonstrated. After Santorum settles on a candidate, the lobbyists present make sure it is known whom the Republican leadership favors.[14]

Santorum's weekly meetings and similar meetings run by Roy Blunt, the House majority whip, were the culmination of the "K Street Strategy," the name Grover Norquist and former House majority leader Tom DeLay gave to their plan to drive Democrats out of lobbying organizations, and give the jobs to loyal Republicans. Part of the purpose of this strategy was to ensure that Republicans received the lion's share of corporate contributions, while Democratic finances were starved—a goal also served by direct pressure. In 1995 DeLay compiled a list of the four-hundred largest political action committees along with the amounts and percentages of money they gave to each party, then called "unfriendly" lobbyists into his office to lay down the law. "If you want to play in our revolution, you have to live by our rules," he told the *Washington Post*.[15] Equally important, however, the takeover of the lobbies helped enforce loyalty within the Republican Party, by providing a huge pool of patronage jobs—very, very well-paid patronage jobs—that could be used to reward those who toe the party line.

The various institutions of movement conservatism create strong incentives for Republican politicians to take positions well to the right of center. It's not just a matter of getting campaign contributions, it's a matter of personal financial prospects. The public strongly believes that Medicare should use its bargaining power to extract lower drug prices—but Rep. Billy Tauzin, a Democrat-turned-Republican who was the chairman of the House Energy and Commerce Committee from 2001 to 2004, pushed through a Medicare bill that specifically prohibited negotiations over prices, then moved on to a reported seven-figure salary as head of the pharmaceutical industry's main lobbying group. Rick Santorum was clearly too far right for Pennsylvania, but he had no trouble finding a nice think tank job after his defeat—whereas Lincoln Chafee, the moderate Rhode Island Republican who lost his Senate seat the same year, had to make do with a one-year teaching appointment at Brown.

Lincoln Chafee's defeat brings me to another aspect of how the institutions of movement conservatism control the GOP: they don't just support Republican politicians who toe the line, they punish those who don't. Chafee faced a nasty primary challenge from his right. His opponent, Steve Laffey, received more than a million dollars in support from the Club for Growth, which specializes in disciplining Republicans who aren't sufficiently in favor of cutting taxes. "We want to be seen as the tax-cut enforcer," declared Stephen Moore, the club's president at the time, in 2001.

The club had high hopes of taking out Chafee: Two years earlier a candidate sponsored by the Club for Growth almost defeated Sen. Arlen Specter, another relatively moderate Republican, in the Pennsylvania primary. And these challenges are effective. As one Republican congressman said in 2001, "When you have 100 percent of Republicans voting for the Bush tax cut, you know that they're looking over their shoulder and not wanting to have Steve Moore recruiting candidates in their district."

Specter was first elected to the Senate in 1980, which makes him a holdover from the days when the GOP still had room for moderates.

Younger Republican politicians have, by and large, grown up inside a party defined by movement conservatism. The hard right had already taken over the College Republicans by 1972, when none other than Karl Rove was elected the organization's chairman. Other notable College Republican alumni include Rick Santorum, Grover Norquist, Ralph Reed, and Jack Abramoff. Movement conservatives run the Republican National Committee, which means that they are responsible for recruiting congressional candidates; inevitably they choose men and women in their own image. The few remaining Republican moderates in Congress were, with rare exceptions, first elected pre-Reagan or, at the latest, before the 1994 election that sealed the dominance of the Gingrich wing of the party.

One last point: The institutions of movement conservatism ensure a continuity of goals that has no counterpart on the other side. Jimmy Carter tried to establish a national energy policy that would reduce dependence on imported oil, and that was that; nobody expected Bill Clinton to pick things up where Carter left off. Ron-

ald Reagan tried and failed to slash Social Security benefits; movement conservatives took that as merely a tactical setback. In a
now-famous 1983 article, analysts from the Cato Institute and the
Heritage Foundation called for a "Leninist strategy" of undermining support for Social Security, to "prepare the political ground
so that the fiasco of the last 18 months is not repeated."[16] That
strategy underlay George W. Bush's attempt to privatize the system—and until or unless movement conservatism is defeated as
thoroughly as pre–New Deal conservatism was, there will be more
attempts in future.

Why Did It Happen?

The mechanics of the widening partisan divide are clear. Bitter
partisanship has become the rule because the Republicans have
moved right, and the GOP has moved right because it was taken
over by movement conservatives. But there's still the question of
ultimate cause. Wealthy families who hate taxes, corporate interests that hate regulation, and intellectuals who believe that the
welfare state is illegitimate have always been with us. In the fifties
and sixties, however, these groups were marginal, treated by both
parties as cranks. What turned them into a force powerful enough
to transform American politics?

Movement conservatives themselves, to the extent that they
think about the reasons for their rise at all, see it as a tale of good
ideas triumphing over bad. The story goes something like this: The
Great Depression, combined with leftist propaganda, misled people into believing that they needed a big government to protect
them. The institutions of big government, in turn, became self-
perpetuating. But brave men, from Milton Friedman to Ronald
Reagan, gradually taught Republicans that government is the prob-

lem, not the solution. And the partisan divide is there only because some people still haven't seen the light.

At the opposite extreme from this heroic account of political change is the almost mechanistic view that growing economic inequality is the root cause of movement conservativism's rise. As I explained in chapter 1, I began working on this book with that view, which goes something like this: Money buys influence, and as the richest few percent of Americans have grown richer thanks to unequalizing forces like technical change, they have become rich enough to buy themselves a party. In this view, the rise of movement conservatism is a by-product of rising inequality.

It's certainly more plausible to think that the drastic rise in income inequality since the 1970s transformed American politics than to attribute it all to the brilliance of a few intellectuals. But the hypothesis that the rising concentration of income empowered the economic elite, driving the rightward shift of the GOP, runs up against a problem of timing. The sharp rightward shift of the Republican Party began before there was any visible increase in income inequality. Ronald Reagan was nominated in 1980, a year in which the rich were no richer, relative to the average American, than they had been during the Eisenhower years. In Congress the political shift began with the 1976 and 1978 elections. As Edsall points out, "the hard core of junior, ideologically committed Republican senators" grew from four in 1975 to eleven in 1979, with a corresponding shift also taking place in the House.[17] The takeover of the College Republicans by movement conservatives took place even earlier: Karl Rove was elected chairman in 1972. And the key institutions of movement conservatism were created at about the same time. For example, the Heritage Foundation was created in 1971. The Business Roundtable, which merged several loosely organized groups into a powerful lobby on behalf of procorporate politics—eventually forming the basis of Santorum's K Street meetings—was formed in 1972, and the U.S. Chamber of Commerce was reborn as a significant lobbying force shortly after.

Add to this the evidence I laid out in chapter 7, that changes in institutions and norms lay behind much of the rise in inequality and that political change is what led to those changes in institutions and norms, and the mechanistic view that inequality moved the Republicans to the right loses most of its plausibility. It's likely that rising income concentration reinforced the rightward trend of the GOP, as the number and wealth of donors able to lavish funds on suitably hard-line politicians grew. But something else must have gotten the process going.

That something, I believe, is the constellation of forces described in chapters 6 and 7. To recapitulate the story: In the late 1950s and early 1960s, the "new conservatives," the narrow, elitist group centered around the *National Review*, grew into a serious movement by merging with other factions unhappy with the moderate, middle-class America of the postwar years. Fervent anticommunists found in movement conservatism kindred spirits who shared their fears. People outraged by the idea of other people receiving welfare found a movement that could make their resentment politically respectable. Businessmen furious at having to deal with unions found a movement that could turn their anger into effective political action.

This convergence of forces was strong enough to nominate Barry Goldwater, but only because the Republican establishment was caught by surprise. And Goldwater lost the election by a landslide. Nonetheless the movement went on, and learned. Reagan taught the movement how to clothe elitist economic ideas in populist rhetoric. Nixon, though not a movement conservative, showed how the dark side of America—cultural and social resentments, anxieties over security at home and abroad, and, above all, race—could be exploited to win elections.

That last part was crucial. The ability to turn hard-right positions into a winning strategy, not a futile protest, brought in the large-scale funding that created the movement conservative institutions—the "vast right-wing conspiracy" we know today.

That, however, brings us to the second puzzle I identified early in this chapter: Why have advocates of a smaller welfare state and regressive tax policies been able to win elections, even as growing income inequality should have made the welfare state more popular? That's the subject of the next chapter.

9

WEAPONS OF MASS DISTRACTION

Voters don't vote solely in their own self-interest—in fact a completely self-interested citizen wouldn't bother voting at all, since the cost of going to the polling place outweighs the likely effect of any individual's vote on his or her own well-being. Some people may vote against "big government" on principle, even though they're likely to be net beneficiaries of government programs, while others may support generous social programs they themselves aren't likely to need. Yet we would expect the preferences of voters to reflect their self-interest to some extent. And they do: Voters in the bottom third of the income distribution are considerably more likely to favor higher government spending, government job programs, and so on than are voters in the top third.[1] For "big government"—the welfare state—does two things. First, it's a form of insurance: It protects people from some of the risks of life, assuring them that whatever happens they won't starve in their later years or, if they're over sixty-five, be unable to afford an operation. Second, it broadly redistributes income downward.

Consider, for example, the effects of Medicare. Medicare is a very effective form of social insurance. It provides peace of mind even to those who end up paying more into the system, in taxes and premiums, than they receive in benefits. Quite a few Americans in their late fifties or early sixties think of themselves as trying to hang on until they reach Medicare—paying health insurance premiums they can't afford, or living anxiously without insurance hoping not to get seriously ill, until they finally reach the magical sixty-fifth birthday.

But there's another reason Medicare is popular. Although it's rarely advertised as such, it's a redistributive program that takes from an affluent minority and gives to the less affluent majority. The benefits guaranteed by Medicare are the same for everyone, but most of the taxes that support the program—which are more or less proportional to income[2]—are paid by no more than 25 percent of the population. Remember, in terms of income the United States is Lake Wobegon in reverse: Most of the people are below average. So a government program that taxes everyone while providing benefits to everyone is bound to look like a good deal to most Americans.

The redistributive aspect of Medicare is characteristic of the welfare state as a whole. Means-tested programs like Medicaid and food stamps obviously redistribute income, but so do middle-class entitlements. Americans in the bottom 60 percent of earners can expect to receive significantly more in Social Security benefits than they paid in FICA taxes, while those in the top 20 percent can expect to receive less than they paid.[3]

Given this, we should expect public opinion to move left as income inequality increases—that is, voters should become more supportive of programs that tax the rich and provide benefits to the population at large. This is to some extent borne out by polling: Even as the Republican Party was moving far to the right, public opinion surveys suggest that the public, if anything, moved slightly to the left.

The main source of information on long-term trends in U.S. public opinion is American National Election Studies, an organization that has been asking consistent questions in public polls going back, in some cases, to the 1950s. The most revealing are three questions that bear more or less directly on the size of government and the generosity of the welfare state.

One question addresses medical care, asking people to place themselves on a scale of 1 to 7, with 1 representing strong support for a government plan that covers medical costs, and 7 support for relying on private payments and insurance companies. In 1972, 37 percent of those surveyed answered 1, 2, or 3, showing support for government health insurance, while 35 percent answered 5, 6, or 7. In 2004 support for government health insurance was up to 42 percent, while opposition was down to 27 percent.

A second question asks whether the government should "see to it that every person has a job and a good standard of living." In 1972, 28 percent thought the government should do that, while 40 percent thought the government "should just let each person get ahead on their own." In 2004 those numbers were 31 and 42 percent respectively—there were fewer fence-sitters or undecided, but the average position was unchanged.

Finally, a third question asks whether the government should provide more or fewer services and spending. Unfortunately, that question only goes back to 1982, when 32 percent wanted smaller government, 25 percent bigger. By 2004 only 20 percent wanted smaller government, while 43 percent wanted bigger government.

These data suggest that the electorate has, if anything, moved
to the left. Maybe it hasn't moved leftward as much as one might
have expected given rising inequality. But public opinion, unlike
the Republican Party, hasn't shifted sharply to the right. Yet the
fact is that the Republicans keep winning elections—an observation that lost some but by no means all its force after the 2006
midterm. What explains the GOP's electoral success?

Kansas on Our Minds

A movement that seeks to cut taxes while dismantling the welfare state has inherent problems winning mass public support. Tax
cuts, especially the kind of tax cuts movement conservatives want,
deliver most of their benefits to a small minority of the population,
while the pain from a weakened safety net hits far more widely.
Organization and money can to some extent make up for the
inherent unpopularity of conservative policies—but winning elections normally requires that movement conservates find some way
to change the subject.

In his famous 2004 book, *What's the Matter with Kansas?* Thomas
Frank offered a bleak picture of working-class voters easily duped,
again and again, by sideshows:

> The trick never ages, the illusion never wears off. *Vote* to stop
> abortion; *receive* a rollback in capital-gains taxes. *Vote* to make
> our country strong again; *receive* deindustrialization. *Vote* to
> screw those politically correct college professors; *receive* elec-
> tricity deregulation. *Vote* to get government off our backs;
> *receive* conglomeration and monopoly everywhere from media
> to meatpacking. *Vote* to stand tall against terrorists; *receive*

Social Security privatization efforts. *Vote* to strike a blow against elitism; *receive* a social order in which wealth is more concentrated than ever before in our lifetimes, in which workers have been stripped of power and CEOs rewarded in a manner beyond imagining.[4]

How true is this picture? I was bowled over by Frank's book when it appeared, and I still think it's a masterfully written essay on movement conservatism's genius at exploiting emotional issues and its hypocrisy on governing priorities. But political scientists, notably my Princeton colleague Larry Bartels—who wrote a scholarly response titled "What's the Matter with *What's the Matter with Kansas?*"—have called into question the extent to which working-class voters really *have* been duped.

The reality is that voting has become more, not less, class-based over time, which is just what you'd expect given the change in the nature of the Republican Party. In the fifties and sixties the GOP was run by men following Eisenhower's doctrine of "modern Republicanism," men who accepted the legacy of the New Deal. In those decades high-income whites were barely more likely to consider themselves Republicans, or vote for Republican candidates, than were low-income whites. Since movement conservatism took over the GOP, however, a strong class division has emerged. The affluent increasingly vote Republican, while lower-income whites, especially outside the South, are actually more likely to vote Democratic than they were half a century ago.

Still, *something* has allowed movement conservatism to win elections despite policies that should have been unpopular with a majority of the voters. So let's talk about the noneconomic issues that conservatives have exploited, starting with the issue that Frank oddly didn't mention in that glorious rant: race.

Philadelphia

Ask the man or woman in the street to free-associate on the name Ronald Reagan, and he or she will probably answer "tax cuts" or "defeating communism." But Reagan didn't start his run for the presidency with rallies on economic or foreign policy. During his 1976 bid for the Republican nomination, he made his mark by grossly exaggerating a case of welfare fraud in Chicago, introducing the term "welfare queen."[5] He didn't mention the woman's race; he didn't need to. He began his 1980 campaign with a speech on states' rights at the county fair near Philadelphia, Mississippi, the town where three civil rights workers were murdered in 1964. Everyone got the message.

Considering how much has been written about the changes in American politics over the past generation, how much agonizing there has been about the sources of Democratic decline and Republican ascendancy, it's amazing how much of the whole phenomenon can be summed up in just five words: Southern whites started voting Republican.

Before I discuss this political shift, let's get some historical perspective. The United States has been politically to the right of other advanced countries for a long time. Spending on subsidies and transfers—basically, welfare state spending—has been a smaller share of GDP in the United States than in Europe since the nineteenth century. By 1937 European countries were already spending as much on welfare-state programs, relative to the size of their economies, as the United States would be spending in 1970, after the creation of Medicare and Medicaid.

What explains this difference? That's an old question, going back at least to Werner Sombart's 1906 book, *Why Is There No Socialism in the United States?* The difference has been attributed to everything from high wages—"All socialist utopias come to grief," wrote Sombart, "on roast beef and apple pie"[6]—to underlying cultural attitudes. But the most systematic recent assessment, by Alberto Alesina, Edward Glaeser, and Bruce Sacerdote, three Harvard economists, concluded that the most important factor in America's enduring exceptionalism is probably race:

> Racial discord plays a critical role in determining beliefs about the poor. Since minorities are highly over-represented amongst the poorest Americans, any income-based redistribution measures will redistribute particularly to minorities. The opponents of redistribution have regularly used race based rhetoric to fight left-wing policies. Across countries, racial fragmentation is a powerful predictor of redistribution. Within the US, race is the single most important predictor of support for welfare. America's troubled race relations are clearly a major reason for the absence of an American welfare state.[7]

This conclusion is borne out both by the history of political fights over key welfare-state programs and by the shape of regional politics today.

Start with the New Deal reform that didn't happen: universal health insurance. Every advanced country except the United States has a universal health care system; how did we miss out? Perhaps the best opportunity to create such a system came in the late 1940s, when Harry Truman attempted to create a system that would have looked essentially like Medicare for the whole population. Opinion polls suggested overwhelming public support for universal care (as they do today). But as described in chapter 4, Truman's bid failed in the face of opposition from two crucial groups: the American Medical Association and Southern whites, who would have gained from the program because of their low incomes but who opposed it out of fear that it would lead to racially integrated hospitals.[8]

The effects of race on support for the welfare state are also clear from a comparison across U.S. states. Alesina, Glaeser, and Sacerdote show that there's a strong correlation between a state's racial makeup and its policies: Broadly, the higher the black fraction of a state's population, the lower its social spending per person. To some extent this may reflect the fact that Southern states are, despite the northward migration of African Americans and the convergence of regional incomes, both blacker and poorer than the rest of the United States. But it's more than that: Even after taking levels of income into account, the correlation remains.

To make the point more concrete, suppose we compare politics and policy in Massachusetts and Virginia. The two states are roughly comparable both in average and in median income per capita—which tells us that the states have similar levels of income and that there aren't big differences in the extent to which income is concentrated at the top. Yet the politics are dramatically different: Massachusetts is famously liberal, while Virginia has long been deeply conservative. (That may now be changing, but the blue-ing of Virginia is a very recent phenomenon.) You can do similar pairwise comparisons between other states of the old Confederacy and their Northern economic counterparts; in most though not all cases the more southerly, blacker state is far more conservative. It's hard not to conclude that race is the difference.

Yet the New Deal coalition included the South, for reasons discussed in chapter 4. There was raw self-interest: The South was long a poor region, which gained disproportionately from the welfare state. There was history: The Republican Party remained, in Southern minds, the party of Lincoln. And there was the initial willingness of Northern liberals to make a bargain with the devil, tacitly accepting Jim Crow in return for Southern support on the broader welfare-state agenda.

Eventually, however, the marriage between Southern whites and the rest of the Democratic Party broke down over irreconcilable differences. The process began with Barry Goldwater, who took a strong states' rights position and came out against the Civil Rights Act of 1964. Aside from Arizona, all the states Goldwater won in the 1964 election were in the South. In 1968 much of the South went for George Wallace, but Nixon picked up several border states. By 1980 Reagan could win Southern states with thinly disguised appeals to segregationist sentiment, while Democrats were ever more firmly linked to civil rights and affirmative action. In fact the real mystery is why it took so long for the South's congressional delegation to flip.

What share of the political rise of movement conservatism can be attributed to the Southern switch? What the numbers suggest is that the switch accounts for *all* of the conservative triumph—and then some.

Compare the makeup of the House of Representatives on two dates half a century apart. After the 1954 election Democrats had just begun what would turn out to be a forty-year dominance of the House, holding 232 out of 435 seats. After the 2004 election Republicans had exactly the same number of seats the Democrats had had in 1954, giving them the largest majority they ever achieved in their twelve-year rule. So where did the Republicans gain their advantage? The answer is that the Democrats actually *gained* seats outside the South. More than all of the Democratic net loss to the Republicans came from the Southern switch.

The Southern switch reflects a change in the voting behavior of white Southerners. In 1954 Southern whites at all levels of income were vastly more likely to vote Democratic than were their counterparts in the North. By 2004 low-income Southern whites were no more Democratic than low-income whites elsewhere in the country, while middle- and upper-income Southern whites were disproportionately Republican. In the 2000 and 2004 presidential elections whites outside the South favored Bush, but only by modest margins. In the South they voted for Bush by margins of 35 or more percentage points, enough to outweigh the overwhelmingly Democratic vote of Southern blacks.[9] Without those Southern white votes Bush wouldn't have gotten anywhere near chad-and-butterfly range of the White House.

The overwhelming importance of the Southern switch suggests an almost embarrassingly simple story about the political success of movement conservatism. It goes like this: Thanks to their organization, the interlocking institutions that constitute the reality of the vast right-wing conspiracy, movement conservatives were able to take over the Republican Party, and move its policies sharply to the right. In most of the country this rightward shift alienated voters, who gradually moved toward the Democrats. But Republicans were nonetheless able to win presidential elections, and eventually gain control of Congress, because they were able to exploit the race issue to win political dominance of the South. End of story.

Or maybe that isn't quite the end of the story. Even before the 2006 election, some analysts—notably Tom Schaller, a political scientist at the University of Maryland—suggested that the Republicans had overreached, and had themselves become vulnerable to a regional flip comparable to the one that drove the Democrats from power.[10] Just as the Democrats continued to hold many Southern congressional seats long after the historic marriage of convenience between New Dealers and Dixiecrats had broken down, relatively moderate districts in the rest of the country continued to send Republicans to Congress long after the GOP congressional delegation had become, in practice, a solid right-wing voting bloc. Indeed, a number of those Republicans finally lost their seats in 2006. After the 2006 election 42 percent of the seats still held by Republicans were in the South—not far short of the 47 percent Southern share of Democratic seats in 1954.[11]

All that said, one thing remains something of a puzzle: What do Southern whites think they're actually getting out of the GOP? Republicans in Washington haven't made the world safe for segregationists again—and to be fair, it's doubtful whether many Southerners would seek a return to Jim Crow even if the feds allowed it. What Reagan offered in Philadelphia, Mississippi, was mainly symbolism—a stick in the eye of censorious Yankees—rather than a real prospect of rolling back the achievements of the civil rights movement. Maybe Frank's book should have been called *What's the Matter with Dixie?* and the rant should have gone like this: "*Vote* for the good old days of Southern pride; *receive* Social Security privatization." And when Bush did in fact try to use his 2004 "mandate" to privatize Social Security, the South was almost as opposed to the proposal as the rest of the country.[12]

Race, then, was essential to the ability of conservatives to win elections in spite of economic policies that favored a minority over the majority. But what about other forms of distraction?

Evil Empires and Evildoers

"Conservatives saw the savagery of 9/11 in the attacks and prepared for war; liberals saw the savagery of the 9/11 attacks and wanted to prepare indictments and offer therapy and understanding for our attackers." So declared Karl Rove, George Bush's chief political strategist, in a 2005 speech.[13]

Rove was, we now know, fighting the last, um, war: By 2005 the debacle in Iraq was rapidly eroding the public's perception that Republicans are better than Democrats at protecting the nation. But where did that perception come from, and how much did it help Republicans win elections?

It's often asserted that the Republican national security advantage dates back to the Vietnam War, and specifically to Richard Nixon's landslide 1972 victory over George McGovern. But as so often happens when we look closely at the real political history of this country, it's far from clear that what everyone knows is true. Rick Perlstein has argued that the even the 1972 election was more of a personal defeat for McGovern than a rejection of the Democrats, who actually gained in the Senate and suffered only modest losses in the House.[14]

More to the point, the available polling evidence does *not* indicate that the public viewed Democrats in general as weak on national security in the years immediately following the fall of Saigon. As late as October 1979 a poll commissioned by the Republican National Committee, asking which party would do a better job of "maintaining military security," found 29 percent of voters naming the Republicans, 28 percent the Democrats, and 21 percent saying both would do a good job.[15] The perception that Democrats are weak on national security—a perception that made the partisan exploitation of 9/11 possible—didn't really settle in until the 1980s. And it had very little to do with the realities of defense or foreign policy. Instead it was a matter of story lines, and above all about the Rambofication of history.

Defeat is never easy to acknowledge. After World War I many Germans famously came to believe in the *Dolchstoßlegende*, the myth that German forces had been "stabbed in the back" by weak civilian leaders. And from the fall of Saigon onward there were Americans who, like their counterparts in post–World War I Germany, became receptive to stab-in-the-back theories, to the claim that the military could have won the war if only civilians hadn't tied its hands. When memories of the Vietnam War in all its horror and futility were still fresh, however, they were a small if vocal minority.

If there was a moment when these theories went mainstream, it was with the success of the 1982 film *First Blood*, the first Rambo movie, in which Rambo declares, "I did what I had to do to win. But somebody wouldn't let us win." He also rails against "those maggots at the airport, protesting, spitting, calling me baby-killer"— and images of protesters spitting on returning servicemen have become ingrained in popular culture. There's no evidence that this ever actually happened; there are no credibly documented cases of returning veterans having been spat upon or called baby killers. Nonetheless, the myth of liberals disrespecting the troops became fixed in the public's mind.

After the stab in the back came the revenge fantasies. *Uncommon Valor* (1983), *Missing in Action* (1984), and *Rambo: First Blood Part II* (1985)—which reinvented the deranged, damaged vet of the first movie as an action hero—tapped into a market for fantasies in which rebellious military men in effect refought the war, and won it.

The newly belligerent mood of the nation clearly worked to the advantage of conservatives. The actual record of liberals in opposing the Vietnam War probably wasn't that important: By the 1980s the realities of what happened had largely slipped from public memory. What mattered, instead, was the way movement conservatives' fear and loathing of communism resonated with the desires of a nation rebounding from post-Vietnam syndrome. When Reagan described the Soviet Union as an "evil empire," liberals and moderates tended to scoff—not because they were weak on national security, but because they were pragmatic about what it took to achieve security. But many Americans loved it.

Movement conservatism's efforts to identify itself as the nation's defender were aided by the fact that the military itself, always a conservative institution, became much more so after the mid-seventies. In 1976 a plurality of military leaders identified themselves as independents, while a third identified themselves as Republicans. By 1996 two-thirds considered themselves Republicans.[16] This shift in political identification probably had several causes. One was that military leaders, who were less able than civilians to put the Vietnam defeat behind them, may have been especially susceptible to the stab-in-the-back myth. It may also have had something to do with budgets: Carter presided over the post-Vietnam shrinkage of the military, Reagan vastly increased military spending, then Clinton presided over another decline, this time after the fall of the Soviet Union. Regional politics also played a role. As one account[17] put it:

> [The shift of the military toward Republicans] also resulted from changed recruitment and base-closing policies, combined with the steady Republicanization of the American South. The period since the late 1960s saw the closure of many northeastern ROTC programs and the expansion of those programs in the South. By the late 1990s, more than 40% of all ROTC programs were in the South—mainly at state universities—though the South is home to fewer than 30% of the nation's college students. Similar patterns in base closures have meant that disproportionate numbers of military personnel are now stationed at bases in the South and Southwest.

Last but not least, there may also have been a "values" component: As American society became more permissive, the military—where adultery is still considered a crime under certain circumstances—grew increasingly alienated. The sexual revolution, which we usually associate with the sixties, didn't go mass-market until the seventies, a point emphasized by the title of one of John Updike's many novels about adultery and the human condition, *Memories of the Ford Administration*.

As movement conservatism gained power, then, it was increasingly able to wrap itself in the flag—to claim to be stronger on national security than the other side, and to claim the support of a large majority of military leaders.

It's hard to make the case, however, that the perceived Republican advantage on national security played a crucial role in any national election before 9/11. That perception did hurt Democrats on several occasions: The image of Michael Dukakis in a tank helped lose the 1988 election, and the fracas over gays in the military contributed to the 1994 Republican takeover of Congress. Military votes made the difference in 2000, but so did many other things: In an election that close any factor that gave the GOP a few thousand votes can be called decisive.

It was only with the 2002 and 2004 elections that national security became a true election-winning issue. Faced with business scandals, a weak economy, and the normal tendency for the president's party to lose seats in midterm elections, Republicans should have lost ground in 2002, ending up with Democratic control of the Senate and, quite possibly, of the House as well. But the nation rallied around George Bush, as he promised to punish the "evildoers" responsible for 9/11 and bring in Osama dead or alive. And Bush's party engaged in raw political exploitation of the atrocity, including ads in which the faces of Democrats morphed into Saddam Hussein. The result was a big victory for the GOP.

By the 2004 election doubts about the Iraq War were growing, but much of the electorate was still in a state of denial. On the eve of the election a majority of voters still believed that the United States did the "right thing" in invading Iraq, was on a path to victory, or both.[18] And national security almost certainly gave Bush his winning margin.

In the immediate aftermath of the 2004 election, there were many pronouncements to the effect that the perceived Republican advantage on national security would help cement a permanent Republican majority. Thus Thomas Edsall, whom I've already credited for his prophetic 1984 book, *The New Politics of Inequality*, argued in his 2006 book *Building Red America* that national security would prove an enduring source of GOP advantage: "Any weakness on national defense that dogs the Democratic Party is substantially amplified in the context of a 'long war.' "[19]

Yet there is a good case to be made that the successful exploitation of security in 2002 and 2004 was an inherently limited, perhaps inherently self-defeating strategy. Unless the United States is actively engaged in major warfare, national security tends to recede as an issue. The elder George Bush learned that in 1992: The 1991 Gulf War temporarily gave him an 80 percent approval rating, but a year later the public's attention had shifted to economic concerns, and the Democrats regained the White House in spite of public perceptions that they were weak on defense issues.

The same thing initially seemed to be happening to the younger Bush: By the summer of 2002 his approval rating had descended from the stratosphere, and public attention was shifting to corporate scandals and the weak economy. Then came the buildup to war with Iraq. We may never know exactly why the administration wanted that war so badly, but military adventurism does have the effect of giving national security, an issue that the Republicans thought they owned, continuing salience.

The problem, which eventually became all too apparent, is

that keeping concerns about national security on the front burner means picking fights with people who shoot back—and in real life the bad guys have better aim than they did in the Rambo movies. The quagmire in Iraq wasn't an accident: Even if the Iraqis had welcomed us with flowers and sweets, there would have been a bigger, worse quagmire down the line. "Everyone wants to go to Baghdad. Real men want to go to Tehran," a British official told *Newsweek* in 2002.[20]

What's more, movement conservatism and major war efforts don't mix. Any major military mobilization prompts calls for equal sacrifice, which means tax increases, a crackdown on perceived profiteering, and more. Both world wars led to a rise in union membership, an increase in tax progressivity, and a reduction in income inequality—all anathema to conservatives. Much has been written about the disastrous lack of planning for post-invasion Iraq. What isn't emphasized enough is that the Bush administration *had* to believe that the war could be waged on the cheap, because a realistic assessment of the war's cost and requirements would have posed a direct challenge to the administration's tax-cutting agenda. Add to this the closed-mindedness and inflexibility that come from the bubble in which movement conservatives live, the cronyism and corruption inherent in movement conservative governance, and the Iraq venture was doomed from the start.

The national security issue seems to have given movement conservatism two election victories, in 2002 and 2004, that it wouldn't have been able to win otherwise, extending Republican control of both Congress and the White House four years beyond their natural life span. I don't mean to minimize the consequences of that extension, which will be felt for decades to come, especially on the Supreme Court. But defense does not, at this point, look like an enduring source of conservative advantage.

The Moral Minority

We believe that the practice of sodomy tears at the fabric of society, contributes to the breakdown of the family unit, and leads to the spread of dangerous, communicable diseases. Homosexual behavior is contrary to the fundamental, unchanging truths that have been ordained by God, recognized by our country's founders, and shared by the majority of Texans.

So declares the 2006 platform of the Texas Republican Party, which also pledges to "dispel the myth of the separation of church and state."

There are two different questions about the role of religion and moral values in the politics of inequality. One is the extent to which believers who don't accept the separation of church and state—what Michelle Goldberg, in her hair-raising book *Kingdom Coming*, calls Christian nationalists—have taken over the Republican Party.[21] The other is the Tom Frank question: The extent to which mobilization of "values voters," and the use of values issues to change the subject away from bread and butter issues, have allowed the GOP to pursue an antipopulist economic agenda.

On the first question, the influence of the Christian right on the Republican Party, the answer is clear: It's a very powerful influence indeed. That Texas Republican platform doesn't represent fringe views within the party, it represents what the activist base thinks but usually soft-pedals in public. In fact it's surprising how long it has taken for political analysts to realize just how strong the Christian right's influence really is. Partly that's because the Bush administration has proved so adept at sending out messages that only the intended audience can hear. A classic example is Bush's description of himself as a "compassionate conservative," which most people heard as a declaration that he wasn't going to rip up the safety net. It was actually a reference to the work of Marvin Olasky, a Christian right author. His 1992 book, *The Tragedy of American Compassion*, held up the welfare system of nineteenth-century America, in which faith-based private groups dispensed aid and religion together, as a model—and approvingly quoted Gilded Age authors who condemned "those mild, well-meaning, tender-hearted criminals who insist upon indulging in indiscriminate charity."[22]

In the spring of 2007 the Bush administration's management of the Justice Department finally came under close scrutiny, and it became clear that the department had, in important respects, been taken over by the Christian right. A number of key posts had gone to graduates of Regent University, the school founded and run by evangelist Pat Robertson; the Civil Rights Division had largely shifted its focus from protecting the rights of minority groups to protecting the evangelizing efforts of religious groups. At the Food and Drug Administration, Bush appointed W. David Hager, the coauthor of *As Jesus Cared for Women*—a book that recommends particular scriptural readings as a treatment for PMS—to the Reproductive Health Advisory Committee; Hager played a key role in delaying approval for the "morning-after" pill.[23] Bush's 2006 choice to head family-planning services at the Department of Health and Human Services, Dr. Eric Keroack, worked at a Christian pregnancy-counseling center that regards the distribution of contraceptives as "demeaning to women."[24] And there are many more examples.

The Christian right we're talking about here isn't merely a group of people who combine faith with conservative political leanings. As Goldberg puts it in *Kingdom Coming*, Christian nationalism seeks "dominion." It's a "totalistic political ideology" that "asserts the Christian right to rule."[25] The influence of this ideology on the modern Republican Party is so great today that it raises the question of who's using whom. Are movement conservatives using religion to distract the masses, as Thomas Frank argued, or are religious groups co-opting corporate interests on their way to dominion?

The important thing for our current discussion is to keep a sense of perspective on the *electoral* significance of the religious right. It's a well-organized group that can play a crucial role in close elections—but it's not large enough to give movement conservatives the ability to pursue wildly unpopular economic policies. Whites who attend church frequently have voted Republican by large margins since 1992, which wasn't the case before. But there are two qualifications to this observation. First, a lot of this shift represents the switch of the South, a far more religious region than the rest of the country, to the GOP. Second, the divergence between the highly religious and the less devout reflects movement in both directions: The secular minded and those who wear their faith lightly have shifted toward the Democrats. That's why whatever mobilization of religious voters has taken place hasn't been enough to prevent white voters outside the South from trending Democratic.

Again, mobilized evangelical voters can swing close elections. Without the role of the churches, Ohio and hence the nation might have gone for Kerry in 2004. But religion doesn't rise nearly to the level of race as an explanation of conservative political success.

Disenfranchised Workers

Another factor needs to be brought into the mix of explanations for conservative political success: The typical voter is considerably better off than the typical family, partly because poorer citizens are less likely than the well-off to vote, partly because many lower-income residents of the United States aren't citizens. This means that economic policies that benefit an affluent minority but hurt a majority aren't necessarily political losers from an electoral point of view. For example, the nonpartisan Tax Policy Center has produced several estimates of the ultimate effect on different income classes of the Bush tax cuts, assuming that the lost revenue is made up somehow, say by cuts in social programs. One estimate assumes "lump-sum" financing—that is, each American suffers the same loss of government benefits, regardless of income. On this assumption everyone with an income below about $75,000 is a net loser. That's about 75 percent of the population. The losses would be modest for people in the $50,000 to $75,000 range. Even so, however, the tax cuts ought to be very unpopular, since 60 percent of the population has incomes below $50,000 a year. But Census Bureau data tell us that fewer than 40 percent of *voters* have incomes below $50,000 a year. So maybe the tax cuts aren't such a political loser after all.

McCarty, Poole, and Rosenthal present data suggesting that the upward bias of voters' incomes, as compared with the incomes of all U.S. residents, has increased substantially since the early 1970s. One reason may be the decline of unions, which formerly did a lot to mobilize working-class voters. Another is the rapid rise of the immigrant population, especially since 1980.[26]

Over the longer term, immigration will help undermine the political strategy of movement conservatism, for reasons I'll explain at length in chapter 10. In brief, movement conservatives cannot simultaneously make tacitly race-based appeals to white voters and court the growing Hispanic and Asian share of the electorate. Indeed, the problems created for the GOP by the intersection of immigration and race were already manifest in the 2006 election. For the past twenty-five years, however, immigration has helped empower movement conservatism, by reducing the proportion of low-wage workers who vote.

As I pointed out in chapter 2, large-scale immigration helped sustain conservative dominance during the Long Gilded Age, by ensuring that a significant part of the low-wage workforce was disenfranchised. The end of large-scale immigration in the 1920s had the unintended consequence of producing a more fully enfranchised population, helping shift the balance to the left. But the resurgence of immigration since the 1960s—dominated by inflows of low-skilled, low-wage workers, especially from Mexico—has largely re-created Gilded Age levels of disenfranchisement. The charts in McCarty, Poole, and Rosenthal suggest that immigration is a significant but not overwhelming factor in low voting by people with low income, that it's a contributing factor to conservative success, but not the core one. The disenfranchisement effect is, however, something liberals need to think hard about when confronting questions about immigration reform.

Block the Vote

One last, unavoidable question is the issue of fraud. To what extent does the political strategy of movement conservatism rely on winning elections by cheating? We can dismiss objections of the form "How can you suggest such a thing?" Voting fraud is an old American tradition, as I explained when describing Gilded Age politics. And movement conservatism is and always has been profoundly undemocratic. In 1957 the *National Review* praised Francisco Franco, who overthrew Spain's elected government and instituted a reign of terror, as a "national hero." In 2007 the Conservative Political Action Committee was addressed by all the major Republican presidential candidates except John McCain. After former Mas-

sachusetts governor Mitt Romney spoke to the gathering, he gave
a warm welcome to the next speaker, the columnist Ann Coulter,[27]
who has declared that we need to "physically intimidate liberals."
Given this history there's no reason to believe that leading figures
in the movement would balk on principle at stealing elections.

In fact there's no question that vote suppression—the use of
any means available to prevent likely Democratic voters, usually
African Americans, from casting legitimate ballots—has been
a consistent Republican tactic since the party was taken over by
movement conservatives. In 2000 Florida's Republican Secretary
of State, Katherine Harris, conducted what the New York Times
called a "massive purge of eligible voters," disproportionately black,
who were misidentified as felons. Without that purge George W.
Bush would not have made it to the White House.[28] In Georgia
the Republican legislature passed a voter identification law in 2005
that a team of lawyers and analysts at the Justice Department rec-
ommended rejecting because it was likely to discriminate against
black voters—but the team was overruled the next day by political
appointees.[29] And this was part of a broader strategy that—characteristically for movement conservatism—involved the collaboration
of political appointees within the government and private-sector
operations with funding from the usual sources, in this case the
"American Center for Voting Rights," which was founded by the
general counsel for the Bush-Cheney 2004 campaign, and suddenly
disappeared in 2007 when the firing of U.S. attorneys who refused
to go along with bogus voter-fraud charges became a major scandal. Here's how McClatchy Newspapers described the strategy:

> McClatchy Newspapers has found that this election strategy
> was active on at least three fronts:
> • Tax-exempt groups such as the American Center and the

Lawyers Association were deployed in battleground states
to press for restrictive ID laws and oversee balloting.

- The Justice Department's Civil Rights Division turned traditional voting rights enforcement upside down with legal
  policies that narrowed rather than protected the rights of
  minorities.
- The White House and the Justice Department encouraged
  selected U.S. attorneys to bring voter fraud prosecutions,
  despite studies showing that election fraud isn't a widespread problem.[30]

So vote suppression is a part of the movement conservative political strategy. It can be decisive in close elections, which means that
as a quantitative matter vote suppression is in the same class as the
mobilization of the religious right—but not in the same class as the
exploitation of white racial backlash, which remains at the heart of
movement conservatism's ability to achieve electoral success.

The truly frightening question is whether electoral cheating has
gone or will go beyond vote suppression to corruption of the vote
count itself. The biggest concern involves touch-screen electronic
voting machines. In August 2007 the state of California sharply
restricted the use of touch-screen machines after an audit by University of California researchers confirmed voting activists' worst
fears: Machines from Diebold, Sequoia, and other major suppli-
ers are, indeed, extremely vulnerable to hacking that alters election results. This raises the question—which I won't even try to
answer—of whether there was in fact electronic fraud in 2002 and
2004, and possibly even in 2006. More important, there is the disturbing possibility that the favorable political trends I'll discuss in
the next chapter might be offset by increased fraud. And given
the history of movement conservatism, such worries can't simply

be dismissed as crazy conspiracy theories. If large-scale vote stealing does take place, all bets are off—and America will be in much
worse shape than even pessimists imagine.

The Limits of Distraction

So what's the matter with America? Why have politicians who advocate policies that hurt most people been able to win elections? The
view that movement conservatives have found sure-fire ways to distract the public and get people to vote against their own interests
isn't completely false, but it's been greatly overstated. Instead the
ability of conservatives to win in spite of antipopulist policies has
mainly rested on the exploitation of racial division. Religion and
invocations of moral values have had some effect, but have been
far less important; national security was decisive in 2002 and 2004,
but not before. And there are indications that most of the ways
movement conservatism has found to distract voters are losing their
effectiveness. Racism and social intolerance are on the decline,
and the Iraq debacle has gone a long way toward discrediting the
GOP on national security. Meanwhile concerns about inequality
and economic insecurity are on the rise. This is, in short, a time of
political opportunity for those who think we've been going in the
wrong direction. The remainder of this book lays out the dimen-
sions of that opportunity, and what we should do with it.

10

THE NEW POLITICS OF EQUALITY

The Democratic victory in the 2006 midterm election came as a shock to many, even though it had been telegraphed by polls well in advance. Many analysts had invested themselves emotionally and professionally in the idea of overwhelming Republican political superiority. I have a whole shelf of books from 2005 and 2006 explaining, in sorrow, triumph, or simply awe, how the superior organization of the GOP, the enthusiasm of its supporters, its advantage in money, its ownership of the national security issue, and—by some accounts—its ability to rig elections made it invincible. Believing that Republicans had a lock on power, some couldn't believe what the polls were saying—namely, that the American people had had enough.

Even after the election results were in, there was a visible reluctance to acknowledge fully what had happened. For months after the vote many news analyses asserted one of two things: that it was only a narrow victory for the Democrats, and/or that the Democrats who won did so by being conservative. The first claim was just false, the second mostly so.

The new Democratic margin in the House of Representatives wasn't narrow. In fact, it was wider than any Republican majority during the GOP's twelve-year reign. The new Democratic majority in the Senate *was* paper thin, but achieving even that starting from a five-seat deficit was something of a miracle, because only a third of the Senate is elected at a time. As it was, Democrats and independents allied with the Democrats won twenty-four of the thirty-three Senate seats at stake. The Democrats also took six governorships, and gained control of eight state legislative chambers.

The claim that Democrats won by becoming conservative is only slightly less false. Some of the new faces in Congress were Democrats who won in relatively conservative districts, and were themselves a bit more conservative than the average Democrat. But it remained true that every Democrat was to the left of every Republican, so that the shift in control drastically tilted the political balance to the left.[1] And the truly relevant comparison is between the Democratic majority now and the Democratic majority in 1993–94, the last time the party was in control. By any measure the new majority, which doesn't depend on a wing of conservative Southern Democrats, is far more liberal. Nancy Pelosi, the new Speaker of the House, made headlines by becoming the first woman to hold the position—but she is also the most progressive Speaker ever.

But what did the Democratic victory and the leftward shift in Congress mean? Was it an aberrational event, a consequence of the special ineptitude of the Bush administration? Or was it a sign of fundamental political realignment?

Nobody can be completely sure. In this chapter, however, I'll make the case for believing that the 2006 election wasn't an aberration, that the U.S. public is actually ready for something different—a new politics of equality. But the emergence of this new politics isn't a foregone conclusion. It will happen only if liberal politicians seize the opportunity.

Inequality Bites

"In general, are you satisfied or dissatisfied with the way things are going in the United States at this time?" asked Gallup in June 2007. Only 24 percent were satisfied, compared with 74 percent unsatisfied. As I write this in the summer of 2007, Americans are very unhappy about the country's direction.

A lot of that has to with the quagmire in Iraq. But what's remarkable is how little the national mood seems to have been lifted by what looks, at first glance, like a pretty good economy. Gross domestic product has been rising for almost six years; the unemployment rate is only 4.5 percent, comparable to its levels in the late nineties; the stock market has been hitting new highs. Yet when Gallup asked, "How would you rate economic conditions in this country?" only about a third of the respondents answered "Excellent" or "Good." The proportion was twice as high in the late nineties.

Conservatives, looking for someone to blame, complain that the media aren't reporting the good news about the economy—just as they aren't reporting the good news about Iraq. More seriously, ill-feeling about the war probably bleeds into the public's views on other matters. Still, it's worth noting that consumer confidence in 1968—the year of the Tet offensive, huge antiwar protests, and, as I documented in chapter 5, a pervasive sense that things were falling apart—was much higher than it is in the summer of 2007.[2] This suggests that there are limits on the extent to which dismay about other aspects of the national situation can color perceptions of how the economy is doing, which in turn suggests that public unhappiness with the economy isn't just a projection of bad feelings about the war. And there's one more crucial point: It actually makes perfect sense for most people to be unhappy about the state of the economy. Due to rising inequality, good performance in overall numbers like GDP hasn't translated into gains for ordinary workers.

The current disconnect between overall economic growth and the fortunes of typical Americans is, as far as I can tell, unprecedented in modern U.S. history. Inequality was high during the Long Gilded Age, but because inequality was stable, most workers saw their standard of living improve steadily as the economy grew. Growth in the great postwar boom that ended in 1973 was broadly shared. Even after inequality began rising at the end of the 1970s, a growing economy continued to translate into gains for almost everyone. Thus inequality was rising in the 1980s, but the expansion of the economy from 1982 onward was still strong enough to let Reagan declare "Morning in America" in 1984, and to get the first George Bush elected in 1988. Inequality continued to rise during the 1990s, but there was still a dramatic improvement in public sentiment as the economy recovered from the 1990–92 slump.

Now, however, the stagnation of wages and median income in the face of overall economic expansion has become so clear that public perceptions of how the economy is doing no longer seem linked to standard measures of economic performance. That is, the years since 2001 have been Bill Gates walking into a bar: The average has gone up, but that means nothing to most people. Or to be less metaphorical, corporate profits have soared—they're now at their highest level, as a percentage of GDP, since 1929—and so have incomes at the top of the scale. But the wages of

most workers have barely kept up with inflation. Add in a growing sense of insecurity, especially because of the crumbling health
insurance system (of which much more in chapter 11), and it's
perfectly reasonable for most people to feel pessimistic about the
economic situation.

Polls also suggest that the public both understands the role of
growing inequality and supports government action to do something about it. A massive Pew survey of trends in public opinion
found that the fractions of the public agreeing that the rich are
getting richer while the poor get poorer, that the government has a
responsibility to help those in need, that everyone should be guaranteed enough to eat and a place to live, have all risen to levels
not seen since the early 1990s.[3] All this suggests that there's an
opportunity for a major push toward policies that address inequality and/or economic insecurity.

The fact that polling numbers today resemble those from the early
1990s may raise some warning flags. After all, economic discontent
got Bill Clinton elected in 1992, but when he tried to push through
health care reform—which, as I'll argue at length in chapter 11, has
to be the centerpiece of any progressive reform agenda—he failed
utterly. This legislative defeat was followed by electoral defeat, in
the 1994 rout that put Republicans in control of Congress. This
raises the question of whether history will repeat itself.

There are, however, several reasons to think that it won't, or at
least doesn't have to.

The first is that Clinton's failure on health care looks, even in retrospect, far from inevitable. Better leadership, better communica-
tion with Capitol Hill and the public, and Clinton might well have
been able to go into 1994 with a major domestic policy achievement under his belt. Even after the initial Clinton push had run
aground, a group of moderate Democrats and Republicans offered

a compromise that would have covered 85 percent of the unin-sured, but Hillary Clinton rejected their overtures.

A more fundamental point is that today's economic discontent is much less likely to be replaced by other concerns than that of the early 1990s. Americans were depressed about the economy in 1992 in large part because the economy as a whole was depressed, with an unemployment rate well over 7 percent. Once the economy recovered, the economic issue lost much of its force. Among other things, as more people got jobs with health care benefits, pressure for health care reform faded away. (There was also a secondary rea-son for declining concern: For much of the 1990s HMOs seemed to be containing costs. Again, more on this in chapter 11.) Today, however, people are worried about their finances and the state of the economy even after years of fairly good economic growth, with the unemployment rate not far off historic lows. It seems likely that demands that the government do something for working Ameri-cans will grow more, not less, intense.

Meanwhile, something else has changed: both long-term trends in American society and recent events have damaged the ability of movement conservatives to change the subject, to mask the reality that they are on the side of the privileged by turning the nation's attention to other issues. One major source of that change is the way Bush has damaged the right's credibility on national security.

Iraq and the New Politics of National Security

As Chris Hedges documented in his 2002 book, *War Is a Force That Gives Us Meaning*, even the Argentine junta of the early 1980s, a government that presided over hyperinflation and economic collapse, became briefly popular when it started a senseless war with Britain by invading the Falkland Islands.[4] George W. Bush's extremely high approval ratings after 9/11 reflected the same rally-around-the-flag effect: Governments always get an initial boost in public support when they go to war, no matter how incompetent and corrupt the government and no matter how foolish the war.

Still, it's doubtful that a Democratic president would have received as big a political boost as Bush did. During the Reagan and Bush I years, Republicans had solidified a reputation as being stronger then Democrats on national security. Never mind the question of whether that reputation ever had any justification; the point is that 9/11 fitted in with a preexisting script. Questions about whether Bush had ignored warnings about the threat were brushed aside. Initial success in Afghanistan was treated as a huge achievement for the Bush administration, as if tipping the balance of power in a third-World civil war were the equivalent of D-day. Minor details like Osama bin Laden's escape from the mountains of Tora Bora were ignored.

In the normal course of events, the national security issue would gradually have receded in political salience, much as it did after the first Gulf War. But Bush and those around him found a way to keep the war psychology going. We have a fairly clear picture of how the Bush administration sold America on war with Iraq: cherry-picked intelligence, insistent rhetorical linkage of Iraq with 9/11, and so on. What's less clear is why the administration wanted to attack a regime that had nothing to do with 9/11. It seems almost certain, however, that the perceived domestic political advantages of a splendid little war played an important role in the decision to invade. The now infamous "Mission Accomplished" photo op, with Bush's staged landing on an aircraft carrier, was, to a large extent, what the war was all about. And the war worked to Bush's advantage for a surprisingly long time. In spite of the failure to find WMD and the rising U.S. death toll, it took more than two years into the war before a majority of Americans began consistently telling pollsters that invading Iraq was a mistake.

At this point, however, public disgust with the Iraq War has become the central fact of American politics. That could be just a short-term phenomenon; the question for this book is whether the Iraq debacle will have a longer-term influence in changing the political landscape. I think it will.

Ideally the public will conclude from the debacle that if you want to win a war, don't hire a movement conservative. Hire a liberal, or at least an Eisenhower-type Republican. Failure in Iraq may have been inevitable, but whatever slim chances of success the United States might have had were dissipated by errors that were inherent to movement conservatism. In particular the Bush administration's overoptimism and its attempt to fight a war on the cheap, with minimal numbers of ground troops, flowed naturally from its commitment to cutting taxes. A frank admission that war is a risky, expensive business would have prompted calls for shared sacrifice; remember, taxes on the rich went up and inequality declined during both world wars. But the Bush administration planned to use the war to further its inequality-enhancing domestic agenda. The script called for a blitzkrieg, a victory parade, and then another round of tax cuts. This required assuming that everything would be easy, and dismissing warnings from military experts that it probably wouldn't work out that way.

Beyond that, the cronyism that is an essential part of movement conservatism played a key role in the failure of Iraqi reconstruction. Key jobs were given to inexperienced partisan loyalists. Shoddy work by politically connected contractors, like the construction of a new police training center in which excrement drips from the ceiling, went unpunished.[5] And outright corruption flourished. These failures weren't accidental: The systematic use of political power to hand out favors to partisan allies is part of the glue holding movement conservatism together. To have run the Iraq War with efficiency and honesty, the way FDR ran World War II, would have meant behaving at least a little bit like the New Deal—and that would have been anathema to the people in charge.

Ideally, as I said, the public should come out of this experience understanding that movement conservatives can't actually defend the country. At the very least the Iraq experience should neutralize for a long time to come the ability of conservatives to win elections by striking belligerent poses and talking tough. Voters will remember where that got us under Bush—that the tough-talking, pose-striking leader misled the nation into an unnecessary and disastrous war. And if they don't remember, liberals can remind them. So it should be quite a while before another movement conservative can do what Bush did in 2002 and 2004: use national security to distract the public from the fundamentally elitist, anti-populist nature of his policies.

That said, movement conservatives have repeatedly won elections even in years when the public wasn't focused on national security. The most important, sustained source of this electoral strength has been race—the ability to win over a subset of white voters by catering, at least implicitly, to their fear of blacks. That source of electoral strength hasn't gone away. There is, however, good reason to believe that the race issue is gradually losing its force.

Is Race Losing Its Sting?

In 2002 Ruy Texeira and John Judis published *The Emerging Democratic Majority*, a book intended to emulate Kevin Phillips's prescient 1969 book, *The Emerging Republican Majority*. Like Phillips they argued from demographic trends, which they claimed were running in the Democrats' favor. The Republican victories in 2002 and 2004 made their thesis look all wrong, but the 2006 election gave it new life. In a 2007 article Texeira and Judis argued that "this election signals the end of a fleeting Republican revival, prompted by the Bush administration's response to the September 11 terrorist attacks, and the return to political and demographic trends that were leading to a Democratic and center-left majority in the United States."[6] That's not too far from my own view. But my version is blunter and cruder than theirs. I'd say that the politics of white backlash, which have been integral to the success of movement conservatism, are losing effectiveness for two reasons: America is becoming less white, and many (but not all) whites are becoming less racist.

By "white" I actually mean "non-Hispanic white," and the rapid growth of the Hispanic population, from 6.4 percent of the total in 1980 to 12.5 percent in 2000, is the main reason America's ethnic composition is changing. The Asian population is also growing rapidly, albeit from a lower base: Asians were 1.5 percent of the population in 1980, but 3.8 percent in 2000. Both ethnic groups are growing mainly because of immigration, although Hispanics also have a high birth rate.

The immediate political effect of immigration is, as I pointed out in the discussion of the Long Gilded Age, to disenfranchise low-paid workers, effectively shifting the political balance to the right. When low-wage immigrants make up a large part of the work force, those who have the most to gain from policies that promote equality don't vote, while those who have the most to lose do. If that were the whole story, the changing ethnic mix of the U.S. population would simply be the by-product of a process that helps conservatives and hurts liberals. But it's not the whole story. The new immigrants are nonwhite—or at least are perceived by many native-born whites as nonwhite, which is all that matters. And the interaction of that fact with the politics of race in America creates a dynamic that, I'd argue, ultimately deprives movement conservatism of its most potent political weapon.

To understand this dynamic one must first recognize that immigration is a deeply divisive issue for the coalition that supports movement conservatism. Business interests are pro-immigration because they like an abundant, cheap labor force. But voters who can be swayed by the race issue, and have been crucial to the movement's success, also tend to be strongly nativist. John Judis has described the profile of Republican anti-immigration voters:

> They are very similar to the white working-class voters who became Republicans in the 1970s and 1980s due to opposition to desegregation and the counter-culture. They are, typically, white evangelical Protestants from the South, Midwest, and non-Pacific West with lower incomes and without college degrees. They live in small towns and rural areas—usually away from concentrations of immigrants—and consider themselves to be "conservatives."[7]

The result is bitter division within the movement over immigration policy. And this has a further consequence: The obvious reality that an important wing of the modern Republican Party is bitterly anti-immigrant pushes nonwhite immigrants into the arms of the Democratic Party. This has already happened in California: Pete Wilson, the former Republican governor, won an upset victory in 1994 by making illegal immigration the center of his campaign. In the years that followed, however, California's growing Hispanic population responded by becoming overwhelmingly Democratic, turning the state's politics in a sharply liberal direction. Even Arnold Schwarzenegger's election as governor changed little: Schwarzenegger quickly learned that to be effective he had to govern as a modern version of an Eisenhower Republican, so much so that, like New York mayor Michael Bloomberg (who recently declared himself an independent), he's often described as being a de facto Democrat.

In other words, the political success of movement conservatism depends on appealing to whites who resent blacks. But it's difficult to be antiblack without also being anti-immigrant. And because the rapidly growing number of immigrants makes them an increasingly potent political force, the race issue, which has been a powerful asset for movement conservatives in the past, may gradually be turning into a liability.

Republicans have sought to contain this problem by keeping immigrants and their descendants disenfranchised as long as possible. Some of the bogus voter fraud cases described in chapter 9 were aimed at Hispanics rather than blacks. In 2003, when Justice Department lawyers unanimously concluded that the infamous Texas redistricting plan violated the Voting Rights Act, they emphasized the way it diluted Hispanic voting influence. (The lawyers were, of course, overruled by political appointees, and the plan went through, leading to a five-seat Republican gain in Congress.) Yet the redistricting didn't keep Democrats from sweeping to control of the House in 2006, and it's hard to see such actions, reprehensible as they are, as more than a delaying tactic.

Beyond the blunt, crude fact that America is getting less white, there's a more uplifting reason to believe that the political exploitation of race may be losing its force: As a nation we've become much less racist. The most dramatic evidence of diminishing racism is the way people respond to questions about a subject that once struck terror into white hearts: miscegenation. In 1978, as the ascent of movement conservatism to power was just beginning, only 36 percent of Americans polled by Gallup approved of marriages between whites and blacks, while 54 percent disapproved. As late as 1991 only a plurality of 48 percent approved. By 2002, however, 65 percent of Americans approved of interracial marriages; by June 2007, that was up to 77 percent.

This may not seem directly relevant to politics. After all, nobody is proposing to reinstate the laws that once existed against interracial marriage. But the ability of the right to exploit racial tension has little to do with actual policies, and a lot to do with tapping into primal emotions. If those primal emotions are losing their intensity—and they are—the strategy loses its force.

The ebbing of racism doesn't translate into an immediate political revolution. The deep South, in particular, will probably remain strongly Republican for some time to come. But the Southern strategy is literally fraying at the edges: Border states, a category that now includes Virginia, are becoming increasingly competitive for Democrats. In fact the upset victory of James Webb over George Allen in the 2006 Virginia Senate race was a perfect illustration of the way old-fashioned racism can interact with immigration in a way that undermines movement conservatives. Many people thought so highly of the political talent exhibited by Allen, a California yuppie who had reinvented himself as a Southern good old boy, that they believed he had a good chance of becoming the next Republican presidential nominee. But then came the Macaca incident: Allen began taunting S. R. Sidharth, a dark-skinned aide to Webb who is American born but of Indian ancestry, with what turned out to be an obscure racial epithet. The incident, caught on video (as everything is these days) was enough to put Webb over the top.

The importance of the shifting politics of race is almost impossible to overstate. Movement conservatism as a powerful political force is unique to the United States. The principal reason movement conservatives have been able to flourish here, while people with comparable ideas are relegated to the political fringe in Canada and Europe, is the racial tension that is the legacy of slavery. Ease some of that tension, or more accurately increase the political price Republicans pay for trying to exploit it, and America becomes less distinctive, more like other Western democracies where support for the welfare state and policies to limit inequality is much stronger.

What's Okay with Kansas?

Possibly the most stunning part of that Pew report on long-term trends in attitudes was the section on social and "values" issues. It's startling to realize how intolerant America was, not that long ago, and how much attitudes have changed. For example, in 1987 more than half of respondents believed that schools should have the right to fire homosexual teachers, and 43 percent believed that AIDS might be God's punishment for immoral sexual behavior. By 2007 those numbers were down to 28 and 23 percent, respectively. Or take the question of women's role in society: In 1987 only 29 percent completely disagreed with the proposition that women should return to their traditional roles, but by 2007 that was up to 51 percent.

The extent of the change in attitudes is impressive. The political implications are less clear. As I explained in chapter 9, political scientists are skeptical about the "What's the matter with Kansas?"

thesis: crunching the numbers, they find little evidence that religious and social issues, as opposed to race, have actually led a large number of working-class whites to vote against their economic interests. "Values voters" seem to be decisive only in close races. Nonetheless, to the extent that social and religious intolerance has been exploited by movement conservatives, the scope for that kind of exploitation is clearly diminishing.

Furthermore there are hints of a dynamic on social and religious issues that in some ways resembles the dynamic on race: As the country becomes more tolerant the dependence of the Republican Party on an intolerant base puts it increasingly out of step with the majority. The case in point is Kansas itself, where a number of prominent Republicans became Democrats after the 2004 election in protest over the local GOP's dominance by the religious right. "I got tired of theological debates over whether Charles Darwin was right," declared the former state Republican chairman as he switched parties. The Kansas Republican Party has responded by demanding that members sign a seriously creepy, vaguely Maoist-sounding "unity pledge," in which they declare, "I will, at no point in my political or personal future, find cause to transfer my Party loyalty."[8] At the time of writing, Kansas has a Democratic governor, and Democrats hold two of its four House seats.

Looking for Answers

Americans are worried about an economy that leaves most of them behind, even in supposedly good times. They've become less susceptible to the politics of distraction—appeals to racial and social intolerance, fearmongering on national security. For all these reasons it seems probable that movement conservatism's moment has passed.

Liberals need, however, to stand for more than simply not being as bad as the people who have been running America lately. Think again of the New Deal: The failure of conservative governance made it more or less inevitable that Democrats would win the 1932 election, but it was by no means certain that the victor would leave a lasting legacy. What made the New Deal's influence so enduring was the fact that FDR provided answers to inequality and economic insecurity. These included, first and foremost, the institutions of the American welfare state—above all, Social Security. As we've seen, the New Deal was also remarkably successful at flattening the U.S. income distribution, without adverse effects on economic growth.

Now we're once again a nation disgusted by conservative governance. It's not 1932 all over again, but the odds are pretty good that Democrats—and relatively liberal Democrats, at that—will soon hold both Congress and the White House. The question is whether the new majority will accomplish anything lasting.

They should be able to do it. Liberals today have one big advantage over liberals seventy-five years ago: They know what to do, on at least one important issue. In the next chapter I'll explain the overwhelming case for completing the New Deal by providing Americans with something citizens of every other advanced country already have: guaranteed universal health care.

11

THE HEALTH CARE IMPERATIVE

The United States, uniquely among wealthy nations, does not guarantee basic health care to its citizens. Most discussions of health care policy, my own included, begin with facts and figures about the costs and benefits of closing that gap. I'll get to those shortly. But let me start with a different kind of question: What do we think is the morally right thing to do?

There is a morally coherent argument against guaranteed health care, which basically comes down to saying that life may be unfair, but it's not the job of the government to rid the world of injustice. If some people can't afford health insurance, this argument would assert, that's unfortunate, but the government has no business forcing other people to help them out through higher taxes. If some people inherit genes that make them vulnerable to illness, or acquire conditions at some point in their lives that make it impossible for them to get medical insurance from then on, well, there are many strokes of bad luck in life. The government can't fix them all, and there's no reason to single out these troubles in particular.

Obviously I don't agree with this argument. But I'm not setting it up merely in order to knock it down. My point is, instead, that while there is a morally coherent argument against universal health care, it's an argument you almost never hear in political debate. There are surely a significant number of conservatives who believe that the government has no right to spend taxpayers' money helping the unlucky; the late Molly Ivins was fond of quoting a Texas legislator who asked, "Where did this idea come from that everybody deserves free education? Free medical care? Free whatever? It comes from Moscow. From Russia. It comes straight out of the pit of hell."[1] But national politicians never say things like that in public.

The reason they don't is, of course, that they know voters don't agree. You'd be hard pressed to find more than a relative handful of Americans who consider it right to deny people health care because of preexisting conditions, and polls suggest as well that a large majority believe that all American citizens should be guaranteed health care regardless of income. The moral case for universal health care isn't in dispute.

Instead the opposition to universal health care depends on the claim that doing the morally right thing isn't possible, or at least that the cost—in taxpayer dollars, in reduced quality of care for those doing okay under our current system—would be too high. This is where the facts and figures come in. The fact is that every other advanced country manages to achieve the supposedly impossible, providing health care to all its citizens. The quality of care they provide, by any available measure, is as good as or better than ours. And they do all of this while spending much less per person on health care than we do. Health care, in other words, turns out to be an area in which doing the right thing morally is also a free lunch in economic terms. All the evidence suggests that a more just system would also be cheaper to run than our current system, and provide better care.

There's one more important thing to realize about health care: It's an issue Americans care about, in large part because the system we have is visibly unraveling. Polls consistently suggest that health care is, in fact, the most important domestic issue to likely voters.

Shared values; good economics; importance in voters' eyes—all these should make health care reform a priority. And everything we know about the economics of health care indicates that the only kind of reform that will work is one that is, by any definition, liberal: It would involve government action that would reduce inequality and insecurity. Health care reform is the natural centerpiece of a new New Deal. If liberals want to show that progressive policies can create a better, more just society, this is the place to start.

Before I can get to proposals for health care reform, however, I need to talk a bit about health care economics.

We're Number Thirty-Seven!

If the past is any guide, during the next year half of Americans will have negligible medical expenses. Maybe they'll buy a few bottles of aspirin, maybe they'll have a checkup or two, but they won't get sick, or at least not sick enough to need expensive treatment. On the other hand a minority of Americans will incur huge medical expenses—they'll need a heart bypass operation, or dialysis, or chemotherapy. Overall 20 percent of the population will account for 80 percent of medical costs. The sickest 1 percent of the population will, on average, need more than $150,000 worth of medical care next year alone.[2]

Very few Americans can afford to pay sums that large out of

pocket—especially if costly medical care goes on for years, as it often does. Modern medical care is available to middle-class Americans and their counterparts in other advanced countries only because someone else pays most of the bills if and when the need for expensive care arises.

In the United States, uniquely among wealthy nations, that "someone else" is usually a private insurance company. Everywhere else most health insurance is in effect provided by the government, and ultimately by taxpayers (although the details can be complex). Even in the United States, a taxpayer-funded insurance program—Medicare—covers everyone sixty-five and older, and another government program, Medicaid, covers some but not all of those too poor to afford private insurance. But the great majority of Americans who have health insurance get it from the private sector. That reliance on private insurance also makes the United States the only advanced country in which a large fraction of the population—about 15 percent—has no insurance at all.

A word on terminology: Opponents of government health insurance sometimes call it "socialized medicine," but that's misleading—it's socialized *insurance*, which isn't at all the same thing. In Canada and most European countries, the doctors are self-employed or work mainly for privately owned hospitals and clinics. Only Britain, among major nations, has actual socialized medicine, in which the government runs the hospitals and doctors are government employees.

So how does the U.S. health care system, with its unique reliance on private insurance, stack up against the systems of other advanced countries? Table 7 tells the story. It shows how much different countries spend per person on health care, and compares that spending with average life expectancy, the simplest measure of how well the health care system is functioning. The United States

Table 7. Comparing Health Care in the Western World

	Spending per Person, 2004	Life Expectancy, Years, 2004
United States	$6102	77.5
Canada	3165	80.2
France	3150	79.6
Germany	3043	78.9
Britain	2508	78.5

Source: World Health Organization, http://who.int/research/en/.

spends almost twice as much on health care per person as Canada, France, and Germany, almost two and a half times as much as Britain—yet our life expectancy is at the bottom of the pack.

These numbers are so stark, and such a refutation of the conventional wisdom that the private sector is more efficient than the public sector, that some politicians, pundits, and economists simply deny them. Our health care system is "the best in the world," says Republican presidential candidate Rudy Giuliani—except that the World Health Organization actually rates it as number 37.[3] Europeans face huge hidden costs from delays and from inconvenient or uncomfortable service, says Tyler Cowen, a conservative economist—except that cross-national surveys say that even the British have better overall access to health care than Americans do: they wait longer for discretionary surgery than we do, but they find it easier to see a doctor on short notice, especially after hours or on weekends. And the Germans and French have no significant delays of any kind.[4]

We hear endlessly that Canadians have to wait longer than Americans for hip replacements, which is true. But that's a peculiar example to choose, because most hip replacements in America are paid for by Medicare. Now, Medicare is a government program, although it's not clear if everyone knows that—health policy experts often repeat the story of how former Senator John Breaux was accosted by a constituent who urged him not to let the government get its hands on Medicare. The point, however, is that the hip-replacement gap is a comparison of two government insurance systems, with the U.S. system more lavishly funded. It has nothing to do with the alleged virtues of private enterprise.

More seriously, there is some question about the extent to which the American lifestyle drives up health care expenses. Ezra Klein of *The American Prospect* calls it the "but-we-eat-more-cheeseburgers" doctrine, and it's true that Americans are more prone to obesity than Europeans, which in turn tends to raise medical costs, especially for chronic conditions like diabetes. Attempts to crunch the numbers, however, suggest that different lifestyles, and the diseases to which they make us prone, aren't enough to explain more than a small fraction of the cost gap between the United States and everyone else. A study by McKinsey Global Institute estimates that the difference in disease mix between the United States and other advanced countries accounts for less than $25 billion in annual treatment costs, or less than $100 of the roughly $3,000 per person extra the United States spends on health care each year.[5]

There's one more thing you should know: although America *spends* much more on health care than anyone else, this doesn't seem to buy significantly more care. By measures such as the number of doctors per 100,000 people, the average number of doctors' visits, the number of days spent in the hospital, the quantity of prescription drugs we consume, and so on, American health care does not stand out from health care in other rich countries.[6] We're off the charts in terms of what we pay for care, but only in the middle of the pack in terms of what we actually get for our money.

All of this tells us that the U.S. health care system is wildly inefficient. But how does a can-do country, at the cutting edge of technology in many fields, manage to have such an inefficient health care system? The main answer is that we've stumbled into a system in which large sums of money are spent not on providing health care, but on denying it.

Health Economics 101

Possibly the best way to understand the U.S. health care mess is to look at the difference between what we—by which I mean the great majority of Americans—want our system to do, and what the system, as it currently works, gives the main players an incentive to do.

As I've argued, there's a near-consensus that all Americans should receive basic health care. Those who believe otherwise keep their beliefs private, because saying that it's okay to deny care to someone because he or she was born poor, or with the wrong genes, is politically unacceptable. Private insurance companies, however, don't make money by paying for health care. They make money by collecting premiums while *not* paying for health care, to the extent that they can get away with it. Indeed, in the health insurance industry actual payments for care, such as paying the cost of a major operation, are literally referred to as "medical losses."

Insurance companies try to hold down those unfortunate medical losses in two principal ways. One is through "risk selection," otherwise known, rather obscurely, as "underwriting." Both are euphemistic terms for refusing to sell insurance to people who are likely to need it—or charging them a very high price. When they can, insurers carefully screen applicants for indications that they are likely to need expensive care—family history, nature of employment, and, above all, preexisting conditions. Any indication that an applicant is more likely than average to have high medical costs, and any chance of affordable insurance goes out the window.

If someone who makes it through the process of risk selection nonetheless needs care, there's a second line of defense: Insurers look for ways not to pay. They pick through the patient's medical history to see if they can claim that there was some preexisting condition he or she failed to disclose, invalidating the insurance. More important in most cases, they challenge the claims submitted by doctors and hospitals, trying to find reasons why the treatment offered wasn't their responsibility.

Insurers don't do all this because they're evil people. They do it because the structure of the system leaves them little choice. A nice insurance company, one that didn't try to screen out costly clients and didn't look for ways to avoid paying for care, would attract mainly high-risk clients, leaving it stuck with all the expenses other insurers were trying to avoid, and would quickly go out of business. If the people doing all this aren't evil, however, the consequences are. Remember, there's an almost universal belief that everyone should have adequate health care, which means having adequate insurance—but the way our system works, millions of people are denied insurance or offered it only at unaffordable prices. At the same time insurance companies spend huge sums screening applicants and fighting over payment. And health care providers, including doctors and hospitals, spend huge sums dealing and fighting with insurance companies to get paid. There's a whole industry known as "denial management": Companies that help doctors argue with insurance companies when payment is denied.

None of these costs arise in a universal health care system in which the government acts as insurer. If everyone is entitled to health insurance, there's no need to screen people to eliminate high-risk clients. If a government agency provides insurance, there's no need to fight over who pays for a medical procedure: If it's a covered procedure the government pays. As a result government health insurance programs are much less bureaucratic and spend much less on administration than do private insurers. For example, Medicare spends only about 2 percent of its funds on administration; for private insurers the figure is about 15 percent. McKinsey Global estimates that in 2003 the extra administrative costs of the U.S. health insurance industry, as compared with the costs of the government insurance programs in other countries, ran to $84 billion.

And that literally isn't the half of it. As the McKinsey report acknowledges, "This total does not include the additional administrative burden of the multipayor structure and insurance products on hospitals and outpatient centers. . . . Nor does it include the extra costs incurred by employers because of the need for robust human resources departments to administer health care benefits."[7] One widely cited comparison of the U.S. and Canadian systems that tried to estimate these other costs concluded that in the United States total administrative cost—including both the costs of insurers and those of health care providers—accounts for 31 percent of health spending, compared with less than 17 percent in Canada. That would amount to around $300 billion in excess costs, or about a third of the difference between U.S. and Canadian spending.[8]

Where did the rest of the money go? Unlike other advanced countries, the United States doesn't have a centralized agency bargaining with pharmaceutical companies over drug prices. As a result America actually uses fewer drugs per person than the average foreign country but pays far more, adding $100 billion or more to the overall cost of health care. There are also a variety of subtler inefficiencies in the U.S. system, such as perverse financial incentives that have led to a proliferation of outpatient CT scan facilities where the expensive equipment gets relatively little use.

Finally U.S. physicians are paid more than their counterparts in other countries. This isn't, however, a large source of the difference in costs compared with administration, drugs, and other problems. The authors of that study comparing U.S. and Canadian administrative costs estimate that higher U.S. physicians' salaries account for only about 2 percent of the difference in overall costs.

There's one more terrible defect I should mention in the U.S. system: Insurers have little incentive to pay for preventive care, even when it would save large amounts in future medical costs. The most notorious example is diabetes, where insurers often won't pay for treatment that might control the disease in its early stages but will pay for the foot amputations that are all too often a consequence of diabetes that gets out of control. This may seem perverse, but consider the incentives to the insurer: The insurer bears the cost when it pays for preventive care, but it's unlikely to reap the benefits since people often switch insurers, or go from private insurance to Medicare when they reach sixty-five. So medical care that costs money now but saves money in the future may not be worth it from an individual insurance company's perspective. By contrast, universal systems, which cover everyone for life, have a strong incentive to pay for preventive care.

So far I've made the U.S. system sound like a nightmare, which it is for many people. Nonetheless about 85 percent of Americans do have health insurance, and most of them receive decent care. Why does the system work even that well?

Part of the answer is that even in America the government plays a crucial role in providing health coverage. In 2005, 80 million Americans were covered by government programs, mostly Medicare and Medicaid plus other programs such as veterans' health care. This was less than the 198 million covered by private health insurance—but because both programs are largely devoted to the elderly, who have much higher medical costs than younger people, the government actually pays for more medical care than do private insurers. In 2004 government programs paid for 44 percent of health care in America, while private insurance paid for only 36 percent; most of the rest was out-of-pocket spending, which exists everywhere.

The rest of the reason why the American system works as well as it does is that the great majority of Americans who do have private health insurance get it through their employers. This is partly the result of history—during World War II companies weren't allowed to raise wages to compete for workers, so many offered health benefits instead. It's also in large part the result of a special tax advantage: Health benefits, unlike salary, aren't subject to income or payroll taxes. In order to get this tax advantage, however, an employer has to offer the same health plan to all its employees, regardless of their health history. Employment-based coverage, then, mitigates to some extent the problem of insurers screening out those who really need insurance. Also, large employers to some extent stand up for their employees' rights to treatment.

As a result of these advantages, employment-based insurance has long provided a workable solution to the health care problem for many Americans—a solution that was good enough to head off demands for a fundamental overhaul of the system. But now that solution, such as it was, is breaking down.

A Slow-Motion Crisis

The basic outlines of the U.S. health care system haven't changed much since 1965, when LBJ created Medicare and Medicaid. Government insurance for the elderly and the poor; employment-based insurance for workers with good jobs at good companies; personal insurance, if you can get it, for those not lucky enough to get employment-based coverage; a scary life without insurance for a significant number of Americans. While the outlines have remained the same, however, the numbers have changed. Employment-based insurance is gradually unraveling. Medicaid has taken up some but not all of the slack. And fear of losing health insurance has come to pervade middle-class America.

The slow-motion health care crisis began in the 1980s, went into brief remission for part of the nineties, and is now back with a vengeance. The core of the crisis is the decline in employment-based insurance. As recently as 2001, 65 percent of American workers had employment-based coverage. By 2006 that was down to 59 percent, with no sign that the downward trend was coming to an end.[9] What's driving the decline in employment-based coverage is, in turn, the rising cost of insurance: The average annual premium for family coverage was more than eleven thousand dollars in 2006, more than a quarter of the median worker's annual earnings.[10] For lower-paid workers that's just too much—in fact, it's close to the total annual earnings of a full-time worker paid the minimum wage. One study found that even among "moderate income" Americans, which it defined as members of families with incomes between twenty and thirty-five thousand dollars a year, more than 40 percent were uninsured at some point over a two-year period.[11]

Why is insurance getting more expensive? The answer, perversely, is medical progress. Advances in medical technology mean that doctors can treat many previously untreatable problems, but only at great expense. Insurance companies pay for these treatments but compensate by raising premiums.

The trend of rising medical costs goes back for many decades. Table 8 shows total U.S. health care spending as a percentage of

GDP since 1960; except for one brief episode, of which more later, it has been rising steadily. As long as medical costs were relatively low, however, rising spending posed little problem: Americans shouldered the financial burden, and benefited from medical progress.

By the 1980s, however, medical costs had risen to the point where insurance was becoming unaffordable for many employers. As medical costs continued to rise, employers began dropping coverage for their employees, increasing the number of people without insurance, who often fail to receive even basic care. As Robin Wells and I wrote back in 2006:

> Our health care system often makes irrational choices, and rising costs exacerbate those irrationalities. Specifically, American health care tends to divide the population into insiders and outsiders. Insiders, who have good insurance, receive everything modern medicine can provide, no matter how expensive. Outsiders, who have poor insurance or none at all, receive very little. . . .
>
> In response to new medical technology, the system

Table 8. Health Care Spending

Year	Percentage of GDP
1960	5.2
1970	7.2
1980	9.1
1990	12.3
1993	13.7
2000	13.8
2005	16.0

Source: Centers for Medicare and Medicaid Services, http://www.cms.hhs.gov/NationalHealthExpendData/.

spends even more on insiders. But it compensates for higher spending on insiders, in part, by consigning more people to outsider status—robbing Peter of basic care in order to pay for Paul's state-of-the-art treatment. Thus we have the cruel paradox that medical progress is bad for many Americans' health.[12]

This cruel paradox was well under way in the 1980s, and it led, for a time, to a powerful movement demanding health care reform. Harris Wofford won a surprise victory in Pennsylvania's 1991 special senatorial election, in large part by stressing the problems of health care. Bill Clinton picked up the same theme, and it helped elect him in 1992.

But Clinton's attempt to deliver on his promise failed, and Wofford himself was defeated by Rick Santorum, a full-fledged movement conservative, in 1994. (Santorum, in turn, was defeated solidly in 2006. As I mentioned in chapter 8, he has taken refuge for the time being in a movement think tank, where he is creating a program called "America's Enemies.") Why did health care reform fail under Clinton, and why has its time come again?

Enduring Obstacles to Health Care Reform

There were a few months in 1993 when fundamental health care reform seemed unstoppable. But it failed—and the failure of the Clinton plan was followed by the Republican triumph in the 1994 election, a sequence that haunts and intimidates Democrats to this day. Fear of another debacle is one of the main factors limiting the willingness of major Democrats to commit themselves to universal health care now. The question, however, is what lessons we really should learn from 1993.

I find it helpful to divide the reasons for Clinton's failure into three categories. First, there were the enduring obstacles to reform, which are the same now as they were then. Second, there were aspects of the situation in 1993 that are no longer relevant. Third, there were the avoidable missteps—mistakes Clinton made that don't have to be repeated.

Let's start with the enduring obstacles, of which the most fundamental is the implacable opposition of movement conservatives. William Kristol, in the first of a famous series of strategy memos circulated to Republicans in Congress, declared that Republicans should seek to "kill" the Clinton plan. He explained why in the *Wall Street Journal*: "Passage of the Clinton health care plan *in any form* would be disastrous. It would guarantee an unprecedented federal intrusion into the American economy. Its success would signal the rebirth of centralized welfare-state policy."[13] He went on to argue that the plan would lead to bad results, but his main concern, clearly, was that universal health care might actually work—that it would be popular, and that it would make the case for government intervention. It's the same logic that led to George W. Bush's attempt to privatize Social Security: The most dangerous government programs, from a movement conservative's point of view, are the ones that work the best and thereby legitimize the welfare state.

We don't have to speculate about whether movement conservatives will be equally implacable in their opposition to future health care reforms—they already are at the time of writing, and their arguments are even more over-the-top than they were in 1993. For example, when British authorities found that a ring of Muslim doctors employed by the National Health Service had been planning terrorist attacks, there was a coordinated effort by media outlets such as Fox News and movement conservative pundits to push the idea that national health care foments terrorism. Honest.[14]

It's equally certain that the insurance industry will fiercely oppose reform, as it did in 1993. What most people remember about the Clinton debacle is the highly effective "Harry and Louise" ads run by the insurance lobby, which scared people into believing that the plan would deprive them of medical choice. What they probably don't realize is that the industry's opposition came as a surprise to the Clintons, whose plan tried to co-opt insurance companies by giving them a major role in running the system. All of the leading health care plans now on the table, as described below, similarly preserve an important role for private insurers—but now, as then, that won't diminish the industry's opposition. The fact is that no health care reform can succeed unless it reduces the excess administrative costs now imposed by the insurance industry—and that means forcing the industry to shrink, even if the insurers retain a role in the system. There's really no way to buy their cooperation.

Again, we don't have to speculate about this. The political dynamics are already visible in California, where Arnold Schwarzenegger, a modern version of an Eisenhower Republican, has proposed universal health care at the state level. Schwarzenegger's plan would preserve the role of private insurance companies, but it would regulate them in an attempt to eliminate risk selection. And sure enough, Blue Cross of California, the state's largest insurer, is running Harry and Louise–type ads warning that "ill-considered reforms" could damage the state's health care.

The drug industry will also be a source of fierce opposition—and probably more so than in 1993, because drug spending is a much larger share of total medical costs today than it was fifteen years ago. Like the opposition of insurers, drug industry opposition is essentially unavoidable, because drug companies are part of the problem—U.S. health care is costly partly because we pay much more than other countries for prescription drugs, and sooner or later a universal health care system would try to bargain those prices down.

So far so bad: Some of the major sources of opposition to health care reform in the early nineties will put up equally fierce resistance today. There is, however, a fundamental sense in which the current push for reform is more durable, less likely to be undercut by events, than the push fifteen years ago.

2008 Isn't 1993

As I pointed out in chapter 10, Bill Clinton got elected in large part because the U.S. economy was depressed. The recession of 1990–91 was followed by a long period of slow job growth, the so-called "jobless recovery," that felt to most people like a continuing recession. And the health care crisis seemed particularly acute because people were losing jobs, and losing the health insurance that went with those jobs. The problem for health care reformers was that once the economy began to improve, so did the health insurance situation. By early 1994 William Kristol had persuaded Republicans to fight Clinton's plan, not simply on its own merits but by claiming that there was no crisis in American health care. And as Table 9 shows, the health insurance situation was in fact improving rapidly: The percentage of Americans with employment-based insurance rose sharply in 1994, as newly employed Americans got coverage along with their jobs. Republican stalling tactics worked in large part because by the time the first year of Clinton's presidency had ended, Americans were feeling better about the health care status quo.

That simply isn't going to happen this time around. The early years of this decade were marked by a recession and jobless recovery similar to that of the early 1990s. The job picture began improving in 2003, however, and by 2006 the unemployment rate had fallen to levels not far above its late-nineties low. Yet the health

Table 9. Employment-Based Insurance

Year	Percentage Covered
1987	62.1
1993	57.1
1994	60.9
2000	63.6
2005	59.5

Source: U.S. Bureau of the Census health insurance tables, http://www.census.gov/hhes/www/hlthins/historic/hihistt1.html.

insurance picture continued to get worse. This time there won't be a temporary improvement in the picture that will let obstructionists deny that there's a crisis.

There was also another factor producing temporary relief just as Clinton was trying to sell his health plan: The mid-1990s were the golden age of HMOs. The original idea behind health maintenance organizations was that traditional fee-for-service insurance, in which insurance companies pay any doctor for an allowed procedure, leads to overspending: Doctors call for any procedure that might yield medical benefits, and patients go along since someone else pays. An HMO was supposed to replace this with "managed care," in which doctors who were part of the HMO's network had incentives to take cost into account, leading them to forgo expensive procedures with small expected medical benefits. People would accept these limits, the theory went, because they would lead to much cheaper insurance.

The overall idea of taking cost into account in medical decisions makes a lot of sense. Britain's National Health Service, the one example of true socialized medicine among major advanced countries, has a limited budget. The medical professionals who run the system try to make the most of this budget by rating medical procedures in terms of the medical gain per pound spent, and limiting low-gain spending. In the United States, the Veterans Health Administration, which is a sort of miniature American version of the NHS, does much the same thing. And both the NHS and the VA system do remarkably well at providing effective health care despite having very limited resources.

HMOs, however, are private organizations run by businessmen, not public agencies run by doctors. At first they seemed to deliver on their promise of cost savings: as HMOs spread in the 1990s, the long-term rise in health care costs paused, a pause clearly visible in Table 8. And during the 1990s the combination of HMO cost savings and a booming economy led to the big but temporary improvement in the health insurance picture visible in Table 9.

But in the end HMOs failed to deliver sustained savings for one simple reason: People don't trust them. Patients in Britain's National Health Service are, on the whole, willing to accept some rationing of health care because they understand that the national health system has a limited budget and is run by doctors trying to make the most of that budget. American HMO members are much less willing to accept rationing because they know it's driven by accountants who are trying to maximize a corporate bottom line. Because of this distrust and dissatisfaction, HMO enrollment as a share of the total peaked in the mid-1990s, although other, milder forms of managed care continued to grow. Moreover, a public outcry and congressional hearings have forced insurers to back away from aggressive attempts to hold down costs. As a result U.S. medical costs are once again rising rapidly, and employer-based insurance is again in decline.

All this implies that the case for health care reform is less fragile now than it was in 1993. Clinton had a short window of opportunity to achieve reform, before the public's attention shifted to other things. This time it's hard to envision anything that would diminish the public's sense that something must be done, and let opponents claim that there isn't a crisis.

Yet even in 1993 Clinton might have achieved health care reform if he hadn't made several crucial mistakes.

Mistakes to Avoid Repeating

Much has been written about the personalities involved in the Clinton health care plan and their shortcomings. I won't try to add to all that. Instead let me focus on two things that Clinton clearly did wrong.

First, he just didn't get started soon enough. Matthew Holt, a health care analyst whose blog on health policy has become must reading in the field, has offered a stark comparison between Clinton's failed attempt at reform and LBJ's successful push for Medicare. Johnson actually signed Medicare into law on July 30, 1965, less than nine months after his victory in the 1964 election. Clinton didn't even make his first national speech on health care until September 23, 1993.[15]

The long delay was disastrous for several reasons. By the fall of 1993 any political momentum from the 1992 election had dissipated, and the Clinton administration was already bogged down in petty issues like the role of gays in the military, as well as various fake scandals manufactured by the movement conservative echo chamber. At the same time economic recovery was undermining the demand for health care reform.

Why didn't Clinton move sooner? Partly it was a question of priorities: His initial preoccupation was with budget issues. The creation of the Clinton health plan was also an unwieldy process, involving a huge but secretive task force whose leadership managed to alienate many natural allies. Above all, however, Clinton just wasn't ready. Medicare emerged from years of prior discussion; Clinton came in with a near-blank slate. His presidential campaign hadn't offered any specifics on health care reform, nor had there been a national debate on the subject to prepare the ground.

When the Clinton plan finally emerged, it turned out to have another problem: It was all too easily portrayed as a plan that would deprive Americans of medical choice.

The Clinton plan embraced the theory behind managed care, that restricting spending on expensive but medically marginal procedures would lead to huge cost savings. It was a plan for universal coverage, but it was also a plan to, in effect, channel everyone into HMOs, which would engage in "managed competition." Opponents of the plan quickly homed in on the managed care aspect: The first and most devastating of the "Harry and Louise" ads warned that "the government may force us to choose from a few health care plans designed by government officials."[16]

In order to avoid repeating this unfortunate history, today's health care reformers have to avoid these mistakes. They need to hit the ground running: If and when a progressive president and a progressive congressional majority take office, they must have at least the key elements of a universal health care plan already decided and widely discussed. Thus it's a very good thing that health care reform has become a central issue in the current presidential campaign. They'll also need to offer a plan that reassures Americans that they will retain some choice, that those who currently have good insurance won't be forced into something worse.

Paths to Health Care Reform

When FDR created Social Security and unemployment insurance, he was entering uncharted territory. Such programs had never existed in America, and the welfare state programs of Germany and Britain were both limited and little known in the United States. Nobody could be sure how well the New Deal's plans to protect Americans from risk would work in practice. By contrast, universal health care has existed for decades in most of the Western world, and we already have a very good idea of what works.

Ezra Klein has produced a very good survey of health care systems in other advanced countries, and his opening paragraphs are worth quoting in full:

Medicine may be hard, but health insurance is simple. The rest of the world's industrialized nations have already figured it out, and done so without leaving 45 million of their countrymen uninsured and 16 million or so underinsured, and without letting costs spiral into the stratosphere and severely threaten their national economies.

Even better, these successes are not secret, and the mechanisms not unknown. Ask health researchers what should be done, and they will sigh and suggest something akin to what France or Germany does. Ask them what they think can be done, and their desperation to evade the opposition of the insurance industry and the pharmaceutical industry and conservatives and manufacturers and all the rest will leave them stammering out buzzwords and workarounds, regional purchasing alliances and health savings accounts. The subject's famed complexity is a function of the forces protecting the status quo, not the issue itself.[17]

Consider the French system, which the World Health Organization ranked number one in the world. France maintains a basic insurance system that covers everyone, paid for out of tax receipts. This is comparable to Medicare. People are also encouraged to buy additional insurance that covers more medical expenses—comparable to the supplemental health insurance that many older Americans have on top of Medicare—and the poor receive subsidies to help them buy additional coverage, comparable to the way Medicaid helps out millions of older Americans.

It's worth noting, by the way, that the Canadian system, which is often used as an example of what universal health care in America would look like, has a feature present neither in the French system nor in Medicare: Canadians are not permitted to buy their own care in areas covered by government insurance. The rationale for this restriction is that it's a means of holding down costs by preventing affluent Canadians from bidding away scarce medical resources. However, it clearly isn't an essential feature of universal care. Again, older Americans covered by Medicare, like the French, are free to buy as much health care as they want over and above what the government provides.

The parallels between the French system and Medicare aren't perfect: There are some features of the French system that don't have counterparts in America, at least not yet. Many French hospitals are government owned, although these have to compete for patients with the private sector. France also has a strong emphasis on preventive care. The French government provides full coverage—no co-pays—for chronic conditions such as diabetes and hypertension, so that patients won't skimp on treatment that might prevent future complications.

The key point, however, is that the French health care system, which covers everyone and is considered the best in the world, actually looks a lot like an expanded and improved version of Medicare, a familiar and popular program, extended to the whole population. An American version of the French system would cost more than the French system for a variety of reasons, including the facts that our doctors are paid more and that we're fatter and hence more prone to some costly conditions. Overall, however, Medicare for everyone would end the problem of the uninsured, and it would almost certainly cost less than our current system, which leaves 45 million Americans without coverage.

In a world run by policy wonks, that would be the end of the story. Americans love Medicare; let's give it to everyone. Paying for the expansion would mean higher taxes, but even Americans who currently have insurance would more than make up for that because they wouldn't have to pay such high premiums. Problem solved! Fortunately or unfortunately, however, the world isn't run by policy wonks. Proposals to institute a single-payer system, aka Medicare for all, face several major political roadblocks.

The roadblock one hears about most often is the implacable opposition of the insurance and drug industries to a single-payer system. Reformers should realize, however, that these interest groups will go all out against any serious health care reform. There's no way to buy them off.

It may be possible, however, to finesse two other barriers to change: the need to raise taxes, and the public's fear of losing choice. First, the problem of taxes: Extending Medicare or its equivalent to every American would require a *lot* of additional revenue, probably about 4 percent of GDP. True, these additional taxes wouldn't represent a true financial burden on the country, since they would replace insurance premiums people already pay.

Despite that fact, it would be very challenging to convince people that a large tax increase didn't represent a true net increase in their financial burden, especially in the face of the dishonest opposition campaign such a proposal would inevitably encounter. It would also be difficult to pass tax increases of the size needed, even with a strong progressive majority.

The problem of maintaining patient choice is, in a way, similar. Medicare-type coverage would replace much of the insurance Americans already have, and they would be free to buy additional coverage. But a plan that automatically puts people into a government insurance system could easily be portrayed as a plan that deprives them of choice. The opponents of reform would do their best to promote that misunderstanding.

It's important to bear in mind that these two problems are *political* objections to a single-payer system, not economic objections. In purely economic terms, single-payer is clearly the way to go. A single-payer system, with its low administrative costs and strong ability to bargain over prices, would deliver more health care, at lower cost, than the alternatives. The perfect can, however, be the enemy of the good. It's much better to go with a reform plan that's politically feasible and achieves some of the advantages of single-payer than to hold out for the ideal solution.

Now for the good news: Over the past few years policy analysts and politicians have been evolving an approach to health care reform that seems to be a workable compromise between economic efficiency and political realism. It involves four basic elements:

- Community rating
- Subsidies for low-income families
- Mandated coverage
- Public-private competition

I'll begin by discussing the first three, pause to explain what they accomplish in combination, and then explain the role of the fourth.

Under community rating, insurers are prohibited from charging customers different premiums, or denying coverage altogether, based on their perceived risk of getting sick. "Pure" community rating, which is already the law in New York and Vermont, requires that insurers offer everyone policies at the same premium—end of story. Under "adjusted" community rating, which is already the law in Massachusetts, New Jersey, and elsewhere, premiums can vary by criteria such as age and geography—but not by medical history. The purpose of community rating is to prevent insurers from denying care to people with preexisting conditions and other risk factors; it's also supposed to reduce administrative costs, because the insurance companies no longer devote large sums to identifying risky applicants and rejecting them.

Subsidies are something we already do, under Medicaid. Reform proposals call for extending these subsidies to cover many people who aren't eligible for Medicaid but still can't afford insurance, mainly lower-income working adults.

Mandated coverage says that you must have health insurance, just as car owners must have auto insurance. It's intended to deal with the problem of individuals who could afford insurance but choose to take their chances instead, then end up in emergency rooms, where taxpayers often end up paying the tab, if something goes wrong. Some plans also include an employer mandate, requiring that employers buy health insurance for their employees.

Combining these three elements leads to a universal health care system run through private insurance companies. People who might have been denied insurance because of medical history are guaranteed access through community rating, people who might not otherwise have been able to afford insurance are helped out financially, and people who might have chosen to take their chances aren't allowed to.

Massachusetts introduced a system along these lines in 2006. And Arnold Schwarzenegger's plan for California is similar. Two major candidates for the Democratic nomination, John Edwards and Barack Obama, have announced related plans at the time of writing, although they both also have the fourth feature, which I'll discuss in a moment.

Does such a system, in which universal care is achieved via private insurers, have any fundamental advantages over single-payer? In economic terms, no. In fact it's best viewed as an attempt to *simulate* a single-payer system through regulation and subsidies, and the simulation will be imperfect. I once compared such plans to Rube Goldberg devices, which achieve simple goals in a complicated way. In particular, enforcing community rating and mandates requires substantial government bureaucracy. Ironically, running health care through private insurers requires more intrusive government than a simple government program would.

There are, nonetheless, political advantages to a community-rating-subsidies-and-mandates system. First and foremost, it requires much less additional revenue than single-payer, because most of the cost of insurance continues to be paid in the form of premiums from employers and individuals. All you need is enough revenue to subsidize low-income families. Reasonable estimates suggest that the revenue needed to institute a hybrid universal care system is considerably less than the revenue lost due to the Bush tax cuts, which are scheduled to expire at the end of 2010. So this kind of universal health care plan could be implemented without the need to pass a tax increase. All a Democratic president and Congress would have to do is let some of the Bush tax cuts expire, and devote the revenue gained to health care.

At the same time such a plan would allow people satisfied with their private insurance to keep it. The insurance industry would try to block reform by attacking community rating—in fact, community rating was the target of one of the "Harry and Louise" ads in 1993—but it wouldn't be able to accuse the government of forcing people into managed care.

Although private insurance–based universal health care looks more doable than single-payer, it would forgo some of single-payer's advantages. Administrative costs, in particular, would be higher, there would still be a multiplicity of insurers and a fight over who pays what. Is there any way to fix these problems?

That's where the fourth element comes in. The Edwards and Obama plans allow people to stick with private insurance, but they also allow people to buy into a Medicare-type government insurance plan, at a price that reflects the actual cost to the government. Allowing a buy-in to Medicare creates competition between public and private plans. The evidence suggests that the government plans, which would have lower overhead costs because they wouldn't devote large sums to marketing, would win that competition. When Medicare began requiring that Medicare Advantage plans—taxpayer-supported private plans for seniors—compete with traditional Medicare on an actuarially fair basis, the private plans withered away. (They began expanding again after the 2003 Medicare Modernization Act introduced large subsidies to private plans, averaging about a thousand dollars per recipient each year. But that's another story.) If the government plans consistently outcompeted private insurers, the system would evolve over time into single-payer, as private insurers lost market share. This would, however, represent choice on the part of the public, not a government edict forcing people into government programs.

If a plan along these lines is enacted, the result will be a U.S.

health care system that isn't quite like anyone else's but somewhat resembles the German system, in which health insurance is provided by competing but heavily regulated "sickness funds." The German system, like the French system, costs far less than ours while providing universal coverage and high-quality care. It also performs better than the U.S. system on every dimension of health care access: It's easier to see a doctor on short notice, waits in emergency rooms are shorter, and even elective surgery involves fewer delays than it does here.[18]

There are many, many details to work out, but the important thing is that universal health care looks very doable, from an economic, fiscal, and even political point of view.

The Payoff to Health Care Reform

The principal reason to reform American health care is simply that it would improve the quality of life for most Americans. Under our current system tens of millions lack adequate health care, millions more have had their lives destroyed by the financial burden of medical costs, and many more who haven't yet gone without insurance or been bankrupted by health costs live in fear that they may be next. And it's all unnecessary: Every other wealthy country has universal coverage. Reducing the risks Americans face would be worth it even if it had a substantial cost—but in this case there would be no cost at all. Universal health care would be cheaper and better than our current fragmented system.

There is, however, another important reason for health care reform. It's the same reason movement conservatives were so anxious to kill Clinton's plan. That plan's success, said Kristol, "would signal the rebirth of centralized welfare-state policy"—by which he really meant that universal health care would give new life to the

New Deal idea that society should help its less fortunate members. Indeed it would—and that's a big argument in its favor.

Universal health care could, in short, be to a new New Deal what Social Security was to the original—both a crucially important program in its own right, and a reaffirmation of the principle that we are our brothers' keepers. Getting universal care should be the key domestic priority for modern liberals. Once they succeed there, they can turn to the broader, more difficult task of reining in American inequality.

12

CONFRONTING INEQUALITY

The America I grew up in was a relatively equal middle-class society. Over the past generation, however, the country has returned to Gilded Age levels of inequality. In this chapter I'll outline policies that can help reverse these changes. As I did in discussing health care, however, I'll begin with the question of values. Why should we care about high and rising inequality?

One reason to care about inequality is the straightforward matter of living standards. As I documented at length in chapter 7, the lion's share of economic growth in America over the past thirty years has gone to a small, wealthy minority, to such an extent that it's unclear whether the typical family has benefited at all from technological progress and the rising productivity it brings. The lack of clear economic progress for lower- and middle-income families is in itself an important reason to seek a more equal distribution of income.

Beyond that, however, is the damage extreme inequality does to our society and our democracy. Ever since America's founding, our idea of ourselves has been that of a nation without sharp class distinctions—not a leveled society of perfect equality, but one in which the gap between the economic elite and the typical citizen isn't an unbridgeable chasm. That's why Thomas Jefferson wrote, "The small landholders are the most precious part of a state."[1] Translated into modern terms as an assertion that a broad middle class is the most precious part of a state, Jefferson's statement remains as true as ever. High inequality, which has turned us into a nation with a much-weakened middle class, has a corrosive effect on social relations and politics, one that has become ever more apparent as America has moved deeper into a new Gilded Age.

The Costs of Inequality

One of the best arguments I've ever seen for the social costs of inequality came from a movement conservative trying to argue the opposite. In 1997 Irving Kristol, one of the original neoconservative intellectuals, published an article in the Wall Street Journal called "Income Inequality Without Class Conflict." Kristol argued that we shouldn't worry about income inequality, because whatever the numbers may say, class distinctions are, in reality, all but gone. Today, he asserted,

> income inequality tends to be swamped by even greater social equality. . . . In all of our major cities, there is not a single restaurant where a CEO can lunch or dine with the absolute assurance that he will not run into his secretary. If you fly first class, who will be your traveling companions? You never know. If you go to Paris, you will be lost in a crowd of young people flashing their credit cards.[2]

By claiming that income inequality doesn't matter because we have social equality, Kristol was in effect admitting that income inequality *would* be a problem if it led to social inequality. And here's the thing: It does. Kristol's fantasy of a world in which the rich live just like you and me, and nobody feels socially inferior, bears no resemblance to the real America we live in.

Lifestyles of the rich and famous are arguably the least important part of the story, yet it's worth pointing out that Kristol's vision of CEOs rubbing shoulders with the middle class is totally contradicted by the reporting of Robert Frank of the *Wall Street Journal*, whose assigned beat is covering the lives of the wealthy. In his book *Richistan* Frank describes what he learned:

> Today's rich had formed their own virtual country. . . . [T]hey had built a self-contained world unto themselves, complete with their own health-care system (concierge doctors), travel network (Net Jets, destination clubs), separate economy. . . . The rich weren't just getting richer; they were becoming financial foreigners, creating their own country within a country, their own society within a society, and their own economy within an economy.[3]

The fact is that vast income inequality inevitably brings vast social inequality in its train. And this social inequality isn't just a matter of envy and insults. It has real, negative consequences for the way people live in this country. It may not matter much that the great majority of Americans can't afford to stay in the eleven-thousand-dollar-a-night hotel suites popping up in luxury hotels around the world.[4] It matters a great deal that millions of middle-class families buy houses they can't really afford, taking on more mortgage debt than they can safely handle, because they're desperate to send their children to a good school—and intensifying inequality means that the desirable school districts are growing fewer in number, and more expensive to live in.

Elizabeth Warren, a Harvard Law School expert in bankruptcy, and Amelia Warren Tyagi, a business consultant, have studied the rise of bankruptcy in the United States. By 2005, just before a new law making it much harder for individuals to declare bankruptcy took effect, the number of families filing for bankruptcy each year was five times its level in the early 1980s. The proximate reason for this surge in bankruptcies was that families were taking on more debt—and this led to moralistic pronouncements about people spending too much on luxuries they can't afford. What Warren and Tyagi found, however, was that middle-class families were actually spending *less* on luxuries than they had in the 1970s. Instead the rise in debt mainly reflected increased spending on housing, largely driven by competition to get into good school districts. Middle-class Americans have been caught up in a rat race, not because they're greedy or foolish but because they're trying to give their children a chance in an increasingly unequal society.[5] And they're right to be worried: A bad start can ruin a child's chances for life.

Americans still tend to say, when asked, that individuals can make their own place in society. According to one survey 61 percent of Americans agree with the statement that "people get rewarded for their effort," compared with 49 percent in Canada and only 23 percent in France.[6] In reality, however, America has vast inequality of opportunity as well as results. We may believe that anyone can succeed through hard work and determination, but the facts say otherwise.

There are many pieces of evidence showing that Horatio Alger stories are very rare in real life. One of the most striking comes from a study published by the National Center for Education Statistics, which tracked the educational experience of Americans who were eighth graders in 1988. Those eighth graders were sorted both by apparent talent, as measured by a mathematics test, and by the socioeconomic status of their parents, as measured by occupations, incomes, and education.

The key result is shown in Table 10. Not surprisingly, both getting a high test score and having high-status parents increased a student's chance of finishing college. But family status mattered more. Students who scored in the bottom fourth on the exam, but came from families whose status put them in the top fourth—what we used to call RDKs, for "rich dumb kids," when I was a teenager—were more likely to finish college than students who scored in the top fourth but whose parents were in the bottom fourth. What this tells us is that the idea that we have anything close to equality of opportunity is clearly a fantasy. It would be closer to the truth, though not the whole truth, to say that in modern America, class—inherited class—usually trumps talent.

Isn't that true everywhere? Not to the same extent. International comparisons of "intergenerational mobility," the extent to which people can achieve higher status than their parents, are tricky because countries don't collect perfectly comparable data.

Table 10. Percentage of 1988 Eighth Graders Finishing College

	Score in Bottom Quartile	Score in Top Quartile
Parents in Bottom Quartile	3	29
Parents in Top Quartile	30	74

Source: National Center for Education Statistics, *The Condition of Education 2003*, p. 47.

Nonetheless it's clear that Horatio Alger has moved to someplace in Europe: Mobility is highest in the Scandinavian countries, and most results suggest that mobility is lower in the United States than it is in France, Canada, and maybe even Britain. Not only don't Americans have equal opportunity, opportunity is less equal here than elsewhere in the West.

It's not hard to understand why. Our unique lack of universal health care, all by itself, puts Americans who are unlucky in their parents at a disadvantage: Because American children from low-income families are often uninsured, they're more likely to have health problems that derail their life chances. Poor nutrition, thanks to low income and a lack of social support, can have the same effect. Life disruptions that affect a child's parents can also make upward mobility hard—and the weakness of the U.S. social safety net makes such disruptions more likely and worse if they happen. Then there's the highly uneven quality of U.S. basic education, and so on. What it all comes down to is that although the principle of "equality of opportunity, not equality of results" sounds fine, it's a largely fictitious distinction. A society with highly unequal results is, more or less inevitably, a society with highly unequal opportunity, too. If you truly believe that all Americans are entitled to an equal chance at the starting line, that's an argument for doing something to reduce inequality.

America's high inequality, then, imposes serious costs on our society that go beyond the way it holds down the purchasing power of most families. And there's another way in which inequality damages us: It corrupts our politics. "If there are men in this country big enough to own the government of the United States," said Woodrow Wilson in 1913, in words that would be almost inconceivable from a modern president, "they are going to own it."[7] Well, now there are, and they do. Not completely, of course, but hardly a week goes by without the disclosure of a case in which the influence of money has grotesquely distorted U.S. government policy.

As this book went to press, there was a spectacular example: The way even some Democrats rallied to the support of hedge fund managers, who receive an unconscionable tax break. Through a quirk in the way the tax laws have been interpreted, these managers—some of whom make more than a billion dollars a year—get to have most of their earnings taxed at the capital gains rate, which is only 15 percent, even as other high earners pay a 35 percent rate. The hedge fund tax loophole costs the government more than $6 billion a year in lost revenue, roughly the cost of providing health care to three million children.[8] Almost $2 billion of the total goes to just twenty-five individuals. Even conservative economists believe that the tax break is unjustified, and should be eliminated.[9]

Yet the tax break has powerful political support—and not just from Republicans. In July 2007 Sen. Charles Schumer of New York, the head of the Democratic Senatorial Campaign Committee, let it be known that he would favor eliminating the hedge fund loophole only if other, deeply entrenched tax breaks were eliminated at the same time. As everyone understood, this was a "poison pill," a way of blocking reform without explicitly saying no. And although Schumer denied it, everyone also suspected that his position was driven by the large sums hedge funds contribute to Democratic political campaigns.[10]

The hedge fund loophole is a classic example of how the concentration of income in a few hands corrupts politics. Beyond that is the bigger story of how income inequality has reinforced the rise of movement conservatism, a fundamentally undemocratic force. As I argued in chapter 7, rising inequality has to an important extent been caused by the rightward shift of our politics, but the causation also runs the other way. The new wealth of the rich has increased their influence, sustaining the institutions of movement conservatism and pulling the Republican Party even further into the movement's orbit. The ugliness of our politics is in large part a reflection of the inequality of our income distribution.

More broadly still, high levels of inequality strain the bonds that hold us together as a society. There has been a long-term downward trend in the extent to which Americans trust either the government or one another. In the sixties, most Americans agreed with the proposition that "most people can be trusted"; today most disagree.[11] In the sixties, most Americans believed that the government is run "for the benefit of all"; today, most believe that it's run for "a few big interests."[12] And there's convincing evidence that growing inequality is behind our growing cynicism, which is making the United States seem increasingly like a Latin American country. As the political scientists Eric Uslaner and Mitchell Brown point out (and support with extensive data), "In a world of haves and have-nots, those at either end of the economic spectrum have little reason to believe that 'most people can be trusted' . . . social trust rests on a foundation of economic equality."[13]

Reducing Income Inequality: Aftermarket Policies

In discussing ways to reduce inequality, it's helpful to make a distinction between two concepts of inequality, and two kinds of inequality-reducing policies.

The first concept of inequality is inequality in market income. The United States is, of course, a market economy. Most people get most of their income by selling their labor to employers; people also get income from the market return to assets such as stocks, bonds, and real estate. So one measure of inequality is the inequality of the income people get from selling things. The distribution of market income is highly unequal and getting more so. In fact, market income is now as unequally distributed as it was in the 1920s.

But that's not the end of the story. The government collects part of market income in the form of taxes, and transfers part of that revenue back to the public either in direct payments, like the Social Security checks that are the main source of income for most older Americans, or by paying for goods and services like health care. So another measure of inequality is the inequality of disposable income—income after you take taxes and government transfers into account. In modern America, as in all advanced countries, inequality in disposable income is less than inequality in market income, because we have a welfare state—though a small one by international standards. Taxes and transfers, which somewhat crimp the living standards of the rich while helping out the less fortunate, are the reason America in 2007 doesn't *feel* quite as unequal as America did in the twenties.

Now, one way to reduce inequality in America is to do more of this: to expand and improve our aftermarket policies, which take the inequality of market income as given but act to reduce its impact. To see how this might work, let me describe an example of a country that does vastly more to reduce inequality than we do: France.

If you're going through a rough patch in your life—or if your whole life has been rough—it's definitely better to be French than American. In France, if you lose your job and have to take an inferior one, you don't have to worry about losing your health insurance, because health insurance is provided by the government. If you're out of work for a long time, the government helps keep you fed and housed. If you're financially pinched by the cost of raising children, you get extra money from the state, as well as help with day care. You aren't guaranteed a comfortable life, but your family members, especially your children, are protected against experiencing really severe material deprivation.

On the other hand, if things are going very well for you, being French has its drawbacks. Income tax rates are somewhat higher than they are in the United States, and payroll taxes, especially the amount formally paid by employers but in effect taken out of wages, are much higher. Also, the cost of living is high because France has a high value-added tax, a form of national sales tax. For people with high incomes these burdens aren't fully offset by the advantages of government health insurance and other benefits. So a Frenchman whose compensation (including payroll taxes paid by his employer) is in the range we would consider upper-middle-class or higher has substantially less purchasing power than does an American receiving the same compensation.

In other words, France has extensive aftermarket policies that reduce inequality by comforting the afflicted but somewhat afflict the comfortable. In this France is typical of non-English-speaking Western nations. And even other English speakers do more to reduce aftermarket inequality than we do.

For example, the United States spends less than three percent of GDP on programs that reduce inequality among those under 65. To match what Canada does we'd have to spend an additional 2.5 percent of GDP; to match what most of Europe does would require an extra 4 percent of GDP; to match the Scandinavian countries, an additional 9 percent.[14] U.S. programs reduce poverty among the nonelderly by 28 percent, compared with 54 percent in Canada, 61 percent in Britain, and 78 percent in Sweden.[15] And these numbers actually understate the difference between the United States and everyone else, because they don't take account of the unique American failure to guarantee health care to all.

One "easy" way for the United States to reduce inequality

beyond the effective reduction we'd achieve with universal health care would be for America to do considerably more to help the unlucky through public aid of various kinds, paid for with higher taxes on the well off. The additional spending would probably consist largely of expanding programs we already have: an expanded earned income tax credit, a more generous food stamp program, bigger housing aid, and so on. It could also include other items such as child support and help with day care. I'll talk about where the additional revenue could come from later in this chapter.

But don't high taxes and an extensive welfare state remove the incentives to work and innovate? Gross domestic product per capita in France is only 74 percent of GDP per capita in the United States. Isn't that a compelling argument against moving in a French direction? Well, France and other countries with generous social programs do have serious economic problems. Those problems are not, however, as simple or as closely related to the generosity of social programs as you might think.

France does have much lower GDP per person than the United States. That's largely because a smaller fraction of the population is employed—French GDP per *worker* is only 10 percent lower than in the United States.[16] And that difference in GDP per worker, in turn, is entirely because French workers get much more time off: On average French workers put in only 86 percent as many hours each year as U.S. workers.[17] Worker productivity per hour appears to be slightly higher in France than in the United States.

The real question is which aspects of the French difference represent problems, and which simply represent different and possibly better choices. The lower number of hours per worker in France seems to fall in the second category. In the United States vacations are very short, and many workers get no vacation at all. France has essentially made a decision, enforced by legal requirements on vacation time as well as union settlements, to trade less income for more time off. And there's some evidence that this decision actually makes most people better off. As one recent study of the difference in working hours between Europe and the United States points out, polls suggest that people would like to work shorter hours, and international comparisons of reported "life satisfaction" seem to say that working less improves the quality of life even if it reduces income. Yet it's very difficult for any individual, operating on his or her own, to trade less income for more leisure. French rules and regulations that solve this problem by requiring that employers provide vacation may actually be a good thing, even though they reduce GDP.[18]

In addition to working fewer hours than Americans, the French are less likely to work at all. To be more specific: In France the young and old tend not to be employed. About 80 percent of French prime-age adults, those between the ages of twenty-five and fifty-four, are employed, which is almost exactly the same as the U.S. number. However, only 25 percent of French residents aged fifteen to twenty-four are employed, compared with 54 percent in the United States, and only 41 percent of those aged fifty-five to sixty-four are employed, compared with 62 percent here.[19] The question is whether these low employment rates should be viewed as a problem.

The low rate of employment among young people in France is less of a problem than it may appear. It does to some extent reflect regulations that make it hard for employers to fire workers, and therefore make them reluctant to hire workers in the first place. A close examination, however, reveals that other reasons for low employment of young people in France are probably more important. The French are more likely than Americans to stay in school: 92 percent of French residents aged from fifteen to nineteen are in school, and 45 percent of those aged twenty to twenty-four, compared with 84 and 35 percent, respectively, in the United States. And only about 10 percent of French students hold jobs at the same time, compared with about 20 percent in the United States. Presumably, in France the combination of free education and public financial support lets young people from lower-income families concentrate on their studies, while in America they either have to drop out of school or work their way through. This sounds like a virtue, not a vice, of the French system.[20]

Once they reach prime working age, as we've seen, the French are just as likely to be employed as we are—a fact that's very much at odds with the picture of a largely idle work force often painted in U.S. news reports. The only place where the French have a serious problem—and just to be clear, it's a very important problem—is in the low employment and labor-force-participation rates of older workers. This reflects some major policy mistakes—especially the decision, a quarter century ago, to lower to sixty the age at which workers were entitled to full pension benefits. This both encouraged early retirement and imposed large burdens on taxpayers.

So the French make mistakes. But saying, "France has mismanaged its pension policies" is very different from saying, "The French economy has been crippled by an oversize welfare state." It's deeply misleading to use the French example to argue against doing more to help the poor and unlucky.

The Arithmetic of Equalization

Suppose we agree that the United States should become more like other advanced countries, whose tax and benefit systems do much more than ours to reduce inequality. The next question is what that decision might involve.

In part it would involve undoing many of the tax cuts for the wealthy that movement conservatives have pushed through since 1980. Table 11 shows what has happened to three tax rates that strongly affect the top 1 percent of the U.S. population, while having little effect on anyone else. Between 1979 and 2006 the top tax rate on earned income was cut in half; the tax rate on capital gains was cut almost as much; the tax rate on corporate profits fell by more than a quarter. High incomes in America are much less taxed than they used to be. Thus raising taxes on the rich back toward historical levels can pay for part, though only part, of a stronger safety net that limits inequality.

The first step toward restoring progressivity to the tax system is to let the Bush tax cuts for the very well off expire at the end of 2010, as they are now scheduled to. That alone would raise a significant amount of revenue. The nonpartisan Urban-Brookings Joint Tax Policy Center estimates that letting the Bush tax cuts expire for people with incomes over two hundred thousand dollars would be worth about $140 billion a year starting in 2012. That's enough to pay for the subsidies needed to implement universal health care. A tax-cut rollback of this kind, used to finance health care reform, would significantly reduce inequal-

Table 11. Three Top Tax Rates (Percentages)

	Top Tax on Earned Income	Top Tax on Long-Term Capital Gains	Top Tax on Corporate Profits
1979	70	28	48
2006	35	15	35

Source: Urban-Brookings Tax Policy Center, http://taxpolicycenter.org/tax facts/tfdb/tftemplate.cfm.

ity. It would do so partly by modestly reducing incomes at the top: The Tax Policy Center estimates that allowing the Bush tax cuts to expire for Americans making more than two hundred thousand dollars a year would reduce the aftertax incomes of the richest 1 percent of Americans by about 4.5 percent compared with what they would be if the Bush tax cuts were made permanent. Meanwhile middle- and lower-income Americans would be assured of health care—one of the key aspects of being truly middle class.[21]

Another relatively easy move from a political point of view would be closing some of the obvious loopholes in the U.S. system. These include the rule described earlier that allows financial wheeler-dealers, such as hedge fund managers, to classify their earnings as capital gains, taxed at a 15 percent rate rather than 35 percent. The major tax loopholes also include rules that let corporations, drug companies in particular, shift recorded profits to low-tax jurisdictions overseas, costing billions more; one recent study estimates that tax avoidance by multinationals costs about $50 billion a year.[22]

Going beyond rolling back the Bush cuts and closing obvious loopholes would be a more difficult political undertaking. Yet there can be rapid shifts in what seems politically realistic. At the end of 2004 it seemed all too possible that Social Security, the centerpiece of the New Deal, would be privatized and effectively phased out. Today Social Security appears safe, and universal health care seems within reach. If universal health care can be achieved, and the New Deal idea that government can be a force for good is reinvigorated, things that now seem off the table might not look so far out.

Both historical and international evidence show that there is room for tax increases at the top that go beyond merely rolling back the Bush cuts. Even before the Bush tax cuts, top tax rates in the United States were low by historical standards—the tax rate on the top bracket was only 39.6 percent during the Clinton years, compared with 70 percent in the seventies and 50 percent even *after* Reagan's 1981 tax cut. Top U.S. tax rates are also low compared with those in European countries. For example, in Britain, the top income tax rate is 40 percent, seemingly equivalent to the top rate of the Clinton years. However, in Britain employers also pay a social insurance tax—the equivalent of the employer share of FICA here—that applies to all earned income. (Most of the U.S. equivalent is levied only on income up to a maximum of $97,500.) As a result very highly paid British employees face an effective tax rate of almost 48 percent. In France effective top rates are even higher. Also, in Britain capital gains are taxed as ordinary income, so that the effective tax rate on capital gains for people with high income is 40 percent, compared with 15 percent in the United States.[23] Taxing capital gains as ordinary income in the United States would yield significantly more revenue, and also limit the range of tax abuses like the hedge fund loophole.

Also, from the New Deal until the 1970s it was considered normal and appropriate to have "super" tax rates on very-high-income individuals. Only a few people were subject to the 70 percent top bracket in the 70s, let alone the 90 percent-plus top rates of the Eisenhower years. It used to be argued that a surtax on very high incomes serves no real purpose other than punishing the rich because it wouldn't raise much money, but that's no longer true. Today the top 0.1% of Americans, a class with a minimum income of about $1.3 million and an average income of about $3.5 million, receives more than 7 percent of all income—up from just 2.2 percent in 1979.[24] A surtax on that income would yield a significant amount of revenue, which could be used to help a lot of people. All in all, then, the next step after rolling back the Bush tax cuts and implementing universal health care should be a broader effort to restore the progressivity of U.S. taxes, and use the revenue to pay for more benefits that help lower- and middle-income families.

Realistically, however, this would not be enough to pay for social expenditures comparable to those in other advanced countries, not even the relatively modest Canadian level. In addition to imposing higher taxes on the rich, other advanced countries also impose higher taxes on the middle class, through both higher social insurance payments and value-added taxes—in effect, national sales taxes. Social insurance taxes and VATs are not, in themselves, progressive. Their effect in reducing inequality is indirect but large: They pay for benefits, and these benefits are worth more as a percentage of income to people with lower incomes.

As a political matter, persuading the public that middle-income families would be better off paying somewhat higher taxes in return for a stronger social safety net will be a hard sell after decades of antitax, antigovernment propaganda. Much as I would like to see the United States devote another 2 or 3 percent of GDP to social expenditure beyond health care, it's probably an endeavor that has to wait until liberals have established a strong track record of successfully using the government to make peoples' lives better and more secure. This is one reason health care reform, which is tremendously important in itself, would have further benefits: It would blaze the trail for a wider progressive agenda. This is also the reason movement conservatives are fiercely determined not to let health care reform succeed.

Reducing Market Inequality

Aftermarket policies can do a great deal to reduce inequality. But that should not be our whole focus. The Great Compression also involved a sharp reduction in the inequality of market income. This was accomplished in part through wage controls during World War II, an experience we hope won't be repeated. Still, there are several steps we can take.

The first step has already been taken: In 2007 Congress passed the first increase in the minimum wage within a decade. In the 1950s and 1960s the minimum wage averaged about half of the average wage. By 2006, however, the purchasing power of the minimum wage had been so eroded by inflation that in real terms it was at its lowest point since 1955, and was only 31 percent of the average wage. Thanks to the new Democratic majority in Congress, the minimum is scheduled to rise from its current $5.15 an hour to $7.25 by 2009. This won't restore all the erosion, but it's an important first step.

There are two common but somewhat contradictory objections often heard to increasing the minimum wage. On one hand, it's argued that raising the minimum wage will reduce employment and increase unemployment. On the other it's argued that raising the minimum will have little or no effect in raising wages. The evidence, however, suggests that a minimum wage increase will in fact have modest positive effects.

On the employment side, a classic study by David Card of Berkeley and Alan Krueger of Princeton, two of America's best labor economists, found no evidence that minimum wage increases in the range the United States has experienced led to job losses.[25] Their work has been furiously attacked both because it seems to contradict Econ 101 and because it was ideologically disturbing to many. Yet it has stood up very well to repeated challenges, and new cases confirming its results keep coming in. For example, the state of Washington has a minimum wage almost three dollars an hour higher than its neighbor Idaho; business experiences near the state line seem to indicate that, if anything, Washington has gained jobs at Idaho's expense. "Small-business owners in Washington," reported the *New York Times*, "say they have prospered far beyond their expectation. . . . Idaho teenagers cross the state line to work in fast-food restaurants in Washington."

All the empirical evidence suggests that minimum wage increases *in the range that is likely to take place* do not lead to significant job losses. True, an increase in the minimum wage to, say, fifteen dollars an hour would probably cause job losses, because it would dramatically raise the cost of employment in some industries. But that's not what's on—or even near—the table.

Meanwhile minimum wage increases can have fairly significant effects on wages at the bottom end of the scale. The Economic Policy Institute estimates that the worst-paid 10 percent of the U.S. labor force, 13 million workers, will gain from the just-enacted minimum wage increase. Of these, 5.6 million are currently being paid less than the new minimum wage, and would see a direct benefit. The rest are workers earning more than the new minimum wage, who would benefit from ripple effects of the higher minimum.

The minimum wage, however, matters mainly to low-paid workers. Any broader effort to reduce market inequality will have to do something about incomes further up the scale. The most important tool in that respect is likely to be an end to the thirty-year tilt of government policy against unions.

I argued in chapter 8 that the drastic decline in the U.S. union movement was not, as is often claimed, an inevitable result of globalization and increased competition. International comparisons show that the U.S. union decline is unique, even though other countries faced the same global pressures. Again, in 1960 Canada and the United States had essentially equal rates of unionization, 32 and 30 percent of wage and salary workers respectively. By 1999 U.S. unionization was down to 13 percent, but Canadian unionization was unchanged. As I discussed in chapter 8, the sources of union decline in America lie not in market forces but in the political climate created by movement conservatism, which allowed employers to engage in union-busting activities and punish workers for supporting union organizers. Without that changed political climate, much of the service economy—especially giant retailers like Wal-Mart—would probably be unionized today.

A new political climate could revitalize the union movement—and revitalizing unions should be a key progressive goal. Specific legislation, such as the Employee Free Choice Act, which would reduce the ability of employers to intimidate workers into rejecting a union, is only part of what's needed. It's also crucial to enforce labor laws already on the books. Much if not most of the antiunion activity that led to the sharp decline in American unionization was illegal even under existing law. But employers judged, correctly, that they could get away with it.

The hard-to-answer question is the extent to which a newly empowered U.S. union movement would reduce inequality. International comparisons suggest that it might make quite a lot of difference. The sharpest increases in wage inequality in the Western world have taken place in the United States and in Britain, both of which experienced sharp declines in union membership. (Britain is still far more unionized than America, but it used to have more than 50 percent unionization.) Canada, although its economy is closely linked to that of the United States, appears to have had substantially less increase in wage inequality—and it's likely that the persistence of a strong union movement is an important reason why. Unions raise the wages of their members, who tend to be in the middle of the wage distribution; they also tend to equalize wages among members. Perhaps most important, they act as a countervailing force to management, enforcing social norms that limit very high and very low pay even among people who aren't union members. They also mobilize their members to vote for progressive policies. Would getting the United States back to historical levels of unionization undo a large part of the Great Divergence? We don't know—but it might, and encouraging a union resurgence should be a major goal of progressive policy.

A reinvigorated union movement isn't the only change that could reduce extreme inequalities in pay. As I mentioned in chapter 8, a number of other factors discouraged very high paychecks for a generation after World War II. One was a change in the political climate: Very high executive pay used to provoke public scrutiny, congressional hearings, and even presidential intervention. But that all ended in the Reagan years.

Historical experience still suggests that a new progressive majority should not be shy about questioning private-sector pay when it seems outrageous. Moral suasion was effective in the past, and could be so again.

Another Great Compression?

The Great Compression, the abrupt reduction in economic inequality that took place in the United States in the 1930s and 1940s, took place at a time of crisis. Today America's state is troubled, but we're not in the midst of a great depression or a world war. Correspondingly, we shouldn't expect changes as drastic or sudden as those that took place seventy years ago. The process of reducing inequality now is likely to be more of a Great Moderation than a Great Compression.

Yet it is possible, both as an economic matter and in terms of practical politics, to reduce inequality and make America a middle-class nation again. And now is the time to get started.

13

THE CONSCIENCE OF A LIBERAL

One of the seeming paradoxes of America in the early twenty-first century is that those of us who call ourselves liberal are, in an important sense, conservative, while those who call themselves conservative are for the most part deeply radical. Liberals want to restore the middle-class society I grew up in; those who call themselves conservative want to take us back to the Gilded Age, undoing a century of history. Liberals defend long-standing institutions like Social Security and Medicare; those who call themselves conservative want to privatize or undermine those institutions. Liberals want to honor our democratic principles and the rule of law; those who call themselves conservative want the president to have dictatorial powers and have applauded the Bush administration as it imprisons people without charges and subjects them to torture.

The key to understanding this paradox is the history I described in this book. As early as 1952—and, it turned out, somewhat prematurely—Adlai Stevenson declared that

> The strange alchemy of time has somehow converted the Democrats into the truly conservative party in the country—the party dedicated to conserving all that is best and building solidly and safely on these foundations. The Republicans, by contrast, are behaving like the radical party—the party of the reckless and embittered, bent on dismantling institutions which have been built solidly into our social fabric.[1]

What he meant was that the Democrats had become the defenders of Social Security, unemployment insurance, a strong union movement—the New Deal institutions, which created and sustained a middle-class society—while the Republicans were trying to tear those institutions down.

Stevenson's characterization of the Republicans was off by a few years. In the years that followed his speech Eisenhower's "modern" Republicans took control of their party away from the old guard that was still fighting the New Deal, and for the next two decades the GOP was mostly led by men who accepted the New Deal's achievements. With the rise of movement conservatism, however, the assault on those achievements resumed. The great domestic policy struggles of the last fifteen years—Newt Gingrich's attempt to strangle Medicare, George W. Bush's attempt to privatize Social Security—were exactly what Stevenson described: the party of the reckless and embittered trying to dismantle institutions that are essential parts of modern America's social fabric.

And the struggle has been about preserving our democracy as well as our social fabric. The New Deal did more than create a middle-class society. It also brought America closer to its democratic ideals, by giving working Americans real political power and ending the dominant position of the wealthy elite. True, the New Deal relied on an alliance of convenience with Southern segregationists—but in the end, inevitably, the New Deal ethos turned the Democrats into the party of civil rights and political rights. The Social Security Act of 1935 led, by a natural progression, to the Voting Rights Act thirty years later. Liberalism, in other words, isn't just about the welfare state: It's also about democracy and the rule of law. And those who call themselves conservative are on the other side, with a political strategy that rests, at its core, on exploiting the unwillingness of some Americans to grant equal rights to their fellow citizens—to those who don't share their skin color, don't share their faith, don't share their sexual preferences.

As I've documented in this book, movement conservatism has been antidemocratic, with an attraction to authoritarianism, from the beginning, when the *National Review* praised Francisco Franco and defended the right of white Southerners to disenfranchise blacks. That antidemocratic, authoritarian attitude has never gone away. When liberals and conservatives clash over voter rights in America today, liberals are always trying to enfranchise citizens, while conservatives are always trying to block some citizens from voting. When they clash over government prerogatives, liberals are always the defenders of due process, while conservatives insist that those in power have the right to do as they please. After 9/11 the Bush administration tried to foster a deeply un-American political climate in which any criticism of the president was considered unpatriotic—and with few exceptions, American conservatives cheered.

I believe in a relatively equal society, supported by institutions that limit extremes of wealth and poverty. I believe in democracy, civil liberties, and the rule of law. That makes me a liberal, and I'm proud of it.

Liberalism and the Progressive Movement

Many people deeply involved in actual politics share the beliefs I've just described, yet prefer to describe themselves as progressives rather than liberals. To some extent that's a response to the decades-long propaganda campaign conducted by movement conservatives, which has been quite successful in making Americans disdain the *word* "liberal" but much less successful in reducing support for liberal policies. Polls generally show that relatively few Americans, usually less than 30 percent, identify themselves as liberals. On the other hand, large majorities of Americans favor policy positions we would normally call liberal, such as a guarantee of health insurance for every American.

Yet "progressive" isn't simply a new word for what "liberal" used to mean. The real distinction between the terms, at least as I and many others use them, is between philosophy and action. Liberals are those who believe in institutions that limit inequality and injustice. Progressives are those who participate, explicitly or implicitly, in a political coalition that defends and tries to enlarge those institutions. You're a liberal, whether you know it or not, if you believe that the United States should have universal health care. You're a progressive if you participate in the effort to bring universal health care into being.

One of the important changes in the U.S. political scene during the Bush years has been the coalescence of a progressive movement that in some—but only some—respects resembles movement conservatism. Like movement conservatism it's a collection of institutions that is associated with, but not the same as, a major political party: Many Democrats are progressives, and most progressives support Democrats, but the movement extends well beyond the party. It includes parts of the old New Deal coali-

THE CONSCIENCE OF A LIBERAL

tion, notably organized labor, a variety of think tanks, and novel entities like the "netroots," the virtual community held together by bloggers and progressive Web sites like Daily Kos, which now attracts regular postings from leading Democratic politicians. In other respects, however, there are sharp differences between the progressive movement and movement conservatism. There's far less centralization: Although right-wingers see the hidden hand of George Soros behind everything, the reality is that there's nothing comparable on the left to the coordinated funding of movement conservatism. Correspondingly, there's nothing like the monolithic unity of views enforced by the funders, the implicit oath of loyalty sworn by movement conservatives.

What makes progressive institutions into a movement isn't money, it's self-perception. Many Americans with more or less liberal beliefs now *consider* themselves members of a common movement, with the shared goals of limiting inequality and defending democratic principles. The movement reserves its greatest scorn for Democrats who won't make a stand against the right, who give in on Social Security privatization or escalation in Iraq.

During the Clinton years there wasn't a progressive movement in this sense—and the nation paid a price. Looking back, it's clear that Bill Clinton never had a well-defined agenda. In a fundamental sense he didn't know what he was supposed to do. When he arrived in office, his advisers were obsessed with the idea of a trade confrontation with Japan, something that never made much sense, was never thought through, and had no real base behind it. There were many reasons Hillary Clinton's health care plan failed, but a key weakness was that it wasn't an attempt to give substance to the goals of a broad movement—it was a personal venture, developed in isolation and without a supporting coalition. And after the Republican victory in 1994, Bill Clinton was reduced to making marginal policy changes. He ran the government well, but he didn't advance a larger agenda, and he didn't build a movement. This could happen again, but if it does, progressives will rightly feel betrayed.

The Progressive Agenda

To be liberal is in a sense to be a conservative—it means, to a large extent, wanting us to go back to being a middle-class society. To be a progressive, however, clearly implies wanting to move forward. This may sound like a contradiction, but it isn't. Advancing the traditional goals of liberalism requires new policies.

Take the case of adding prescription drugs to Medicare, which was arguably a conservative policy that maintained the program's original mission. Medicare was always supposed to cover major health expenses. Drugs weren't included in the original program, because at the time they weren't a big expense. When drug treatment for chronic diseases became a huge cost for many of the elderly, Medicare's original focus on hospital coverage was out of step with its mission—and adding prescription drugs became necessary to maintain the program's original intent.

You can say something similar, with a little less force, about universal health care. The Social Security Act of 1935 established retirement benefits and a federal-state system of unemployment insurance, but its larger purpose, says the Social Security Administration's official history, was "to meet some of the serious problems of economic insecurity arising in an industrial society."[2] Protecting families against severe health care costs fits in very well with that purpose. In fact, FDR considered including health insurance in the act but backed off for political reasons. Achieving universal care would, then, be a completion of FDR's legacy. Furthermore, health care is to social insurance as drugs are to Medicare: It was once a relatively small expense, but today insecurity over medical expenses is arguably the single biggest financial risk working Americans face. And if we consider our goal to be sustaining a middle-class society, guaranteed health insurance is essential: Employment-based insurance may have been good enough for most people thirty years ago, but it's woefully inadequate today. A society in which 40 percent of the population either has no insurance or has inadequate insurance that forces them to postpone medical care because of its cost isn't middle-class.[3]

A progressive agenda, then, would require major changes in public policy, but it would be anything but radical. Its goal would be to complete the work of the New Deal, including expansion of social insurance to cover avoidable risks that have become vastly more important in recent decades. And as an economic matter, achieving that agenda would be eminently doable. It would amount to giving U.S. citizens no more than the level of protection from financial risk and personal misfortune that citizens of other advanced countries already have.

In fact, to survey the current political scene is to be struck by just how well formulated the progressive agenda is—and how intellectually decrepit movement conservatism has become. As this book was being written, Democratic presidential candidates were discussing plans for universal health care, new approaches to poverty, options for helping troubled home buyers, and more. Meanwhile, Republican contenders offered no concrete proposals at all—they seemed to be competing over who sounded most like Ronald Reagan, and who was most enthusiastic about torture. To the extent that the Democratic Party represents the progressive movement, the Democrats have become the party of ideas.

On Being Partisan

The progressive agenda is clear and achievable, but it will face fierce opposition. The central fact of modern American political life is the control of the Republican Party by movement conservatives, whose vision of what America should be is completely antithetical to that of the progressive movement. Because of that control, the notion, beloved of political pundits, that we can make progress through bipartisan consensus is simply foolish. On health care reform, which is the first domestic priority for progressives, there's no way to achieve a bipartisan compromise between Republicans who want to strangle Medicare and Democrats who want guaranteed health insurance for all. When a health care reform plan is actually presented to Congress, the leaders of movement conservatism will do what they did in 1993—urge Republicans to oppose the plan in any form, lest successful health reform undermine the movement conservative agenda. And most Republicans will probably go along.

To be a progressive, then, means being a partisan—at least for now. The only way a progressive agenda can be enacted is if Democrats have both the presidency and a large enough majority in Congress to overcome Republican opposition. And achieving that kind of political preponderance will require leadership that makes opponents of the progressive agenda pay a political price for their obstructionism—leadership that, like FDR, welcomes the hatred of the interest groups trying to prevent us from making our society better.

If the new progressive movement succeeds, the need for partisanship will eventually diminish. In the 1950s you could support Social Security and unions and yet still vote for Eisenhower in good conscience, because the Republican Party had eventually (and temporarily) accepted the New Deal's achievements. In the long run we can hope for a return to that kind of politics: two reasonable parties that accept all that is best in our country but compete over their ability to deliver a decent life to all Americans, and keep each other honest.

For now, being an active liberal means being a progressive, and being a progressive means being partisan. But the end goal isn't one-party rule. It's the reestablishment of a truly vital, competitive democracy. Because in the end, democracy is what being a liberal is all about.

Notes

---

1 THE WAY WE WERE

1. Much of what we know about long-term trends in inequality comes from the pioneering work of Thomas Piketty and Emmanuel Saez, "Income Inequality in the United States, 1913–1998," *Quarterly Journal of Economics* 118, no. 1 (Feb. 2003), pp. 1–39.

2. Nolan McCarty, Keith Poole, and Howard Rosenthal, *Polarized America: The Dance of Ideology and Unequal Riches* (MIT Press, 2006).

3. Claudia Goldin and Robert Margo, "The Great Compression: The Wage Structure in the United States at Mid-Century," *Quarterly Journal of Economics*, 107, no. 1 (1992), p. 1–34.

4. See, in particular, Ian Dew-Becker and Robert Gordon, "Where Did the Productivity Growth Go?" Inflation Dynamics and the Distribution of Income," *Brookings Papers on Economic Activities*, no. 2 (2005), pp. 67–127, and Frank Levy and Peter Temin, "Inequality and Institutions in 20th-Century America" (MIT Department of Economics working paper, no. 07-17, June 2007).

5. Thomas Piketty and Emmanuel Saez, "The Evolution of Top Incomes: A Historical and International Perspective" (National Bureau of Economic Research working paper no. 11955, Jan. 2006).

6. William Greider, "Rolling Back the 20th Century," *The Nation* (May 12, 2003).

2 THE LONG GILDED AGE

1. Bradford DeLong, "Robber Barons," econ161.berkeley.edu/Econ_Articles/car negie/DeLong_Moscow_paper2.html.

2. Vito Tanzi and Ludger Schuhknecht, *Public Spending in the 20th Century* (Cambridge University Press, 2000).

3. Wilson was considered a Bourbon before his presidential run but made his peace with Bryan before the election. In practice he did move the government somewhat to the left, adopting a relatively tolerant attitude toward unions and instituting the income tax. But he was no FDR.

4. Election finance statistics from *Historical Statistics of the United States,* Series Y 187–188 (US Bureau of the Census, 1975).

5. For an overview of the evidence, see Peter H. Argersinger, "New Perspectives on Election Fraud in the Gilded Age," *Political Science Quarterly* 100, no. 4 (Winter 1985–86), pp. 669–87.

6. "Col. Dudley's Letter: 'Divide the Floaters into Blocks of Five,' *New York Times,* Nov. 3, 1888, p. 1.

7. A detailed set of tables on immigrants and their role in the population may be found in "Historical Census Statistics on the Foreign-born Population of the United States: 1850–1990" (U.S. Census Population Division working paper no. 29, 1999).

8. Thomas E. Watson, "The Negro Question in the South," *The Arena* 6 (Oct. 1892), pp. 540–50.

9. Arthur M. Schlesinger, Jr., *The Crisis of the Old Order* (Houghton Mifflin, 1957), pp. 94–100.

10. Ibid., pp. 126–29.

11. Jacob Metzer, "How New Was the New Era? The Public Sector in the 1920s," *Journal of Economic History* 45, no. 1 (Mar. 1985), pp. 119–26.

12. Quoted in David Khoudour-Casteras, "The Impact of Bismarck's Social Legislation on German Emigration Before World War I" (photocopy, University of California, Berkeley, 2004).

13. David M. Cutler and Richard Johnson, "The Birth and Growth of the Social-Insurance State: Explaining Old-age and Medical Insurance Across Countries," *Kyklos* 57, no. 4 (2004), 475–504.

14. Schlesinger, *Crisis of the Old Order,* pp. 126–27.

15. Quoted in Ibid., p. 303.

3 THE GREAT COMPRESSION

1. Alvin Josephy, "The U.S.: A Strong and Stable Land," *Time,* Sept. 14, 1953.

2. "The Glittering Domains of LI's Royalty," http://www.newsday.com/entertainment/localguide/north-shore-nassau/ny-dligold,0,7095725.story?cool =ny-explore-nsn-utility.

3. Piketty and Saez "Income Inequality."

4. Income for the middle fifth of families from *Historical Statistics of the United*

States, Series G 328, adjusted by consumer price index data from the Bureau of Labor Statistics, bls.gov.

5. *Historical Statistics*, B 402, ibid.

4 THE POLITICS OF THE WELFARE STATE

1. Dwight D. Eisenhower to Edgar N. Eisenhower, Nov. 8, 1954, http://eisenhower memorial.org/presidential-papers/first-term/documents/1147.sfn.

2. See Schlesinger, *Crisis of the Old Order*, p. 136.

3. J. J. Wallis, P. Fishback, and S. Kantor, "Politics, Relief, and Reform: The Transformation of America's Social Welfare System during the New Deal" (National Bureau of Economic Research Working Paper no. 11080, January 2005).

4. Jan Leighley and Jonathan Nagler, "Unions, Voter Turnout, and Class Bias in the U.S. Electorate, 1964–2000," *Journal of Politics* 69, no.2 (May 2007), pp. 430–41.

5. The actual process of estimation is considerably more sophisticated than what I've described, but is similar in spirit. See McCarty, Poole, and Rosenthal, *Polarized America*.

6. See John R. Petrocik, "Reformulating the Party Coalitions: The 'Christian Democratic' Republicans" (paper prepared for Center for Research in Society and Politics, Aug. 1, 1998), table 2.

5 THE SIXTIES: A TROUBLED PROSPERITY

1. "Economic Mobility: Is the American Dream Alive and Well?" (Pew Economic Mobility Project, May 2007).

2. Levy and Temin, "Inequality and Institutions."

3. An online version is available at http://www.wadsworth.com/history_d/tem plates/student_resources/0534607411/sources/old/ch29/29.4.nixon.html.

4. Steven Levitt, "Understanding Why Crime Fell in the 1990s," *Journal of Economic Perspectives* 18, no. 1 (2004), pp. 163–90.

5. This phenomenon was first noted by John F. Kain, "Housing Segregation, Negro Employment, and Metropolitan Decentralization." *Quarterly Journal of Economics* 82 (1968) 175–97, although really strong statistical evidence for the effect becomes clear only after 1970.

6. Ronald Reagan, *An American Life* (Simon & Schuster, 1990), p. 147.

7. In 1970, after a decade of rapid growth, AFDC payments totaled $4.9 billion, compared with $39 billion in payments to Social Security beneficiaries. Data from the Social Security Administration, http://www.ssa.gov/policy/docs/statcomps/ supplement/2005/9g.html.

8. Ibid.

9. *Time*, Nov. 23, 1970.

10. Mickey Kaus, "The Ending of the Black Underclass," Slate.com, Nov. 3, 1999. http://slate.com/id/1003938/.

11. Harris Poll, January 1971, http://www.ropercenter.uconn.edu/data_access/ipoll/ipoll.html.

12. Speech at http://www.watergate.info/nixon/silent-majority-speech-1969.shtml.

13. Philip Klinkner and Thomas Schaller, "A Regional Analysis of the 2006 Election," *Forum* 4, no. 3 (2006), http://www.bepress.com/forum/vol4/iss3/art9.

6 MOVEMENT CONSERVATISM

1. Editorial, *National Review,* Aug. 24, 1957.

2. William F. Buckley, "Yes, and Many Thanks, But Now the War Is Over," *National Review*, Oct. 26, 1957.

3. Paul Preston, *"The Conqueror of His Country,"* *New York Times*, Dec. 27, 1987.

4. Speech delivered by Senator Joseph McCarthy before the Senate on June 14, 1951, from *Congressional Record: Proceedings and Debates of the 82nd Congress, First Session*, vol. 97, part 5 (May 28, 1951–June 27, 1951), pp. 6556–603.

5. Richard Hofstadter, "The Paranoid Style in American Politics," *Harper's Magazine*, Nov. 1964, pp. 77–86.

6. The term comes from Lisa McGirr, *Suburban Warriors: The Rise of the New American Right* (Princeton University Press, 2001).

7. Peter Viereck, "The New Conservatism: One of Its Founders Asks What Went Wrong," *New Republic*, Sept. 24, 1962.

8. Jacob Hacker, *The Divided Welfare State*, Cambridge University Press, 2002.

9. http://www.time.com/time/time100/builder/profile/reuther2.html.

10. Rick Perlstein, *Before the Storm: Barry Goldwater and the Unmaking of the American Consensus* (Hill & Wang, 2001), chap. 1.

11. Paul Krugman, "Who Was Milton Friedman?" *New York Review of Books*, Feb. 15, 2007.

12. Irving Kristol, "American Conservatism, 1965–1995," *The Public Interest* (Fall 1995), pp. 80–96.

13. Ibid.

14. Dan Balz, "Team Bush: The Iron Triangle," *Washington Post*, July 23, 1999, p. C1.

15. Franklin Foer, "Swimming with Sharks," *New Republic*, Oct. 3, 2005, p. 20.

16. As posted at the Huffington Post, http://www.huffingtonpost.com/rick-perlstein/i-didnt-like-nixon-_b_11735.html, Dec. 5, 2005.

7 THE GREAT DIVERGENCE

1. "Public Says Work Life Is Worsening, but Most Workers Remain Satisfied with Their Jobs," Pew Center for People and Press, Labor Day, 2006, http://pewresearch.org/assets/social/pdf/Jobs.pdf.

2. Dean Baker of the Center for Economic Policy Research estimates that "usable" productivity growth—the increase in the net value produced per U.S. worker-hour

adjusted for rising consumer prices—was 47.9 percent between 1973 and 2006. However, nonwage labor costs rose due to rising payroll taxes, rising health care costs, and other factors, so that the amount available for wages rose about 36 percent. Dean Baker, "The Productivity to Paycheck Gap: What the Data Show," at www.cepr.net, Apr. 2007.

3. Edward Lazear, speech given at the Hudson Institute, "The State of the U.S. Economy and Labor Market," Washington, D.C., May 2, 2006.

4. Piketty and Saez, "Income Inequality."

5. Levy and Temin, "Inequality and Institutions."

6. See, for example, Reed Abelson, "Wal-Mart's Health Care Struggle Is Corporate America's, Too," New York Times, October 29, 2005.

7. See Piketty and Saez, "The Evolution of Top Incomes."

8. See Andrea Brandolini and Timothy Smeeding, "Inequality Patterns in Western-Type Democracies: Cross-Country Differences and Time Changes" (Luxembourg Income Study working paper no. 458, Apr. 2007). An attempt to systematize the survey data, yielding results similar to Piketty and Saez, is http://www.tcf.org/list .asp?type=NC&pubid=1403.

9. Carola Frydman and Raven Saks, "Historical Trends in Executive Compensation, 1936–2003," Federal Reserve Bank of New York, 2005.

10. See Xavier Gabaix and Augustin Landier, "Why Has CEO Pay Increased So Much?" (National Board of Economic Research working paper no. 12365), July 2006.

11. Pay Without Performance: The Unfulfilled Promise of Executive Compensation (Harvard University Press, 2004).

12. Michael C. Jensen and Kevin J. Murphy, "CEO Incentives—It's Not How Much You Pay, but How," Harvard Business Review (May/June 1990), pp. 138–53.

13. Ibid.

14. http://money.cnn.com/magazines/fortune/fortune_archive/2001/06/25/305448 /index.htm.

15. Ibid.

16. "U.S.-Style Pay Deals for Chiefs Become All the Rage in Europe," New York Times, June 16, 2006, p. A1.

17. Sherwin Rosen, "The Economics of Superstars," American Economic Review 71, no. 5 (Dec. 1981), pp. 845–58.

8 THE POLITICS OF INEQUALITY

1. At the time Republicans insisted that they were not proposing cuts in Medicare, because the dollar amounts spent per senior would continue to rise under their proposal. But the increases in funding would have fallen well short of increases in medical costs, so they were in effect proposing big cuts. Similar evasiveness marked the 2005 debate over Social Security.

2. After the Washington Post columnist David Broder, the "dean of the Washington press corps," who spent most of the Bush era placing the blame for discord equally on both parties.

3. American National Election Studies, "The ANES Guide to Public Opinion and Electoral Behavior," table 2B-4, http://electionstudies.org/nesguide/toptable/tab2b_4.htm.

4. "Special Message to the Congress Proposing a Comprehensive Health Insurance Plan," February 6, 1974, http://www.presidency.ucsb.edu/ws/index.php?pid=4337.

5. Thomas Edsall, *The New Politics of Inequality* (W. W. Norton, 1984), p. 73.

6. Francis X. Clines, "Watt Asks That Reagan Forgive 'Offensive' Remark About Panel," *New York Times*, September 23, 1993.

7. Decedents, http://www.taxpolicycenter.org/TaxFacts/TFDB/TFTemplate.cfm?Docid=52&Topic2id=60; distribution, http://www.taxpolicycenter.org/TaxFacts/TFDB/TFTemplate.cfm?Docid=50&Topic2id=60.

8. Michael Graetz and Ian Shapiro, *Death by a Thousand Cuts* (Princeton University Press, 2005), pp. 222–24.

9. Robert Dreyfuss, "Grover Norquist: Field Marshal of the Bush Plan," *The Nation*, May 14, 2001.

10. William Greider, "Rolling Back the 20th Century," *The Nation*, May 26, 2003.

11. http://www.sourcewatch.org/index.php?title=National_Center_for_Policy_Analysis.

12. http://www.sourcewatch.org/index.php?title=Ethics_and_Public_Policy_Center; http://www.epcc.org/news/newsid.2818/news_detail.asp.

13. http://www.sourcewatch.org/index.php?title=National_Center_for_Public_Policy_Research.

14. Nicholas Confessore, "Welcome to the Machine," *Washington Monthly*, July/Aug. 2003, cover story.

15. David Maraniss and Michael Weisskopf, "Speaker and His Directors Make the Cash Flow Right," *Washington Post*, November 27, 1995, p. A01.

16. Stuart Butler and Peter Germanis, "Achieving a Leninist Strategy," *Cato Journal* 3, no. 2 (Fall 1983), pp. 547–61.

17. Edsall, *New Politics of Inequality*, p. 74.

9 WEAPONS OF MASS DISTRACTION

1. See Larry Bartels, "What's the Matter with *What's the Matter with Kansas?*"

2. As with almost everything involving government finance, it's a bit more complicated than that. Medicare Part A, which provides hospital care, is financed by a proportional tax on all earned income (but not on capital income such as dividends and capital gains.) The rest of Medicare is paid for out of general revenue, which mostly means the personal income tax, a strongly progressive tax that is mainly paid by the richest 10 percent of households.

3. See Karen Smith and Eric Toder, "Lifetime Distributional Effects of Social Security Retirement Benefits," paper prepared for the Third Annual Joint Conference for the Retirement Research Consortium, "Making Hard Choices About Retirement," May 17–18, 2001, Washington, D.C.

4. Thomas Frank, *What's the Matter with Kansas? How Conservatives Won the Heart of America* (Henry Holt, 2004).

5. "'Welfare queen' Becomes Issue in Reagan Campaign," *New York Times*, Feb. 15, 1976, p. 51.

6. Werner Sombart, *Warum gibt es in den Vereinigten Staaten keinen Sozialismus?* (Mohr, 1906).

7. Alberto Alesina, Edward Glaeser, and Bruce Sacerdote, "Why Doesn't the US Have a European-Style Welfare State?" (National Bureau of Economic Research working paper no. 8524, Oct. 2001).

8. See Jill Quadagno, *One Nation Uninsured: Why the U.S. Has No Health Insurance* (Oxford University Press, 2005).

9. Exit-poll data at http://www.nytimes.com/packages/pdf/politics/20041107_px_ELECTORATE.xls.

10. Thomas Schaller, *Whistling Past Dixie: How Democrats Can Win Without the South* (Simon & Schuster, 2006).

11. Klinkner and Schaller, "A Regional Analysis."

12. See, for example, a *Time* poll taken in March 2005, http://www.srbi.com/time_poll_arc13.html.

13. "Rove Criticizes Liberals on 9/11," *New York Times*, June 23, 2005, p. A13.

14. Rick Perlstein, "Why Democrats Can Stop the War," *Salon*, Jan. 24, 2007, http://www.salon.com/opinion/feature/2007/01/24/perlstein/index_np.html.

15. National Survey for RNC/NRCC, Oct. 21–Nov. 15, 1979, data from Roper Center for Public Opinion Research. Two Harris Polls from 1978 also show the parties closely matched. See http://www.ropercenter.uconn.edu/data_access/ipoll/ipoll.html.

16. Ole R. Holsti, "A Widening Gap Between the U.S. Military and Civilian Society? Some Evidence," 1976–96. *InternationalSecurity* 23 (Winter 1999): pp. 5–44.

17. Rosa Brooks, "Weaning the Military from the GOP," *Los Angeles Times*, Jan. 5, 2007, p. A23.

18. See Christopher Gelpi, Jason Reifler, and Peter Feaver, "Iraq the Vote" (photocopy, Duke University, 2005).

19. Thomas Edsall, *Building Red America* (Basic Books, 2006), p. 21.

20. "Periscope," *Newsweek*, Aug. 19, 2002, p. 4.

21. Michelle Goldberg, *Kingdom Coming: The Rise of Christian Nationalism* (W. W. Norton, 2006).

22. Marvin Olasky, *The Tragedy of American Compassion* (Regnery, 1992), p. 227.

23. Goldberg, *Kingdom Coming*, p. 150.

24. "Bush Choice for Family-Planning Post Criticized," *Washington Post*, Nov. 17, 2006, p. A01.

25. Goldberg, *Kingdom Coming*, p. 7.

26 McCarty, Poole, and Rosenthal, *Polarized America*, p. 124.

27. http://www.pfaw.org/pfaw/general/default.aspx?oid=1625.

28. "How America Doesn't Vote," *New York Times*, Feb. 15, 2004, sec. 4, p. 10.

29. "Criticism of Voting Law Was Overruled," *Washington Post*, Nov. 17, 2005, p. A01.

30. "Was Campaigning Against Voter Fraud a Republican Ploy?" McClatchy Washington Bureau, July 1, 2007, http://www.mcclatchydc.com/homepage/story/17532.html.

10 THE NEW RULES OF EQUALITY

1. Update by McCarty, Poole, and Rosenthal at http://voteview.com/hou110.htm.

2. See Sydney Ludvigson, "Consumer Confidence and Consumer Spending," *Journal of Economic Perspectives* 18, no. 2 (Spring 2004), pp. 29–50. Current data from www.pollingreport.com.

3. *Trends in Political Values and Core Attitudes, 1987–2007* (Pew Research Center for People and the Press, Mar. 2007), http://people-press.org/reports/pdf/312.pdf.

4. Chris Hedges, *War Is a Force That Gives Us Meaning* (PublicAffairs, 2002).

5. The best overview of the follies of reconstruction is Rajiv Chandrasekaran, *Imperial Life in the Emerald City: Inside Iraq's Green Zone* (Knopf, 2006). On the police academy, "Heralded Police Academy a 'disaster'," *Washington Post*, Sept. 28, 2006, p. A01.

6. Ruy Texeira and John Judis, "Back to the Future: The Re-emergence of the Emerging Democratic Majority," *American Prospect*, June 2007.

7. John Judis, "Continental Divide: Why the Immigration Bill Will Never Become Law," *New Republic*, May 23, 2007.

8. http://bluetiderising.blogspot.com/2007/07/kansas-republicans-unveil-unity-pledge.html.

11 THE HEALTH CARE IMPERATIVE

1. Molly Ivins, "Bucking the Texas Lockstep," *Washington Post*, May 15, 2003, p. A29.

2. Figure based on Kaiser Family Foundation, *Trends and Indicators in the Changing Health Care Marketplace*, exhibit 1.11. http://www.kff.org/insurance/7031/index.cfm.

3. World Health Organization, *The World Health Report 2000*, available at http://www.who.int/whr/2000/en/index.html.

4. Commonwealth Fund, "Mirror, Mirror on the Wall: An Update on the Quality of American Health Care Through the Patient's Lens," http://www.commonwealthfund.org/publications/publications_show.htm?doc_id=364436.

5. McKinsey Global Institute, *Accounting for the Cost of U.S. Health Care*, Jan. 2007, http://www.mckinsey.com/mgi/rp/healthcare/accounting_cost_healthcare.asp.

6. Gerard F. Anderson et al., "It's the Prices, Stupid: Why the U.S. Is So Different from Other Countries," *Health Affairs* 22, no. 3 (2003), pp. 89–105.

7. McKinsey, *Accounting for the Cost*, p. 18.

8. Steffie Woolhandler, Terry Campbell, and David U. Himmelstein, "Costs of Health Care Administration in the United States and Canada," *New England Journal of Medicine* (Aug. 2003), pp. 768–75.

9. Kaiser Family Foundation, *Employer Health Benefits Annual Survey 2006*, exhibit 3.1, http://kff.org/insurance/7527/index.cfm.

10. Kaiser Family Foundation, op. cit., exhibit 1.11.

11. *Commonwealth Fund Biennial Health Insurance Survey*, 2005, http://www.com monwealthfund.org/surveys/surveys_show.htm?doc_id=367929.

12. Paul Krugman and Robin Wells, "The Health Care Crisis and What to Do About It," *New York Review of Books* 53 no. 5 (Mar. 23, 2006), http://www.nybooks .com/articles/18802.

13. William Kristol, "How to Oppose the Health Care Plan—and Why," *Wall Street Journal*, Jan. 11, 1994, p. A14.

14. For Fox News, see http://thinkprogress.org/2007/07/05/fox-news-universal-health-care-breeds-terrorists/. For pundits' attempts to make the same case, see http://rawstory.com/news/2007/Conservative_bloggers_try_to_link_Michael_0702.html.

15. Matthew Holt, http://www.thehealthcareblog.com/the_health_care_blog/2005/07/policypoltics_w.html.

16. The ads are now available on YouTube, http://youtube.com/watch?v=Dt31 nhleeCg.

17. Ezra Klein, "The Health of Nations," *American Prospect*, May 7, 2007, http://www.prospect.org/cs/articles?article=the_health_of_nations.

18. Commonwealth Fund, *Mirror, Mirror on the Wall: An International Update on the Comparative Performance of American Health Care*, May 2007, http://www .commonwealthfund.org/publications/publications_show.htm?doc_id=482678.

12 CONFRONTING INEQUALITY

1. Thomas Jefferson, Letter to James Madison, Oct. 28, 1785, http://press-pubs .uchicago.edu/founders/documents/v1ch15s32.html.

2. Irving Kristol, "Income Inequality Without Class Conflict," *Wall Street Journal*, Dec. 18, 1997, p. A22.

3. Robert Frank, *Richistan: A Journey Through the American Wealth Boom and the Lives of the New Rich* (Crown Publishers, 2007), pp. 3–4.

4. "Suites for the Sweet," *Newsweek International*, July 2–9, *http://www.msnbc.msn .com/id/19388720/site/newsweek*, part of a special report on "Secret Habits of the Super Rich."

5. Elizabeth Warren and Amelia Warren Tyagi, "What's Hurting the Middle Class," *Boston Review*, Sept./Oct. 2005, http://bostonreview.net/BR30.5/warrentyagi.html.

6. Tom Hertz, *Understanding Mobility in America* (Center for American Progress, 2006), http://www.americanprogress.org/issues/2006/04/b1579981.html.

7. Woodrow Wilson, *The New Freedom* (Doubleday, 1913), Downloaded from Project Gutenberg, http://www.gutenberg.org/files/14811/14811-h/14811-h.htm.

8. "Tax Breaks for Billionaires," Economic Policy Institute Policy Memorandum no. 120, http://www.epi.org/content.cfm/pm120.

9. See, for example, Jessica Holzer, "Conservatives break with GOP Leaders on a Tax Bill," *The Hill*, July 18, 2007, http://thehill.com/leading-the-news/conservatives-break-with-gop-leaders-on-a-tax-bill-2007-07-18.html.

10. "In Opposing Tax Plan, Schumer Supports Wall Street Over Party," *New York Times*, July 30, 2007, p. A1.

11. Eric M. Uslaner and Mitchell Brown, "Inequality, Trust, and Civic Engagement," *American Politics Research* 33, no. 6 (2005), pp. 868–94.

12. *The ANES Guide to Public Opinion and Electoral Behavior*, table 5A.2, http://electionstudies.org/nesguide/toptable/tab5a_2.htm.

13. Uslaner and Brown, "Inequality, Trust, and Civic Engagement."

14. Irwin Garfinkel, Lee Rainwater, and Timothy Smeeding, "Equal Opportunities for Children: Social Welfare Expenditures in the English-speaking Countries and in Western Europe," *Focus* 23, no. 3 (Spring 2005), pp. 16–23.

15. Timothy M. Smeeding, "Public Policy, Economic Inequality, and Poverty: The United States in Comparative Perspective," *Social Science Quarterly* 86, suppl. 1 (Dec. 2005), pp. 955–83.

16. Bureau of Labor Statistics, "Comparative Real Gross Domestic Product per Capita and per Employed Person," ftp://ftp.bls.gov/pub/special.requests/ForeignLabor/flsgdp.txt.

17. See Organization for Economic Cooperation and Development (OECD) Statistical Index, http://dx.doi.org/10.1787/075816831582.

18. Alberto Alesina, Ed Glaeser, and Bruce Sacerdote, "Work and Liesure in the U.S. and Europe: Why So Different?" (National Bureau of Economic Research working paper no. 11278, Apr. 2005).

19. OECD Statistical Index, op. cit.

20. Data from OECD *Education at a Glance*, http://www.oecd.org/dataoecd/46/22/37368734.xls.

21. Tax Policy Center, "Options to Extend the 2001–2006 Tax Cuts, Static Impact on Individual Income and Estate Tax Liability and Revenue ($ billions), 2008-17," Table T07-0126, http://taxpolicycenter.org/TaxModel/tmdb/Content/PDF/T07-0126.pdf.

22. Kimberly A. Clausing, "Multinational Firm Tax Avoidance and U.S. Government Revenue" (working paper, Wellesley College, Wellesley, MA, 2007).

23. OECD Tax Database, http://www.oecd.org/ctp/taxdatabase.

24. Piketty and Saez, 2005 preliminary estimates, http://elsa.berkeley.edu/~saez/TabFig2005prel.xls.

25. David Card and Alan B. Krueger, "Minimum Wages and Employment: A Case Study of the Fast-Food Industry in New Jersey and Pennsylvania," *American Economic Review* 84, no. 4 (1994), pp. 772–93.

13 THE CONSCIENCE OF A LIBERAL

1. Quoted in Viereck, "The New Conservatism."

2. http://www.ssa.gov/kids/history.htm.

3. Results of a *Consumer Reports* survey, September 2007, http://www.consumerreports.org/cro/health-fitness/health-care/health-insurance-9-07/overview/0709_health_ov.htm.

Acknowledgments

First and foremost, thanks to Robin Wells, my wife and frequent coauthor. She was deeply involved in every stage of this project: formulating ideas, doing the research, and drafting the chapters. It's really her book as much as mine.

Thanks also to two historians. Sean Wilentz read an early draft in detail, correcting many of my misconceptions and setting me on the right path. Rick Perlstein talked over some of the basic ideas with me, and let me see an early draft of his terrific forthcoming book *Nixonland*, which vastly improved my understanding of the crucial transition period in postwar political economy.

Thanks also to Drake McFeely of Norton, who both helped the writing and remained preternaturally calm as we made the final dash for the finish line.

Finally, although nobody at the *New York Times* was directly involved in this book, I would like to say a word of thanks to those at the *Times*—especially Gail Collins, the editorial-page editor from 2001 through 2006, who stood by me at a time when there was enormous pressure for critics of the Bush administration to mute their voices.

Index

PENGUIN ECONOMICS

THE ACCIDENTAL THEORIST AND OTHER DISPATCHES FROM THE DISMAL SCIENCE
PAUL KRUGMAN

'Probably the most creative economist of his generation' *Economist*

'Everything Mr Krugman has to say is smart, important and even fun to read…he is one of a handful of very bright, relatively young economists who do everything well' Peter Passell, *New York Times Book Review*

Paul Krugman has made a reputation for himself by telling us the truth about economics, however unlikely it may seem and however little we want to believe it.

In this wonderfully cohesive set of sharp, witty essays, Krugman tackles bad economic ideas from across the political spectrum, giving us clear-eyed insights into unemployment, globalization, economic growth and financial speculation among other topics. The writing here brilliantly combines the acerbic style and clever analysis that has made Krugman famous. Some of the articles have been written in response to particular economic events, but there is no particular orthodoxy in them, only rational common sense.

'Paul Krugman is the heir apparent to Galbraith. Some of these essays will make you smile, some will make you wince, all will make you think. Krugman's words are as sharp as his mind' Alan S. Blinder, Princeton University

'You can learn a great deal, about economics and otherwise, by reading these delightful essays' Robert M. Solow, Nobel Laureate, Massachusetts Institute of Technology

'[Paul Krugman] writes better than any economist since John Maynard Keynes' Rob Norton, *Fortune*

PENGUIN HISTORY

THE ASCENT OF MONEY
NIALL FERGUSON

Bread, cash, dosh, dough, loot: call it what you like, it matters. To Christians, love of it is the root of all evil. To generals, it is the sinews of war. To revolutionaries, it is the shackles of labour. But in *The Ascent of Money*, Niall Ferguson shows that finance is in fact the foundation of human progress. What's more, he reveals financial history as the essential back-story behind all history.

With the clarity and verve for which he is famed, Niall Ferguson explains why the origins of the French Revolution lie in a stock-market bubble caused by a convicted Scots murderer. He shows how financial failure turned Argentina from the world's sixth richest country into an inflation-ridden basket case – and how a financial revolution is propelling the world's most populous country from poverty to power in a single generation.

Yet the most important lesson of financial history is that sooner or later every bubble bursts – sooner or later the bearish sellers outnumber the bullish buyers – sooner or later greed flips into fear. And that's why, whether you're scraping by or rolling in it, there's never been a better time to understand the ascent of money.

He just wanted a decent book to read ...

Not too much to ask, is it? It was in 1935 when Allen Lane, Managing Director of Bodley Head Publishers, stood on a platform at Exeter railway station looking for something good to read on his journey back to London. His choice was limited to popular magazines and poor-quality paperbacks – the same choice faced every day by the vast majority of readers, few of whom could afford hardbacks. Lane's disappointment and subsequent anger at the range of books generally available led him to found a company – and change the world.

'We believed in the existence in this country of a vast reading public for intelligent books at a low price, and staked everything on it'
Sir Allen Lane, 1902–1970, founder of Penguin Books

The quality paperback had arrived – and not just in bookshops. Lane was adamant that his Penguins should appear in chain stores and tobacconists, and should cost no more than a packet of cigarettes.

Reading habits (and cigarette prices) have changed since 1935, but Penguin still believes in publishing the best books for everybody to enjoy. We still believe that good design costs no more than bad design, and we still believe that quality books published passionately and responsibly make the world a better place.

So wherever you see the little bird – whether it's on a piece of prize-winning literary fiction or a celebrity autobiography, political tour de force or historical masterpiece, a serial-killer thriller, reference book, world classic or a piece of pure escapism – you can bet that it represents the very best that the genre has to offer.

Whatever you like to read – trust Penguin.